LENIN

Arthur S. Link, *Princeton University*
GENERAL EDITOR FOR HISTORY

LENIN
TO
GORBACHEV

Three Generations
of Soviet Communists

Joan Frances Crowley
and
Dan Vaillancourt
Mundelein College

Harlan Davidson, Inc.
Arlington Heights, Illinois 60004

Library of Congress Cataloging-in-Publication Data

Crowley, Joan Frances.
Lenin to Gorbachev : three generations of Soviet communists / Joan
Frances Crowley and Dan Vaillancourt.
p. cm.
Bibliography: p.
Includes index.
ISBN 0-88295-863-1
1. Communism—Soviet Union—History. 2. Soviet
Union—Politics and government—20th century.
3. Communists—Soviet Union—
Biography. 4. Communism—History—20th century.
I. Vaillancourt, Dan. II. Title.
HX311.5.C76 1989
335.43'092'2—dc19   88-29960

93 92 91 90 89 EB 2 3 4 5 6 7 8 9 10

CONTENTS

DEFINITIONS, CHARTS, MAPS

Communists have changed more of the world political map in less time than any other group of people in the history of mankind. Before 1917 no one lived in a society controlled by communists. Today one of every three persons in the world lives under a communist banner. Who are the communists? What is communism? An examination of one country, the Union of Soviet Socialist Republics (USSR), provides some answers.

PREFACE

The spread of Marxist communism around the world has been nothing short of phenomenal. A few numbers make this point dramatically. There are today nearly a hundred communist parties active throughout the globe. There are nearly twenty communist countries with a combined population of almost two billion people, more than a third of the people on the planet. Yet communist ideology is only one hundred and fifty years old.* The "bible" of all communist parties and nations, *The Communist Manifesto*, was published in 1848. The first modern-day communist party, the Bolshevik Party, was organized in Russia in 1903. The first communist state, the USSR, appeared in 1917 and remained virtually the only communist nation until the Eastern European states and China became communist following World War II. In the history of mankind, no group of people, be they philosophers, politicians, or members of religious sects, has changed so much of the world in so little time as have the communists.

Who are the communists? In what do they believe?

Communists are members of a political party committed to realizing the kind of society described in the works of Karl Marx. Communists trace their ideological roots to Marx. Although Marx and his lifelong friend and collaborator, Friedrich Engels, gave incomplete and sometimes superficial descriptions of a future communist society, they inspired millions of people with their vision of an international society which would be highly industrialized and which would be controlled by one class of

---

*Communists possess no historical or ideological ties with the so-called "communists" of some primitive societies or religious groups, including first-century Christian sects.

people, namely, workers. All property under communism, Marx declared, would be owned by the workers collectively, and social institutions would support the development of individual talents. Personal freedom would be paramount, consumer goods and services would be bountiful, and traditional repressive agencies of the state such as the army and police would be unnecessary, hence, nonexistent.

The Soviet Union is not a communist society in the true Marxist sense since it has not reached the final stage of history known as communism; but the country is still described as "communist" because it is ruled by a party that is striving to create a communist society. The Union of Soviet Socialist Republics, as its name indicates, is a socialist society. The state owns and regulates, in the name of the people, the major services and industries so that, ostensibly, the population can share the available wealth. Soviet leaders have always asserted that the present socialist stage is a transitional phase between capitalism and communism.

Soviet communists have exerted, for better or worse, a powerful influence in the twentieth century, and they must not be ignored by American students. How can students consider themselves educated if they have not studied the phenomenon of the communist movement? The importance of this question provided the impetus for *Lenin to Gorbachev*. The book endeavors to help American students understand the most important experiment in communism, the Soviet Union.

Before we wrote this book, we formulated this question for ourselves: can the history of the Soviet communists be told by writers whose political and religious values are radically different? Communists cannot be properly understood if examined from the viewpoint of an American value system, which judges the absence of God as damnable and state control of private institutions as tyranny. We are convinced that an understanding of the world view of other peoples and their political systems is a key component of a liberal arts education and can perhaps serve as a modest step toward world peace. Therefore, we answered our question with a strong affirmative. *Lenin to Gorbachev* is our attempt to tell the history of the Soviet communists within the framework of their own value system.

This brief work examines Marx's ideas and the three genera-

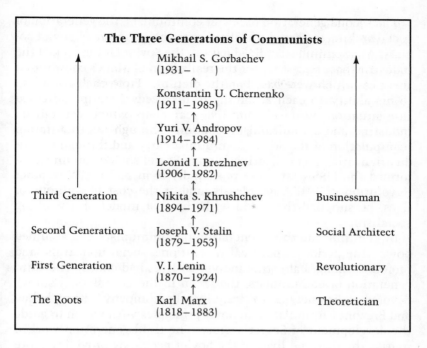

The Three Generations of Communists

	Mikhail S. Gorbachev (1931–) ↑	
	Konstantin U. Chernenko (1911–1985) ↑	
	Yuri V. Andropov (1914–1984) ↑	
	Leonid I. Brezhnev (1906–1982) ↑	
Third Generation	Nikita S. Khrushchev (1894–1971) ↑	Businessman
Second Generation	Joseph V. Stalin (1879–1953) ↑	Social Architect
First Generation	V. I. Lenin (1870–1924) ↑	Revolutionary
The Roots	Karl Marx (1818–1883)	Theoretician

tions of Soviet communists that followed him: the revolutionaries, the social architects, and the businessmen. Karl Marx envisioned a communist society and the forces that he thought would
lead to its emergence, but he did not live to see his ideas transform any society. For Marx's theories to influence national events,
a generation of revolutionaries was needed. V. I. Lenin and his Bolshevik (Communist) Party pitted Marxist principles against the
forces of Russian history. Conventional Marxist theory could not
readily explain events or guide revolutionary action in this vast
autocratic and semiindustrialized country. The pragmatic Lenin
reinterpreted Marx's theories; for example, he doubted whether
the workers, if left to their own resources, would carry out a successful revolution. Because the few Russian workers who existed
were not afire with revolutionary anger, Lenin created a party
of professional revolutionaries to lead the workers in rebellion
against the existing government. The revolution succeeded, and
Lenin and his communists took control of Russia.

The second generation of Soviet communists, the generation of social architects, forced socialism onto the structure of Soviet society. As a semiindustrialized nation, the Soviet Union lacked the industrial base necessary for the realization of Marx's communist theories, which were based on the dictum, "From each according to his ability, to each according to his needs." Stalin addressed this situation by developing five-year plans which centralized industrial and agricultural production. Through his totalitarian manipulation of the Soviet communist party and through the industrialization and collectivization of Soviet society, Stalin transformed the USSR far more profoundly than had the November Revolution of 1917.* Ruthlessly, and at the cost of millions of lives, he supplied the world with the first model of a working socialism.

By the time the third generation of communists had assumed power, the period of political revolutions, social upheavals, and profound changes affecting individual lives had ended. The third generation of communists, the "men in the grey flannel suits," devoted their energies to "running the company." Khrushchev and Brezhnev formulated no novel principles with which to guide the development of Soviet society. The third generation worked to ease the material lives of the Soviet people by providing more and better goods and services. In the 1950s Khrushchev urged that the communist leaders help the people to eat and dress well, but problems like low worker productivity, excessive centralization, and an inefficient bureaucracy handicapped his efforts and those of his successors. Today, Gorbachev with his *glasnost* campaign has opened the doors of the Soviet Union—but to whom and for what? Is *glasnost* an indication of fundamental change in the economic and political structure of the country? It is too soon to tell, but the new man in Moscow is now the world's most interesting politician to watch.

A few words about our methodology. This book does not argue that the three generations of Soviet communists were predestined to succeed one another or were impelled by some irrepressible dialectic. *Lenin to Gorbachev* employs the generational concept

---

* According to the old style Julian calendar, the November Revolution is actually the October Revolution; see explanation on p. 52.

as a tool of organization and description—without suggesting causality. A three-generational structure has several advantages. It organizes into distinct parts a century of complex, convoluted, and at times contradictory history and ideology. Perhaps more important, the three-generational structure focuses the vision onto each part by creating windows of history and ideology, windows that allow a limited view of each historical period. For example, during his life Joseph Stalin wrote a few brief philosophical essays, operated clandestinely as a revolutionary between 1899 and 1917, put many socialist programs in place in Soviet society, and like an efficient businessman developed a complex bureaucracy to keep the socialist system running smoothly in his country. Unfortunately, it is not possible within the limits of this short work to explore all these dimensions of Stalin's life. Instead, *Lenin to Gorbachev* modestly examines Stalin's importance as a social architect, emphasizing his role as the instigator of important programs like collectivized agriculture. The three labels we employ—revolutionary, social architect, and businessman—highlight the contributions of communist leaders during their brief moments in the spotlight of history.

Assistance on this project has come from numerous sources. We express gratitude to the administrators and students of Mundelein College in Chicago. The administrators encouraged us to teach a course on Marxism and communism as a team on a yearly basis; they awarded a Lilly Foundation Grant to the authors during the early stages of the book's development; and they awarded a sabbatical to Dan Vaillancourt to complete the text. Over a thousand students in our "Marxism and Communism" course have responded enthusiastically to our unique approach to the study of this remarkable chapter of twentieth-century history. Their frank criticisms inspired some rewriting, but, more important, encouraged us to bring this text to completion. Finally, we are grateful to Kathy Vaillancourt for invaluable assistance during the manuscript's early drafts, and to Michael Kendrick, assistant editor at Harlan Davidson, Inc., for his adroit editing and for gently guiding us through the final revisions.

"In place of the old bourgeois society,
with its classes and class antagonisms, we
shall have an association, in which the
free development of each is the condition
for the free development of all."

—Karl Marx and Friedrich Engels

1

THE LIFE AND THOUGHT
OF KARL MARX

K arl Marx and Friedrich Engels are rightfully called the fathers
of communism. The collaboration of these two nineteenth-
century Germans produced an ideology which has attracted millions and today challenges seriously capitalist ideology and multiparty liberal democracy throughout the world. Though Marx and
Engels shared a forty-year friendship and co-authored several vital
works such as *The German Ideology* and *The Communist Manifesto,* they played different roles in the formulation of communist
ideology. Engels wielded a clear and popular pen; it was he who
presented the major ideas of communism in digestible, uncompli-
cated language for the common people. He also contributed as an
expert in such specialized fields as military science, natural science, and anthropology, but his primary role was to popularize
communist ideology. The real genius, however, was Karl Marx.
Like no thinker before him, Marx saw the importance of economic conditions in producing class conflict. This class struggle,
Marx reasoned, would continue to be the basic force moving human history toward its inevitable destiny, a communist world.
Engels, a few years after the death of Marx, gave this appraisal of
his friend's work:

> Marx could very well have done without me. What Marx accom-
> plished I would not have achieved. Marx stood higher, saw further,
> and took a wider and quicker view than all the rest of us. Marx was a
> genius; we others were at best talented.[1]

Thus the study of the ideological foundation of Soviet communism is the study of Marx, his life, and his ideas.

Marx: From Exiled Journalist to Nouveau Riche

Karl Marx was born May 5, 1818 in Trier, a city located in the Rhineland province of Prussia (now part of West Germany). He was the oldest son and third of nine children. Both of his parents were descended from a long line of rabbis, though his father, one of the most respected lawyers in Trier, capitulated to the town's anti-Semitism and received a Protestant baptism. Despite his father's conversion, Marx in his formative years felt the presence of Jewish customs and piety, principally through guidance from his mother. But later he voiced a vigorous aversion to religion that continued throughout his life. He believed that religion kept the masses in chains; it was the "opium of the people" because the promise of a next world free of pain and injustice dulled their ability to react against the brutality of their lives.

Marx's father and a neighbor, Baron von Westphalen, exercised important influences on the growing boy. His father read Enlightenment philosophers such as Voltaire and Lessing and recited passages from their works to the young Marx. Thus the boy grew up on a diet of Enlightenment ideals. A nearby neighbor, Baron von Westphalen, whose daughter Jenny would later become Marx's wife, spent much time with the young Marx, introducing him to such classical authors as Homer and Shakespeare and discussing with him the progressive political ideas of the Enlightenment. Since Marx was educated at home until his teens, these influences emphasizing the goodness and power of human reason constituted in large measure his youthful intellectual world. Indeed, Marx never outgrew these childhood influences. Marx himself has been called "the last *philosophe* of the Enlightenment."

After the customary five years at the *Gymnasium* (high school) in Trier, where he graduated eighth in a class of thirty-two, Marx spent the 1835–36 academic year studying law at the University of Bonn. The year was a disaster. Marx's initial fervor for classwork quickly waned. He joined a drinking club, participated in duels, and spent the remainder of his time writing poetry, primarily to his childhood sweetheart, Jenny von Westphalen. (They married in 1843 after a seven-year engagement.) Marx's performance at Bonn angered his father, who was paying the bills. The elder Marx transferred his son to the bigger and more demanding University of Berlin. There Marx turned over a new leaf and spent four years studying philosophy. He earned his doctoral degree in 1841.

In Berlin, Marx took the most significant step of his intellectual career by adopting a system of thought conceived by the German philosopher G. W. F. Hegel. The philosophy of Hegel placed a crucial emphasis on reason. In his major work, *The Phenomenology of Mind*, Hegel referred to reality as essentially spiritual, which he conceptualized by the notion of the "universal mind." Human beings and other conscious beings like animals and plants were particular manifestations of the universal mind. Historically, the universal mind first appeared as individual minds which were conscious but not self-conscious or free. The universal mind would continue its development in history until the individual minds recognized themselves as free and fully self-conscious, that is, until they viewed themselves not only as individuals but also as part of the one universal mind.

Marx gradually moved away from the conclusions of Hegel, but he did retain throughout his life two important elements of the Hegelian system. First, Marx borrowed from Hegel the idea that human history was a unified whole which was in the process of development, and that human beings could attain full knowledge of this history. What Hegel had said about the rational character of the world and of human beings Marx had not forgotten. Second, he adapted Hegel's dialectical method to suit his explanation of the development of human history. Hegel claimed that the spirit or universal mind advanced in its development dialectically, that is, according to the resolution of contradictions. Marx, however, used the dialectical method to explain the contradictions among human beings. In every society, for example, some people were wealthy while others were poverty-stricken. Philosophers and politicians could not eradicate or rationalize this real contradiction. In time, the enmity between the rich and the destitute grew into open conflict that led to a redistribution of wealth and a restructuring of society. Thus one could say that human history developed dialectically.

Marx claimed that Hegel had "found the *abstract, logical, speculative* expression for the movement of history."[2] According to the young thinker, Hegel's vision was fruitful but his conclusions erroneous. History was not the march of abstract reason; it

portrayed the struggle of flesh and blood. Marx turned Hegel's dialectic right side up by emphasizing the concrete over the abstract,
the material over the spiritual.

In 1842 Marx turned to journalism to make a living since he
was unable to obtain a university teaching position. In the 1840s
his pen constantly incensed government officials. During an eight-
year period, Marx was expelled from several western European
countries because of his radical political journalism. Finally in
1849 he settled in London.

Despite his turbulent personal life, Marx established himself as
a powerful and far-ranging thinker. One of his friends described
him in this way:

> You can prepare yourself to meet the greatest, perhaps the only real
> philosopher now living. . . . He combines with the deepest philo-
> sophical earnestness the most biting wit. Imagine Rousseau, Vol-
> taire, Holbach, Lessing, Heine, and Hegel united in one person . . .
> and you have Dr. Marx.[3]

His genius notwithstanding, Marx also developed during this period a working habit that annoyed publishers and friends alike: he
seldom completed his works, "constantly breaking off and plung-
ing anew into an endless sea of books."[4]

One friend who recognized Marx's genius and who helped him
financially and intellectually was Friedrich Engels, son of a rich
Prussian industrialist who owned cotton-spinning enterprises in
Barmen, Prussia and Manchester, England. Passing through Paris
in 1844, Engels sought out Marx because the latter had written to
him in praise of one of his articles. In ten days of constant conver-
sation, Marx and Engels found that they agreed on all theoretical
matters. This fateful encounter marked the beginning of the lifelong friendship and professional collaboration of Engels and Marx.
While working in the Manchester branch of the family business,
Engels helped Marx to relocate in England.

Financial worries preoccupied Marx and his family during their
first fifteen years in London. Although he worked more or less
regularly as the European correspondent for the radical American
newspaper, the *New York Daily Tribune*, and although his wife

Jenny received modest family inheritances, Marx was regularly in financial trouble. In a letter to Engels he graphically described a destitute period in his life:

> My wife is ill. Little Jenny is ill. Lenchen [the maid] has some sort of nervous fever. I could not and cannot call the doctor because I have no money to buy medicine. For the past 8-10 days I have been feeding the *family* solely on bread and potatoes, but whether I shall be able to get hold of any today is doubtful.[5]

Karl and Jenny had little practical sense when it came to money. At one point they were supporting two maids, renting a piano, and paying for their children's private lessons in French, Italian, drawing, and music. Whenever economic survival became impossible for Marx and his family, Engels generously provided ready cash to restore them to solvency.

Despite Marx's need to hack out newspaper articles for income during these years, he produced some serious works. During 1857 and 1858, in six months of furious writing ("I am working like mad all night and every night collating my economic studies . . ."[6]), Marx completed a discursive eight-hundred page manuscript known as the *Grundrisse* (Outlines). This large manuscript contained notes for most of the six parts of a projected, ambitious multivolume work called *Economics*. In the early 1860s he worked in earnest on "Capital," the first part of his magnum opus. He later expanded this part into the three volumes of his famous *Capital*, completing and publishing the first volume in 1867. The other two volumes were never published by Marx, and the other five parts of *Economics* were never even drafted!

Beginning in 1864 Marx climbed gradually from indigency to the financial independence usually associated with upperclass gentlemen. From 1864 to 1869 he received several sizable legacies, and from Engels he obtained an annuity as well as substantial funds to pay off creditors. As financial worries lessened, the philosopher was unable to recapture the imagination and productivity which had characterized his earlier years. Although he was still convinced of the validity of his major ideas, by the 1870s he had eased into the lifestyle of an independent European gentleman: work and correspondence in the morning, a walk after lunch (often with Engels), dinner at six, and company at nine.

Marx's years as a *nouveau riche* were not totally tranquil. His financial woes receded but his health deteriorated. Boils from head to foot debilitated him for years. He also suffered a mild stroke in 1873 and spent much time in recuperation.

Physical problems aside, Marx devoted considerable time and energy to workers' politics during his twilight years. From 1864 to 1872 he was one of the leaders of the International Workingmen's Association (known as the First International), an organization created to unite laborers and promote working-class interests around the world. In the mid-1870s he followed closely the unification of two German working-class parties, which consolidated as the Social Democratic Workers' Party. This new organization included in its ranks several colleagues and disciples of Marx. Unhappy, however, with many points in the program which united the two parties, Marx made his criticisms known in a lengthy letter subsequently published as the *Critique of the Gotha Program*. His criticisms fell on deaf ears, and the new political party supported ideas Marx himself opposed. The German Social Democratic Workers' Party contained an increasing number of activists who called themselves "Marxist" but who corrupted Marx's ideas by transforming them into dogma. This development prompted Marx to proclaim by the end of the 1870s: "All I know is that I am no 'Marxist.'"[7]

The final years were difficult ones for Marx. Money was no longer a problem. Ill health, however, and distorted interpretations of the philosophy to which he had devoted his life continued to plague him until his death on March 13, 1883.

The Materialist Conception of History

The writings of Karl Marx had one ultimate goal: to describe through economic laws the inevitability of worldwide communism, the society constructed by liberated workers.

Marx was not a dreamer. In fact he labelled Charles Fourier, Robert Owen, Henri de Saint-Simon, and many other social critics of the nineteenth century as dreamers, since these thinkers described utopian societies without any systematic means or methods for realizing them. To differentiate himself from these utopian thinkers, Marx declared himself to be a scientific socialist. (Marx used "socialist" and "communist" interchangeably; the words did not have distinct meanings as they do today.)

A few words must be added about Marx's use of the term "scientific." The philosopher never proposed to experiment with history in the way scientists conduct laboratory experiments, predicting outcome x every time conditions a and b prevail—e.g., steam always results when water is heated to 212° F. Marx's understanding of "scientific" was more general and included any serious and systematic study whose foundation was empirical as opposed to imaginative or fictional. In this sense, "scientific" could characterize Hegel's account of universal mind, and Hegel indeed referred to his work as such. Marx used "scientific" to describe his approach to history which, he maintained, followed a detectable pattern that would culminate in the demise of capitalist society and the birth of a communist society.

Although Marx never developed or published a comprehensive and orderly system of his philosophical ideas, he often claimed that his work was a materialist interpretation of history. Briefly, he meant that the way to understand human beings and the societies in which they live could be found in each society's process of production, and in particular its relations of production. Before continuing with Marx's explanation of the materialist conception of history, let us explain the pivotal phrases "process of production" and "relations of production." The process of production includes all the items necessary to make a product, e.g. raw materials, tools, and human labor; it also encompasses the relationships that exist in the making of a product. These relationships are known as the relations of production, and they are twofold. First, there is a relation between human beings and the items necessary for production; in the production of this book, for example, someone bought the paper on which the book was printed. Buying, borrowing, or bartering is a relation of production. Second, after products are made, there is a relation between the persons who own the products and the products themselves. The persons who control the business that manufactured this book can give, sell, barter, lend, or keep the book; they can distribute the book in any

way they wish. The giving, selling, bartering, lending, or keeping
of a product is also a relation of production.

Marx's claim in the materialist conception of history was that
human beings and their societies were influenced by the relations
of production. He even went so far as to use "determined" in
some of his writings, but the word is too strong because Marx
meant that the relations of production, which he viewed as the
economic base or foundation of society, were crucial influences
but not the only ones. Let us explore briefly the influence of the
relations of production on human beings and their societies. In
capitalist society, for example, the relations of production empha-
size the accumulation of profit. This book is sold by its owner,
the capitalist, to earn a profit. (Business owners are capitalists
when their goal is to accumulate more capital.) Marx believed
that this relation of production, this economic foundation, would
encourage the development of an atomistic society in which capitalists displayed greed and competitiveness while the workers
who fabricated the products became mere robots on the assembly line. Since capitalist relations of production were organized
around monetary exchange, the people who lived in capitalist societies centered much of their lives around the accumulation and
the spending of money. Marx cast the understanding of history
within an economic framework. This is what he meant by the
phrase "materialist conception of history." Why did he use the
word "materialist" in writing about economics? To Marx, "materialist" and "economic" meant the same thing; they identified
the material things and tangible relations involved in the manufacture of products. He would never have understood "materialist," as we do today, to describe a lifestyle immersed in the enjoy-
ment of expensive cars, lavish houses, custom-tailored clothing,
and other material "niceties" of contemporary life.

But an understanding of human beings and the societies in
which they lived comprised only part of Marx's historical study.
In 1845 he stated categorically in his epigrammatic "Theses on
Feuerbach": "The philosophers have only *interpreted* the world
in various ways; the point is to *change* it."[8] Marx not only explained the relation between a society's economic base and its
inhabitants and institutions, but he also provided insights into
the dynamics of political change. He was, in fact, a committed

revolutionary, especially during the 1840s. For example, in 1848 Marx spent part of an inheritance from his father to support an armed uprising in Brussels, for which the king of Belgium ordered his arrest and deportation from the country. Marx failed as a revolutionary activist but his writings on revolution, especially *The Communist Manifesto*, exerted a worldwide influence. He explained how a workers' revolution against the capitalists would lead ultimately to a communist society throughout the world. Thus the materialist conception of history provided a thread in Marx's writings that tied together his ideas on human beings, society, revolution, and communism.*

HUMAN BEINGS EXERCISE POWER THROUGH THEIR WORK

In Marx's view people made history. They were concrete beings who distinguished themselves from other forms of nature, particularly animals, by their labor. To Marx, work or labor was any physical activity, not necessarily paid, designed to sustain or fulfill life. Did Marx consider the human thought process as the distinctive characteristic of *homo sapiens*? No, he declared, human beings affirmed their humanness in their production, in their daily work, since they were the only objects of nature who could plan their work before engaging in it. He illustrated the uniqueness of human beings in the famous bee and architect comparison found in his most important work, *Capital*. Although bees construct perfect cells in their honeycomb, Marx stated that architects are different and superior to bees since they raise their structure in imagination before they erect it in reality.[9] Human labor was a powerful activity since laborers, through their work, could transform nature and, with it, themselves. Human labor changed nature and society into a *human* reality. Let us create an example to illustrate Marx's point. In constructing chairs, individuals began with objects from nature (trees), and through work they fash-

---

*Marx devoted considerable energy to detailing the economic forces at work in capitalism. Indeed the three volumes of *Capital*, totalling nearly 2300 printed pages, treated almost exclusively the birth, life, and death of capitalism as an economic system. But these works, other than punctuating dramatically the importance of economic forces, do not alter appreciably the broad strokes of Marx's ideas. The arguments of *Capital* therefore remain beyond the scope of this work.

ioned the trees into a reality of their making (chairs). Human beings through their work could also alter society. Although Marx is
often misunderstood on this point, he asserted unequivocally that
human beings influenced society. In his "Theses on Feuerbach"
he stated:

> The materialist doctrine concerning the changing of circumstances
> and upbringing forgets that circumstances are changed by men. . .[10]

Let us continue with the example of the chairs. After constructing more chairs than they could use, artisans bartered or sold
their surplus to other people; by exchanging chairs for food or in
selling chairs for profit, craftsmen established economic conditions—or patterns—for the exchange or sale of other surplus
items in their society. In this way workers influenced the development of social interaction. (We reserve the words "worker" and
"laborer" for the people who produce the physical goods in a society. Thus in capitalist society, the capitalists hire the workers
and own the products but do not engage in physical labor; therefore, they do not qualify as workers.)

Human beings through their work also affected the conditions
of their own existence. In building chairs, Mr. Smith learned an
important handicraft which helped shape him as an individual
quite distinct from Ms. Baker, who crafted shoes. These individuals viewed their identity in large measure through the work they
did. Moreover, the products they created became extensions of
their personalities. The chairs of Mr. Smith and the shoes of Ms.
Baker, products resulting from their respective labors, became
"Smith chairs" and "Baker shoes." According to Marx, human beings through their work could control their own existence—up to
a point.

ECONOMICS INFLUENCES THE CONSCIOUSNESS OF HUMAN
BEINGS AND THE SOCIETIES IN WHICH THEY LIVE

Marx depicted human beings as free but subject also to the influence of economic forces. People were, in a certain sense, products
of the society in which they lived; they were molded by the rela-

tions of production in a society. In a four-page intellectual autobiography written in 1857, Marx claimed in no uncertain terms that "it is not the consciousness of men that determines their existence, but their social existence that determines their consciousness."[11] Human beings were born into a society that had specific relations of production which colored language and influenced human thought and desires. A contemporary example illustrates this point. Capitalists who manufacture flashlights might give consideration to the service they were providing for other people but, according to Marx, their motives would be attuned to the accumulation of profit for themselves.

Once placed in an economic structure, however, individuals were also able to change that structure. The capitalists who manufactured flashlights might decide at some point to give flashlights away to the employees working the night shift so that they could travel to and from work in greater safety. These capitalists would be introducing a new relation of production: the manufacture of goods for the welfare of people instead of for profit. Thus the influence of economic structures on human beings did not contravene human freedom but indicated rather that all human beings acted within a specific economic context. In sum, human beings, who were shaped by economic forces, could also influence these forces.

In describing humans as both free and influenced by economic forces, Marx was employing a dialectical style of thinking and writing. No singular view of human nature was adequate for him. Humans were pulled in opposite directions—toward freedom and toward determinism—and no explanation could eliminate this tension.

Economic forces also influenced social institutions. In his brief intellectual autobiography, Marx described clearly the influence of the relations of production on the structure of society:

In the social production of their existence, men inevitably enter into definite relations, which are independent of their will, namely *relations of production* appropriate to a given stage in the development of their *material forces of production*. The totality of these relations of production constitutes the economic structure of society, the real foundation, on which arises a legal and political superstructure and to which correspond definite forms of social consciousness. The mode of production of material life conditions the general process of social, political, and intellectual life.[12]

Before examining in more detail the influence of the relations of production on the structure of society, it is important to understand clearly what Marx meant by relations of production and the material forces of production. The productive forces, as the phrase indicated, were the raw materials and the tools and labor required to make a product, whereas the relations of production explained the manner in which the productive forces and products were owned and distributed in a society. In the manufacture of this book, for example, the material forces of production were paper, ink, and printing presses as well as the human labor necessary to operate the presses. The relations of production were capitalist, that is, entrepreneurs owned the productive forces, paid wages to the laborers, and distributed the book in a competitive market to earn a profit.

Marx made three observations about productive forces and relations of production. First, the relations of production must support the development of the productive forces. In *The Poverty of Philosophy*, written in 1847, he clearly outlined this connection: "The hand-mill gives you society with the feudal lord; the steam-mill, society with the industrial capitalist."[13] The significance of the hand-mill was that it enabled serfs to grind more grain in less time than with previous methods. Thus the hand-mill gave the world a society dominated by the feudal lord. The lord enabled manual labor to develop steadily because he allowed the serfs to own tools. He also unwittingly encouraged serfs to use the new tools in producing and processing more grain since, in addition to working a specified number of days on the lord's land, serfs also toiled on land designated for their own use; serfs worked harder when they worked for themselves. Beyond these measures, the lord protected his serfs from marauders so that they could devote their time to production. (The lord was owner and master of a feudal estate which included serfs who worked the land. If a parcel of land was sold, the serf who worked that parcel was transferred with it from one lord to the other.) Relations of production in a society protected and encouraged the development of productive forces in that society.

In his second observation Marx purported that relations of production supported the superstructure of a society, such as its laws, government, religion, science, arts, philosophy, and ideology. The superstructure identified the layer of society that had been influenced by economic forces. To illustrate Marx's point, we turn again to the feudal society. Feudal relations of production promoted the authority of the lord, who demanded obedience and diligent work from the serfs. Dominant in the superstructure was the Roman Catholic Church. Feudal relations of production, which required serfs to work long hours on land they did not own and for a lord with whom they could not negotiate better working conditions, supported a Roman Catholic morality which emphasized obedience to God and the patient fulfillment of onerous duties, even those unjustly demanded, such as the payment of heavy taxes to use the lord's property. Throughout the medieval centuries the morality of the Church mandated obedience with the promise of peace and justice in the world to come.

Productive forces were dynamic, developing and expanding constantly, while relations of production remained relatively fixed. Eventually, the relations of production in a society restrained new productive forces. In his third observation, Marx maintained that a tug of war existed between productive forces and relations of production. Again in his brief intellectual autobiography he said:

> At a certain stage of development, the material productive forces of society come into conflict with the existing relations of production. . . . From forms of development of the productive forces these relations turn into their fetters. Then begins an era of social revolution. The changes in the economic foundation lead sooner or later to the transformation of the whole immense superstructure.[14]

The relations of production of feudalism restricted the growth of the steam-mill, since serfs tied to their land could not readily congregate in small towns to work in factories. The capitalist class that was emerging at the twilight of the feudal period needed workers, and so it turned to the serfs and peasants for assistance in overthrowing the lords in a social revolution. The serfs became free from the land and from the lords and evolved into a potential class of factory workers. Then the capitalist class created relations of production more suitable to the accumulation of profit. Capitalist relations of production, in turn, gave rise to a capitalist superstructure which protected the freedom to purchase and dispose of property and emphasized individual competition and other self-centered interests.

The influence of the economic base on the superstructure has become known in Marxist literature as "the economic interpretation of history" or "economic determinism." Considerable debate exists over the nature of the relationship between relations of production and the superstructure, but one point is clear. Marx did not believe that a causal link existed between the economic base and superstructure. Rather, he suggested that a flexible relationship existed between economic forces on the one hand and the culture and institutions of society on the other.

In his study of history Marx discovered five kinds of relations of production (with their respective productive forces) which generally gave rise to five kinds of society: primitive communal, Asiatic, feudal, capitalist, and communist. Every stage of economic development had to be experienced, and the process was not complete until a global communist society was attained. In a sense, communist society was the inevitable culmination of history. Marx, once again, was not proposing a rigid formula for predicting events but rather presenting a general structural pattern for the interpretation of historical change. Moreover, these five archetypal societies were not abstractions of any individual countries. Each stage of economic development could apply to numerous countries simultaneously. For example, today the capitalist stage of development could characterize France, the United States, Japan, and numerous other countries.

Marx made numerous claims throughout his life. As a scientific socialist, he had discovered economic laws operating in history, and he had developed a thesis to explain what he saw as the progression toward a communist society. These claims were linked to the three observations about relations of production and productive forces: the relations of production must correspond to the productive forces; the relations of production must influence the

The Five Types of Society

Process of Production

Society	Relations of Production	Material Forces of Production
Primitive Communal	Limited ownership of the material forces of production, such as land; production of goods for individual consumption only	Stone tools
Asiatic (slave)	Production of goods by slaves for distribution to slaveowners who own material forces of production	Iron tools; beginning of division of labor
Feudal	Production of goods by serfs who consume part of the harvest and distribute the remainder of the harvest to landlords as payment for the right to farm the land; the landlords own or control material forces of production	Hand-mill; expansion of division of labor in agriculture
Capitalist	Production of goods by workers to be sold for profit by capitalists who own or hire material forces of production	Steam-mill; development of manufacture and industry as machines become more sophisticated and division of labor more expansive
Communist	Planned production for equitable distribution of goods by a democratic society of workers who own and control material forces of production	Highly sophisticated machines for production of goods and services

Note: This linking of the relations of production to material forces of production in each type of society is our interpretation of Marx's ideas.

superstructure; and the widening gap between the constantly
growing productive forces and the stagnant relations of production must lead to social revolution. These statements summed up
the economic laws which Marx believed shaped history, and they
confirmed in his mind his calling as a scientific socialist. In the
next two sections of the chapter, it will become clearer how Marx
thought that the development of economic forces led inexorably
to a communist society.

WORKERS DEFEAT BOURGEOISIE IN THE PROLETARIAN REVOLUTION

At no time in history have the masses been happy or fulfilled with
their labor conditions. During the primitive communal period,
before any extensive division of labor (specialization) had occurred, humans worked with stone tools and weapons to combat a
hostile climate and savage animals and to procure enough food.
Human energies were devoted to one task only—the battle for
survival. With the introduction of the division of labor, when
whole tasks were divided into small, specialized jobs, primitive
peoples began amassing and trading food surpluses, thereby easing
the struggle for survival. But the division of labor created another
kind of problem for human beings, one that afflicted the spirit instead of the stomach. Individuals now experienced alienation,
that is, they felt both estranged from their work and dehumanized
in the work process.

Marx complained in *Capital* that division of labor "attacked
the individual at the very roots of his life,"[15] and also that "it converted the laborer into a crippled monstrosity."[16] Human beings
should develop their talents, and they ought to do it of their own
volition. The division of labor meant that they spent the better
part of each workday in repetitive, boring, and meaningless activity. In the British museum where Marx worked daily, he read
about the skinny and undernourished children in nineteenth-
century England who pulled carts of coal through dark, narrow
mine shafts for a dozen or more hours a day. He also read about
thousands of men and women who worked for capitalists, producing items that did not belong to them, and even treating fellow
workers as rivals rather than as comrades. In the end the enor-

mous potential for self-development was wasted as human beings became self-alienated. In an earlier section our Mr. Smith and Ms. Baker were at least fulfilled in their work since they controlled the labor process from beginning to end. They possessed the freedom to work when they wanted, and they controlled the entire process of production. For instance, Mr. Smith felled a tree for lumber, handcrafted the chair, and oiled it for protection against moisture. His work was not limited to one repetitive activity in some factory, like glueing the legs of a chair to its seat. Finally, our two artisans owned their products upon completion of the work. Self-fulfillment occurred when workers controlled every aspect of production.

Alienation, though experienced individually, was shared collectively by members of an exploited social class, that is, the group of people who did not own the material forces of production and who were conscious of themselves as a class. Marx defined "class" in terms of the economic process, i.e. one class owned the material forces of production and the other produced the products; he also added a psychological dimension to the meaning of class by claiming that a group of people must be aware of their shared condition if they are to consider themselves to be a class. The relations of production of a society (except the primitive communal, which predated the division of labor as well as the evolution of social classes, and the communist, which would support a classless society) gave rise to two main opposing classes. The exploited class surrendered its freedom in order to labor for owners, and the exploiting class owned and directed the productive forces, including the labor of workers. Although Marx acknowledged the multiplicity of classes in each society, he maintained that the class struggle was waged primarily between two main opposing classes. In the Asiatic relations of production, the two contending classes were the slave and master; in the feudal, the serf and lord; in the capitalist, the proletarian and bourgeois classes. (To identify city workers and differentiate them from farmers, Marx used the word *proletarian*. He also referred to capitalists as members of the *bourgeois* class.) The two opposing classes were always related in an inverse proportion: as the exploited class grew larger, poorer, and more alienated, the exploiting class grew smaller, richer, and more corrupted by possessions. The clear de-

marcation between the two classes was paramount since Marx
claimed that a class existed only when it was conscious of itself
as a class, that is, when it saw its interests being oppressed by
other groups and consequently organized to fight for them. The
alienation experienced by individuals of an exploited class gradually awakened a class consciousness which propelled the group
into open hostility against its oppressors. This class struggle,
which frequently erupted in violent revolution, was the instrument of change that transformed one type of society into another.
Marx and Engels explained in *The Communist Manifesto*, their
most dramatic exposition of the class struggle, that "the history
of all hitherto existing society is the history of class struggles."[17]

The class struggle occupying Marx's attention was of course the
city worker-capitalist struggle. He referred to this class struggle
as the proletarian revolution. Though Marx discussed in extensive detail the eventual economic demise of capitalist society, he
could not describe in the same way the proletarian revolution. It
was impossible and "unscientific" to anticipate with any ac-
curacy the historical details of a future proletarian revolution.
Only general observations would do and these would be tentative,
based on perceivable historical trends. At different periods during
his life Marx offered general comments on the nature, combatants, method, location, and time of the proletarian revolution.

Nature. Every revolution in the past had been no more than a
political revolution with one form of state being replaced by another one more suited to protect the new relations of production.
Marx wrote that the state differed from the government. The
latter carried out administrative functions like the collection of
taxes and the building of bridges, activities which were generally
devoid of political overtones. The government performed tasks to
ameliorate the existence of its citizens, whereas the state and its
agencies, the bureaucracy, judicature, police force, and army,
functioned mainly to perpetuate themselves. In other words, the
state existed for the purpose of preserving the interests of the ruling class. Hence every revolution merely substituted one form of
class oppression for another. This point was clearly demonstrated
after the revolutions ending feudalism; the states that were created established laws to protect property and paid little attention
to the food, shelter, and clothing of workers.

The coming proletarian revolution would not only be political but social and international as well. By eliminating the bourgeois state and replacing it with a workers' state, the revolution would be political. It would also be social in the sense that the workers would be emancipated from all class domination and economic exploitation. Freed from the class struggle, the workers would be able to restructure their lives to eliminate alienation and thus develop themselves fully. Finally the revolution would be international because the proletarian movement would be worldwide.

Combatants. Led by a political party of workers, the revolution would be waged by the proletariat against the bourgeoisie. Marx never wavered from his lifelong faith in the proletariat as the only class capable of carrying out the revolution.

To be successful in their battle, the proletarians must be led by an international workers' (or communist) political party, structured democratically to allow for expression and discussion of diverse viewpoints. The party would exercise educational leadership over the workers in two areas: 1) it would remind the workers that the proletarian movement was international, not national, though struggles on the national level would be waged by local working-class parties; 2) it would point out to the workers the necessity of the international movement while they waged local battles against their bourgeoisie. Simply put, communist party members would clearly understand the conditions necessary for proletarian victory. They would function as philosophers, teachers, and military commanders. This eclectic expertise would designate the communist party as "the most advanced and resolute section of the working-class parties of every country."[18]

Method. For the most part Marx advocated violence as the sure means of wresting power from the bourgeoisie. Only in the 1870s did he consider the possibility that workers might obtain power peacefully, using the electoral process to gain a majority in representative bodies. Once elected, they could accomplish through legal means the transformation of capitalist society into a communist society. For the workers to be successful at the ballot box, they must be highly organized politically, and the repressive agencies of the state, especially the bureaucracy and military, must not be extensive. In a very few countries (Britain and the United States, for example) did Marx concede that the workers could transform society at the voting booth. In most cases, however, violent revolution represented the only method by which the proletariat would overcome the bourgeoisie.

Location. Since the proletarian revolution would be international, it could not be confined to any one country. It must erupt simultaneously in many nations, eventually encircling the globe. But the first spark, the origin of the revolution, could occur anywhere in the world. In Europe, especially on the Continent, the advanced industrial countries could kindle the global proletarian revolution as long as the revolutionary flames were not doused by the armies of prosperous countries like England and the United States, whose economic development had attained new heights through colonial exploitation. At the other extreme, underdeveloped countries could also ignite the proletarian revolution. In the conclusion of *The Communist Manifesto* Marx and Engels singled out Germany, still in the feudal stage of development, as the country most likely to witness the outbreak of revolution. They believed that Germany would experience a bourgeois revolution, followed shortly by a proletarian revolution. In 1882, the year before his death, Marx was looking to Russia, primarily a peasant society, for the outbreak of a revolution which could be successful if followed by "a proletarian revolution in the West so that both complement each other."[19] The initial spark of the proletarian revolution could happen anywhere in the world as along as a strong proletarian class fanned the flames until they circled the globe.

Time. Several times throughout his life Marx thought that the proletarian revolution was imminent. In the late 1840s he returned to his native Germany only to be disappointed by the unsuccessful bourgeois and proletarian revolutions. In the early 1850s, he anticipated that a severe European economic crisis would foment a revolution. But in the mid-1850s, in his *Grundrisse,* Marx intimated that capitalism had a long way to go before exhausting its economic possibilities. In this work he forewarned that the revolution could *not* erupt before the full development of capitalism. The economic vitality of capitalism played a major role in determining the time of the revolution.

Marx reasoned that capitalism must mature according to its

own economic laws, much like a tree maturing according to organic laws. Capitalist society had the capacity for more development in at least three areas: the growth of the proletariat, an increased class consciousness, and the development of more complex mechanization. Before revolution would be at hand, the workers must be conscious of themselves as a class and comprise a majority of the population, or at least occupy a strategic position in society. A class-conscious group of workers, if too small, would easily fall before the guns of the bourgeois military. A large group of workers, if unaware of its common suffering, would continue to languish under the capitalist yoke and would entertain no thoughts of revolution. The proletariat could effect change only when the workers were numerous enough to occupy a vital role in society and only when they functioned together as a social unit.

Sophistication of industrial machinery would occur as a natural part of the maturation process of capitalist society. But in the process, mechanization would give birth to opposing communist productive forces. As these forces developed, tension within capitalist society would increase. The productive forces could only grow to a limited extent under capitalist relations of production. In other words, although workers would eventually create, operate, and repair all machinery, they would not control it; capitalists would continue to own industrial machines and other productive forces and to utilize them to manufacture goods for profit. The most efficient manner to develop better and more sophisticated machines would be to grant the workers who operated the machines the autonomy and resources to work on them. Capitalists, however, would never allow such a development and would continue to frustrate the proletariat. Only a revolution would solve the problem. The internal contradiction within capitalism would eventually rend the system asunder. The growth of the proletariat, the increase in class consciousness, and the sophistication of industrial machines, normal developments within a capitalist society, formed the mechanism of an economic clock that ticked inexorably toward the time of the proletarian revolution.

As Marx stated repeatedly, his insights on social development were not formulas for predicting the future. He was not a seer. His

theories identified broad patterns for interpreting history. More
specifically, he detected patterns—specifically, concerning the
nature, combatants, method, location, and time—that anticipated a future proletarian revolution.

DICTATORSHIP OF THE PROLETARIAT PRECEDES
COMMUNIST SOCIETY

After the proletarian revolution, the victorious workers would in-
augurate a socialist society that would serve as a transitional system between capitalist and communist societies. Directing this
socialist society would be a form of government and state known
as "the dictatorship of the proletariat." Though Marx explicitly
referred to the dictatorship only a few times in his correspondence and not at all in his manuscripts for publication, he men-
tioned it as one of his contributions to posterity: "My own contribution was to show . . . that the class struggle necessarily leads to
the *dictatorship of the proletariat.*"[20]

The dictatorship of the proletariat would set as its supreme goal
the abolition of classes and class distinctions. It would realize this
goal both as a state and as a government. As a state, the dictatorship would employ institutions like the police and army
to eradicate any capitalist class remnants which had survived
the revolution. Capitalists would not be permitted to mount a
counterrevolution or to exercise countervailing influences on the
work of the dictatorship. They must embrace the ideals of the proletariat or be destroyed. As a government, the dictatorship would
eliminate class distinctions through socioeconomic programs. As
explained by Marx and Engels in *The Communist Manifesto*, it
would exact all capital from the bourgeoisie, centralize the instruments of production, and increase production as rapidly as
possible. In other words, the dictatorship would in the name of
the workers eventually own and control all land, industry, and
production, thus preventing personal aggrandizement at the expense of the rest of the population. Marx believed these measures
would effectively eliminate classes and class distinctions.

In none of his works did Marx present a detailed description
of the future communist society. To have done so would have violated his thesis that societies were products of the economic

conditions of their time. When it did come, communist society would take on characteristics determined by the prevailing economic conditions. As a consequence, his remarks on communist society, though distributed throughout most of his works, were incomplete and oftentimes merely parenthetical.

Once the communist society had been achieved, the dictatorship of the proletariat would no longer be needed. It would wither away, and in its place would emerge an association of free producers. The association would be an interesting social institution, very different from the governments of today. It would function without an army or perhaps even without a militia since after the revolution peaceful coexistence would reign among nations. There would be no need for a police force or a judicature since the people who disobeyed the law would be so sensitive to the rights of others that they would impose punishment on themselves. And it would not need a bureaucracy since the association would be decentralized, serving the needs and interests of local populations. A central government, however, would remain with a few important functions such as economic planning for the new society. Since people would collectively own the productive forces in the form of local cooperatives, a central plan for the economy would be necessary to guarantee the production of sufficient goods such as food, housing, clothing, and social services including medical care and education to meet without cost the needs of every individual. Communist society could then inscribe on its banner: "From each according to his ability, to each according to his needs."[21]

But classes, class distinctions, and repressive agencies of the state would disappear only with the gradual elimination of the division of labor. Social classes and the state had appeared with the beginnings of the division of labor, and they would fade with it also. Throughout history the ever-multiplying divisions of labor had enabled societies to become increasingly complex and to produce greater quantities of goods and services. How would communist society dispense with division of labor while at the same time creating an economy of abundance? Since it followed capitalism, communist society would be highly industrialized with much menial labor passing from human hands to machines. In addition, communist society through its central planning would produce needed goods and services without waste. It would become a society of bounty with a novel feature, that of a greatly reduced working day. As the quantity of goods and services necessary to satisfy world demand became commensurate with the population, and as communist society became more industrialized, the working day would correspondingly become shorter. During an undoubtedly romantic moment Marx even wondered if unskilled labor would not at one point be abolished!

Without the division of labor, which confined individuals to one repetitive activity and thereby crippled their talents, communist society for the first time in history would make possible the full realization of human potential for everyone—not just a privileged few. For communist society to be viable, however, individuals must possess desires different from those of any other people in history. The question of human desires occupied Marx at some length in *The German Ideology*, an important seminal manuscript written in collaboration with Engels in the mid-1840s. Human desires, Marx advanced, could be divided into two major groups: *constant desires* like the desires to eat and to have sex which "exist under all relations (of production), and only change their form and direction under different . . . relations," and *relative desires* such as the desire to be rich and famous which originate "solely in a particular society, under particular conditions of (production) and intercourse."[22] Marx contended that communist society would satisfy constant desires, and that relative desires like power and avarice created by capitalist relations of production would be destroyed since the economic conditions for their existence would no longer prevail. The communist relations of production would create new relative desires, but Marx did not know which ones they would be. He refused to prognosticate.

Despite Marx's reluctance to sketch future social panoramas, his ideas on communist society were generally clear. Communist society did not represent in any way a return to the days of an idyllic past, if such days ever existed. After the dictatorship of the proletariat, communist society would represent a classless, stateless, industrialized society of cooperative producers united by a common plan for production. The citizens of this society would perform fulfilling work a few hours a day according to their ability and receive in exchange free vital goods and social services. With their leisure time they could pursue personal interests and continue to develop their talents. In the end human beings would enjoy rich, happy existences.

Marx did not live to see his communist society blossom in any part of the world. He was a philosopher, and his role in history was to sow the seed, to articulate communist theory. And this theory remained the focus of much heated debate in Europe after Marx's death. The debate featured classical Marxists like the Czech-born Karl Kautsky, who combined a commitment to proletarian revolution with a belief in universal suffrage and parliamentary democracy. Since the workers would eventually govern themselves democratically, he believed that universal suffrage would help develop the habit of democracy among the proletarians until they were ready for revolution. Until World War I, Kautsky's prestige among Marxists was such that he was often referred to as the "pope" of Marxism. The Marxist debate also featured revisionists like the German thinker Eduard Bernstein, who revised those elements in Marx's work that were incompatible with late nineteenth-century developments in capitalist economics and politics. Bernstein rejected the idea that a deepening economic crisis would bring about the imminent collapse of capitalism. In place of revolution, he advocated the gradual extension of political and economic rights to the proletariat so that it could create socialism peacefully. Appropriately, his major work was entitled *Evolutionary Socialism*.

Both Bernstein and Kautsky were close friends of Friedrich Engels, who survived Marx by twelve years and who enjoyed unrivaled prestige as the interpreter of Marx's work. It was Engels who unwittingly fueled the Marxist debate over the role of revolution in transforming capitalist society when in 1895, in a preface to Marx's *Class Struggles in France*, he argued that the proletariat would gain ascendancy over the capitalists peacefully, since capitalist politics would permit universal suffrage. The workers would vote themselves into the "decisive power in the land." Engels, Kautsky, and the classical Marxists, and Bernstein and the revisionists kept the debate over Marxist revolutionary theory a lively one until V. I. Lenin and his communists brought socialism to Russia in 1917.

Summary and Comment

Karl Marx's ideas revolved around the dignity of human beings, and in particular the dignity of their labor. For one of the first times in the history of Western civilization, work was viewed as an edifying human activity, not as a punishment for violating a divine law in the Garden of Eden. History was on the move, and its climax was a communist society where human beings could finally perform fulfilling labor.

Marx devoted most of his writings to discussing human labor as the quintessential activity of human beings and as the force that propelled historical change. As human beings worked together, their labor established processes of production (productive forces and relations of production). The workers always improved the productive forces, that is, they developed greater skill and more sophisticated tools and techniques. But a ruling social class, which controlled the relations of production, stymied some of these changes. Thus, the rift between the productive forces and relations of production frustrated the workers and encouraged the formation of two opposing social classes. In time, this class struggle led to a revolution that permitted the oppressed class to create a new social order. This process, and here is the point of Marx's writings, occurred because the economic structure of society (the labor of human beings) developed dialectically, through opposites. Workers constantly improved their skills and tools but owners kept the workers in check with production and distribution systems suited to their own desires. Thus the dialectic of economic forces in history led inevitably, according to Marx, to the succession of societies which culminated in the realization of a communist society.

If nothing else, Marx accomplished two things. He brought to public attention the dignity of the labor of the masses. Furthermore, he underscored the importance of economic forces in shaping history.

Further Reading

No thinker in modern times has been the subject of as much attention and scholarship as Karl Marx. There are Marxist exegetes, Marxist societies, Marxist institutes, Marxist teachers, and Marxist journals and presses. The proliferation of groups and publications devoted to the writings of Marx reflects, in part, the failure of the philosopher to complete or edit important manuscripts and to organize a system of thought. His one attempt at conceiving a system was to be called *Economics,* and he completed only one-third (*Capital,* Vol. I) of the first part of a projected six-part work. Marx compounded these difficulties by changing topics of investigation several times throughout his career. In the early and mid-1840s he commented on the German and European philosophical heritage; in the late 1840s and early 1850s he turned his attention to political philosophy, and finally during most of the 1850s and 1860s, his most prolific period, he dissected capitalism. Marx is a challenging, provocative, and difficult writer to digest. This annotated bibliography and the others that follow at the end of each chapter draw the reader's attention to works in English which are highly regarded by scholars.

BY MARX

Marx, Karl, and Frederick Engels. *Karl Marx/Frederick Engels: Collected Works.* New York: International Publishers, 1975–. The works of Marx and Engels will comprise fifty volumes; about half are published at this time. The *Marx/ Engels Collected Works* will represent the first extensive edition of Marx and Engels in English.

Kamenka, Eugene, ed. *The Portable Karl Marx.* New York: Penguin, 1983. This paperback contains documents and letters about Marx the man and selections from the important works in chronological order, including the complete *Communist Manifesto.*

The following five works are fundamental for understanding the variety and complexity of Marx's thought:

Fromm, Eric. *Marx's Concept of Man.* New York: Frederick Un-

gar, 1961. Though bearing Fromm's name, the book contains
extensive selections from Marx's *Economic and Philosophical Manuscripts of 1844* that discuss alienation. Fromm's
eighty-three page introduction sheds important light on a
difficult work.

Marx, Karl. *A Contribution to the Critique of Political Economy.*
London: Lawrence & Wishart, 1971. The 1859 work signals
Marx's transition from politics to economics. The preface is
the only summary Marx ever wrote of his own ideas.

————. *Capital, A Critique of Political Economy,* 3 volumes.
New York: International Publishers, 1967. This major work
represents an important contribution to economic theory.

Marx, Karl, and Friedrich Engels. *The German Ideology.* Moscow:
Progress Publishers, 1976. This work (1845–46) is felt to be
Marx's first mature work. The first chapter expounds the
materialist conception of history.

————. *The Communist Manifesto.* Middlesex, England: Penguin, 1967. After the Bible, the *Manifesto* (1848) is the most
widely read book in the Western world. This edition contains an excellent introduction by A. J. P. Taylor.

ON MARX

McLellan, David. *Karl Marx, His Life and Thought.* New York:
Harper and Row, 1973. This full-scale biography covers the
personal, political, and intellectual facets of Marx's life.

Padover, Saul K. *Karl Marx, An Intimate Biography.* New York:
McGraw-Hill, 1978. This work examines Marx the human
being—lover, husband, friend, fighter, father.

Popper, Karl R. *The Open Society and Its Enemies.* Vol. 2, *High
Tide of Prophecy, Hegel, Marx, and the Aftermath.* New
York: Harper and Row, 1963. Popper presents one of the
most convincing philosophical refutations of Marx.

Singer, Peter. *Marx.* Oxford: Oxford University Press, 1980. Singer
succeeds in presenting a good, brief introduction to Marx's
thought.

Tucker, Robert. *Philosophy and Myth in Karl Marx.* New York:
Cambridge University Press, 1961. The work examines the

notion of alienation and portrays Marx as a moralist rather
than as an economist.

REFERENCE TOOLS

Bochenski, Joseph M., and others, eds. *Guide to Marxist Philosophy, An Introductory Bibliography.* Chicago: Swallow Press,
1972. This annotated bibliography guides the beginning student through the maze of philosophy books written by and
on Marxist thinkers.

Drachkovitch, Milorad M., ed. *Yearbook on International Communist Affairs.* Stanford: Hoover Institution Publications,
1966–. This is the authoritative yearly source of statistics,
events, and changes concerning individual communist
countries throughout the world.

Lachs, John. *Marxist Philosophy: A Bibliographical Guide.*
Chapel Hill: University of North Carolina Press, 1967. This
source lists 1500 titles organized into thirty-six bibliographical chapters with helpful introductions.

Leonhard, Wolfgang. *Three Faces of Marxism, the Political Concepts of Soviet Ideology, Maoism, and Humanist Marxism.*
Trans. Ewald Osers. New York: Holt, Rinehart and Winston,
1974. The book details the intellectual progress of Marxism
as a political movement from Marx through Mao based on
the writings of the leaders.

"Give us an organization of revolutionaries and we will overturn Russia."

—V. I. Lenin

2

THE FIRST GENERATION OF COMMUNISTS: VLADIMIR ILYICH LENIN, REVOLUTIONARY

The work of Marx, with its confident and stirring account of the inevitability of communist society, captured the interest and imagination of many Western and Eastern thinkers. Communist ideology was seen as an exciting alternative to a world convulsed in the agonies of capitalism, which was enriching the few and enslaving the many.

But Marx had created a *theory* of historical development. Now, people of action would be needed to make a revolution. In Russia, Marxists like V. I. Lenin and Leon Trotsky would lead the world's first proletarian revolution and then take the initial steps toward the construction of a socialist state. The undisputed leader of this first generation of communists was Vladimir Ilyich Ulyanov, better known as Lenin. Fellow Marxist Paul Axelrod wrote of him:

> There is not another man who for twenty-four hours of the day is taken up with the revolution, who has no other thoughts but thoughts of revolution, and who, even in his sleep, dreams of nothing but revolution.[1]

Lenin: From Country Lawyer to Marxist in Exile

In 1870, the same year during which Marx was promoting working-men's politics as a leader of the First International, a second son was born to a couple in the sleepy provincial town of Simbirsk (now Ulyanov) in the middle Volga region of the Russian Empire. He was named Vladimir in honor of the Russian saint credited with bringing Christianity to Russia. This Vladimir Ulyanov, who later adopted the pseudonym Lenin as a way of avoiding detection by the Tsar's secret police, would bring his own gift to his native land, a gift that would dramatically change the course of world history.

The young Lenin enjoyed an almost idyllic childhood. One of six children born to a minor official in the Russian educational bureaucracy, Lenin grew to adolescence in a home where the serious pursuit of learning was given high priority but where a healthy amount of mischief and play was also tolerated. The children's father, Ilya, despite a humble background, had advanced steadily in the Russian educational system to the position of inspector of schools for the province of Simbirsk. Although he was a typical patriarchal figure in the household, he apparently influenced his children through example rather than force, and he was loved, admired, and respected by the entire family. The children's mother, Maria, was the heart of the home and overseer of the young ones' education since her husband was frequently away on inspection tours.

In 1886 the sudden death of the father rocked the calm of family life. The following year the family again received a shattering blow, this time with the shocking news of the execution of the eldest son Alexander. He died on the gallows for his part in an unsuccessful plot on the life of the Tsar. Soviet hagiographers have attempted to link Alexander's death with Lenin's conversion to Marxism. The effect of Alexander's death on Vladimir, however, can only be surmised since Lenin apparently did not discuss the execution of his brother with any friends.

The Russian Patronymic

In spoken Russian the formal given name plus the patronymic or father's name is used. This is the polite, respectful form of address. For instance Lenin's family and friends addressed him as "Vladimir Ilyich."

The patronymic is formed from a father's given name and an ending such as "-ovich" or "-ich" (son of) and "-ova" or "-ovna" (daughter of). Since the elder Ulyanov's given name is Ilya, Vladimir's patronymic is "Ilyich" while that of his sister is the slightly irregular "Ilyinichna."

Western usage, omitting the patronymic, will be employed throughout the text.

In the same year of that family tragedy, the teenage Lenin left home to enroll at the University of Kazan. His goal was a law degree. Within four months his academic life came to an abrupt halt with his unjust expulsion from school. Although charged with "deceit, dereliction, and even discourtesy,"[2] he apparently was a victim of his brother's tainted name. Trotsky in later years aptly commented that Lenin was expelled from the University of Kazan into the University of Marxism!

But Lenin's path to Marxism was not as direct as Trotsky's witty remark suggested. His entrance into the company of Russia's radicals was by way of Populism, a peculiarly Russian form of socialism which based its revolutionary hopes on the country's suffering peasants. Only in his late teens, in 1888, did Lenin begin a serious study of Marx's *Capital*. He became increasingly attracted to the German philospher's scientific formulation of communist theory. Avidly devouring this detailed work as well as the *The Communist Manifesto*, Lenin now wholeheartedly embraced the principles espoused by Marx. Convinced that urban workers rather than peasants would bring about revolutionary change, and convinced of the inevitability of communist society, he studied and interpreted Marxism and converted many who would later work with him in transforming Russian society. This determined apostle of Marx even mastered German and translated into Russian several works important to the Marxist cause, such as *The Communist Manifesto*, completed in 1890. In the early 1890s he also made contact with clandestine Marxist groups operating in St. Petersburg.

Lenin's mother hoped to remove her son from the dangers of revolutionary activity by interesting him in the peaceful lifestyle at the family's small country estate on the Volga river. During these days in the country Lenin enjoyed picnics, berry-picking expeditions, and daily swims in the placid Volga. This lifelong rapport with nature and outdoor sports accounted for Lenin's hardy physique and gave him treasured moments of peace and satisfaction throughout his turbulent life. His mother's hopes were not to be realized, however. For Lenin these country days also offered an opportunity to deepen his probe of Marx's thought, to observe the peasant agricultural problem firsthand, and to dream of revolutionary action.

In addition to his devotion to Marxism, Lenin had continued his private study of law. Nearly three years after his expulsion from the University of Kazan, Lenin received permission from the Education Ministry to present himself for the bar examinations upon completion of his private study of law, primarily due to the persistent pleas of his mother. He studied intensely for little more than a year and then took the law exams. He scored highest on the examinations, which covered a four-year university curriculum. This feat revealed the intelligence, tenacity, and diligence of this remarkable man.

In 1892 his mother's incessant pleas opened another door when Lenin was granted the requisite Certificate of Loyalty and Good Character that made him eligible to practice law. For a short time the man who would later overturn Russian society worked within the system as a respectable citizen of the state. He practiced law for nearly two years in provincial Samara, representing peasants accused of petty theft, and defending them for the most part unsuccessfully!

Lenin would not remain within the good graces of the Tsar's government for long. Moving to St. Petersburg in 1893, he became an active Marxist. He established contact with factory workers, and he attacked Populist doctrinaires who refused to acknowledge the increasing revolutionary potential of the proletariat. Populists, according to Lenin, also misunderstood the peasantry. While the Populists dismissed the peasants' desire to own individual plots of land as naivete, Lenin believed the peasants were displaying a deep rooted petit-bourgeois mentality. Events would later prove Lenin's interpretation to be the correct one. Peasants would confiscate landlords' estates, not to create common ownership under socialism but to obtain land for planting their own grain and to establish family ownership.

Following a severe bout with pneumonia in 1895 and after European travel where he met emigré Russian Marxists, Lenin was arrested by the Tsar's police for his subversive activities in organizing the St. Petersburg League of Struggle for the Liberation of the Working Class. The prison conditions he experienced provided an ironic contrast to the harsh, inhumane treatment political prisoners would one day be accorded in the Soviet gulag. Tsarist prisons were often accommodating to men like Lenin. Contacts with friends and relatives were permitted, and books, both licit and illicit, were not too difficult to acquire. After a year's imprisonment in 1896, Lenin served the remainder of his term, until 1900, in exile in western Siberia. The pseudonym "Lenin"—man from Lena—was adopted during this time, inspired by the Lena River which flowed a few hundred miles from the revolutionary's place of exile. The authorities also allowed fellow conspirator and fiancée, Nadzheda Krupskaya, to join Lenin as his bride.

The years of Siberian exile were peaceful and productive ones for the young couple. They enjoyed free use of a good library, and Lenin completed his first major theoretical work, *The Development of Capitalism in Russia*. One of more than thirty works Lenin wrote during his Siberian exile, this important book described statistically the rise of capitalism in Russia. The study showed that Russia was taking giant strides toward capitalism and that the peasants were not aspiring to socialism but to the private ownership of land. In analyzing the development of capitalism in Russia, Lenin was emulating his master, Marx, who had also examined capitalism in one country. The focus of Marx's study was England; for Lenin, it was Russia. And in pointing to the petit-bourgeois mentality of peasants, which placed great value on land ownership, Lenin, like Marx, was declaring that the peasantry was reactionary; it wanted to go backward toward land ownership, instead of forward toward socialism and the communal ownership of property. But Marx, in *The Communist Manifesto* and *Capital*, had dismissed summarily the problem of the peasantry, whereas Lenin in *The Development of Capitalism in Russia* was presenting the problem of the peasantry as a major issue.

His term in exile completed, Lenin returned to St. Petersburg where after a few confrontations with police for probation violations, he and his wife received permission to go abroad. Between 1900 and 1917 Lenin and Krupskaya spent lonely but fruitful years in and out of European exile. In Paris, Lenin organized a workers' school and delivered more than fifty lectures to the laborers; in Cracow, where the couple lived for two years prior to the beginning of World War I, Lenin took advantage of Austrian Poland's proximity to Russia and directed the revolutionary activities of his comrades. Financially, these years in exile were lean ones for the two emigrés. Lenin's mother regularly supplied them with funds from her small estate, but it was not enough. Lenin supplemented his allowance by giving language lessons and by doing translations.

When World War I broke out, the couple returned to neutral Switzerland. Lenin believed the war would strengthen bourgeois hegemony at the expense of the proletariat, and so he denounced it. The only way to exploit the war for the Marxist cause would be to transform it from an imperialist war into a civil war. He hoped civil war would lead to the seizure of government by workers throughout the world. But Lenin apparently did not expect to see this workers' victory in the near future. As late as January 1917, less than three months before his triumphant return to Russia after the fall of Tsar Nicholas II, the exiled Marxist told a Zurich audience that "we of the older generation may not live to see the decisive battles of this coming revolution."[3]

The Long Road to Revolution

PEASANTS AND WORKERS EKE OUT AN EXISTENCE IN LATE NINETEENTH-CENTURY RUSSIA

What was this colossus known as the Russian Empire that Lenin and other revolutionaries dreamed of destroying? As it entered the twentieth century, Russia could aptly be described as a nation in turmoil.

The recently emancipated peasants who constituted more than 90 percent of the population experienced little satisfaction with their so-called freedom. In 1861 Tsar Alexander II, after his Empire had suffered a crushing defeat at the hands of the more industrially advanced western European countries, namely, England and France, in the Crimean War (1854–56), had a blunt message for his serf-owning nobility. Russia, he claimed, had lost the war because of its backwardness. Illiterate serfs, increasingly rebellious at their lot in life, and in poor physical condition, made indifferent soldiers and had been a major contributing factor in the defeat. If the Empire was not to suffer further humiliation at the hands of European powers, radical change was necessary. And if a

---

Russian Society—From Tsar to Peasant

Tsar: King or Emperor

nobleman: Member of aristocracy, a hereditary class possessing immense social and political power. The nobility was usually wealthy, owned most of the land, and lived off the work of serfs.

intelligentsia: Estranged group of intellectuals advocating sweeping reforms in Russia's political and social system.

serf: Person bound to the soil and required to render service to the landowner. If the land was sold or exchanged according to a seldom-obeyed law, the serf was transferred with it from one owner to the other.

peasant: Free person tilling the soil as a small landowner or hired laborer (farm worker). Most peasants were poor and uneducated.

---

rebellion of these suffering serfs was to be avoided, emancipation from their near-slave status had to be carried out quickly.

Forced by the Tsar, committees of noblemen worked out the resultant Emancipation of 1861. Ironically, the emancipated serfs became the chief victims of the edict intended to free them. Instead of personal freedom and the piece of land they coveted, the former serfs remained confined by law to their native village and were free to till only the piece of land allotted to them by the village elders. They also shouldered the heavy tax levied on the village in the form of redemption payments. In assuming this heavy tax burden, payable over a forty-nine year period, the serfs were reimbursing the government for the land given to them in the Emanicpation agreements. (In 1905 the government would recognize the serious financial plight of the peasants by cancelling these burdensome payments.) In effect the liberated serfs were paying a ransom for the freedom grudgingly granted them after centuries of oppression. The Emancipation of 1861 had eliminated serfdom in name only.

While turmoil was brewing in the Russian countryside, discontent was growing in the cities. In the latter half of the nineteenth century, Russian industrial output was increasing by leaps and bounds. In the year of Emancipation, for example, the Empire produced approximately 352,100 tons of pig iron; by 1900 this figure had increased to 3,233,900 tons. In 1861 its coal output was

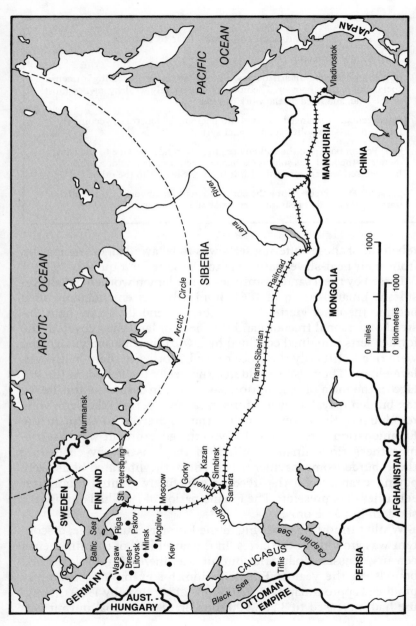

The Russian Empire: 1914

just 424,325 tons; by 1900 it had jumped to 17,809,125 tons. Similar advances occurred in cotton and other textile industries. As an augur of the future, Russia's railroad trackage extended during this period from 1400 to 33,000 miles. The completed Trans-Siberian Railroad extended from Moscow to Vladivostok, linking for the first time in the country's history its European and Siberian regions. Despite significant industrial development, the Empire at the turn of the century could claim only a relatively small working class, with some 800,000 railroad workers, 1 million miners, and 3 million factory workers in a country of 125 million people. Like the western European proletariat, which had endured cruel exploitation during the early years of the Industrial Revolution, the small, weak Russian working class suffered from pitiable wages and inhuman working and living conditions.

As Russia entered the twentieth century, the peasants experienced for the most part deep dissatisfaction with their lot and would need only the right pretext to erupt into violent revolutionary action. The burgeoning proletariat, laboring in despair in factories and mines throughout the Empire, also existed in a similarly explosive atmosphere.

MARXISM COMES TO RUSSIA

In the history of the Russian revolutionary tradition, the beginning of the twentieth century marked one hundred years of restless questioning of Russia's past. Prince Alexander Radishchev's *Journey From St. Petersburg to Moscow*, written at the close of the eighteenth century, had fired the first salvo against the institution of serfdom. Radishchev suffered disgrace and exile by order of Empress Catherine for his courageous portrayal of the terrible plight of the serfs. In the nineteenth century, poets like Pushkin and Lermontov as well as novelists such as Gogol, Dostoevsky, Turgenev, and Tolstoy continued to illuminate the appalling social conditions of the masses and the corruption of the governing bureaucracy. The beauty and power of their works prompted admiring Westerners to describe the era as a golden age of literature which at that time was unequalled throughout the world.

This same century also signalled the appearance of writers who, eschewing the form of novel and poem, wrote bluntly about the nation's problems and called for bold solutions. For some of the critics, collectively called the *intelligentsia*, the answer to Russia's ills could be found in Western political institutions modelled after the British constitutional monarchy or even the American democratic system. Other intellectuals saw salvation in a Slavic consciousness untainted by foreign ideas and ways of life. These Slavophiles believed that the country's spiritual foundation was the Orthodox Church and that a return to Slavic virtues and faith would overcome the contamination caused by Western ideas about industry, government, and morals. Slavophiles and Westernizers, in their separate ways, advocated political reform and an amelioration of peasant hardships.

Among the groups that looked to the West for inspiration was a radical wing known as the Populists. For this group, socialism as interpreted by western European thinkers offered a system of societal relationships well suited to Russia's peasant population. For centuries peasant communes and producers' cooperatives had existed in scattered parts of the Empire. This indigenous peasant socialism appealed to nineteenth-century Populists as a workable foundation on which to build a just social order. Unfortunately for their cause, these proponents of Russian socialism could agree on nothing beyond the goal of socialism itself. Quarrels and pettiness effectively defused their revolutionary potential. Out of this seemingly hopeless situation, however, a new revolutionary movement was developing, one that would eventually overrun the old Russian state.

The year 1883 witnessed both the death of Karl Marx and the birth of the Liberation of Labor, Russia's first Marxist organization. Although the group was founded in Geneva, Switzerland, it was nonetheless a truly Russian Marxist organization. Its brilliant founder, G. V. Plekhanov, had supported the Russian Populist movement during his student days. He had also edited *Black Partition*, a Populist newspaper. When the newspaper folded and when peasants failed to respond to Populist agitation, Plekhanov retreated to Switzerland. As Populists in Russia turned to terrorist activities, the young intellectual broke with them and began his lifelong espousal of Marxism. Lenin claimed that it was Plekhanov who reared the first group of Russian Marxists.

With the assistance of Vera Zasulich, Paul Axelrod, and others, Plekhanov worked zealously to spread Marx's gospel and to at-

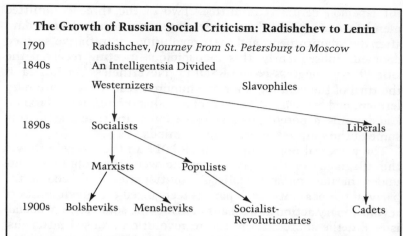

The Growth of Russian Social Criticism: Radishchev to Lenin

1790   Radishchev, *Journey From St. Petersburg to Moscow*

1840s   An Intelligentsia Divided

Westernizers   Slavophiles

1890s   Socialists   Liberals

Marxists   Populists

1900s   Bolsheviks   Mensheviks   Socialist-   Cadets
                                                Revolutionaries

Note: Early in the 1900s the Marxists, Populists, and Liberals evolved from elitist groups into national political parties and adopted new names. Respectively they became the Russian Social Democratic Labor Party (RSDLP), the Socialist-Revolutionary Party, and the Constitutional Democratic Party (Cadets). In 1903 the RSDLP split into two groups, the Bolsheviks and Mensheviks.

tract new followers to the cause. By the mid–1890s the ideas of Marx had reached captivated audiences throughout most of Russia's rapidly expanding cities. In St. Petersburg, for example, Lenin and six other Marxists united some twenty different Marxist groups in a new organization called the St. Petersburg League of Struggle for the Liberation of the Working Class. For his involvement in this group, Lenin spent time in prison and in Siberian exile.

With Marxist and other workers' groups sprouting throughout Russia's cities, the need for a central organization to coordinate their work became acute. In 1898 nine Marxist and socialist leaders secretly assembled in the little town of Minsk in western Russia (now Belorussia) to create a national laborers' party. They patterned their organization on the growing European social democratic movement and named the new group the Russian Social Democratic Labor Party (RSDLP). The Party's deliberations lasted only three days and produced little of substance other than an agreement on the need for a nationwide party and the election of a three-person central committee. Two of the three committee members and eight of the nine delegates were arrested a few days after the adjournment, and their revolutionary initiative seemed doomed. Subsequently, this inauspicious meeting received the title "First Congress of the RSDLP." Nevertheless, in Russia at the turn of the century, after one hundred years of revolutionary ferment and less than fifty years of socialist orientation, Marxism had become a potentially explosive force, its tenets attracting some of the Empire's most brilliant minds.

The principal opponents of the RSDLP in the struggle to win the allegiance of the Russian people were the Populists who, under the new name Socialist-Revolutionaries, had become the party of the peasants. Both parties recognized the inevitability of revolutionary action as a means of achieving some form of social-ism. But the source of the future revolution aroused bitter dis-agreement between the two groups. In the estimation of the Socialist-Revolutionary Party, Russia was an agricultural state and its population overwhelmingly peasant; socialism would tri-umph with this class only. To Social Democrats, this view was a serious misreading of the situation. Marx had clearly outlined the unalterable path to communist society. The nation's only hope for revolutionary change lay with the oppressed city workers.

A third group that would exercise political influence in the first decades of the twentieth century was the Constitutional Demo-cratic Party, or Cadets. Members of this party agreed that the au-tocracy must go, but they disagreed on the form of government that should replace it. Some favored a constitutional monarchy similar to England's while others simply wanted to modify the powers of the Tsar. On one point all Cadets agreed: revolution was not the method for bringing about social and political reform; they preferred peaceful, legislative means.

As the government's police agents monitored the activities of these political groups, the small Russian Social Democratic Labor Party was beginning to struggle with an identity problem. The di-visive issues involved standards for membership and a debate over the role of Marxism in Russia's immediate future. In particular, Lenin began to question the tenets of his mentor Plekhanov. Be-cause of the worldwide recognition accorded to Lenin, the impor-tance of Plekhanov to the birth and growth of Russian Marxism often goes unnoted. Yet Plekhanov, not Lenin, was the dominant figure early in the movement's history, his intellectual superiority unchallenged by Lenin or Trotsky. Both were content to sit at his feet as eager pupils. Only at the turn of the century did quarrels gradually break up a close relationship. For the young Lenin, revolution was the goal, and it must be attained as quickly as possible. He insisted on the organization of an elite professional leadership to direct proletarian revolutionary action. Plekhanov and his followers, on the other hand, saw the need for further industrial development in Russia before the country would be ripe for revolution. They also believed that Lenin's idea of elite leadership was an abhorrent dictatorial tendency. The differences between the two leaders became irreconcilable when Lenin expounded his views in more detail in the seminal work *What Is To Be Done?*

LENIN ASKS "WHAT IS TO BE DONE?"

Any attempt to trace Russian revolutionary theory from thought to action must take special note of the pamphlet *What Is To Be Done?*, completed by Lenin early in 1902. The title had a special and indeed double significance for Lenin. Generations of Russian radicals had become familiar with the provocative question, which first appeared in the 1860s as the title of a novel written by an uncompromising critic of Russian society, Nikolai Chernyshevsky. The book was peopled with larger-than-life heroes and heroines who willingly sacrificed personal happiness to further the cause of Russian socialism. It could hardly be considered a masterpiece, however. The characters lacked human qualities, and the writing style was dull, moralistic, and pedantic. Nevertheless, Chernyshevsky's story had an enormous effect on many of Russia's radicals, among them Lenin and his older brother Alexander. Commenting on the book's impact Lenin said:

> It captivated my brother, and it captivated me. It *made me over completely*. . . . It's something that charges you up for the whole of your life.[4]

But Lenin's *What Is To Be Done?* had an influence which far outweighed that of Chernyshevsky's on Russian socialism. Though written in haste and replete with names which today are forgotten, Lenin's pamphlet put forward in unmistakable detail the plans necessary for revolutionary takeover in Russia. In essence the brief work made four points.

First, Lenin reminded his fellow Marxists that "without revolutionary theory there can be no revolutionary movement."[5] He was distraught at the growing tendency of some members of the newly formed RSDLP to struggle for petty reforms like wage increases instead of working for outright revolution.

Second, he argued that revolutionary consciousness must be brought to workers from outside their ranks. Left to themselves, workers would not develop a Social Democratic or revolutionary consciousness.

> The history of all countries shows that the working class, exclusively by its own effort, is able to develop only trade-union consciousness, i.e., the conviction that it is necessary to combine in unions, fight the employers, and strive to compel the government to pass necessary labor legislation, etc.[6]

Marx's contention that the proletariat would spontaneously develop revolutionary consciousness through the gradual maturation of the capitalist system had been erroneous. As capitalism had matured, the proletariat had combined in unions and had bargained successfully for higher wages and improved working conditions. A more comfortable material life had quelled any thoughts of revolution among the proletariat.

Third, an organization of professional revolutionaries must assume responsibility for bringing revolutionary consciousness to workers. Lenin outlined in this part of his pamphlet the characteristics he hoped the RSDLP would possess. It must be an organization of stable leaders with a highly selective membership that was professionally engaged in revolutionary activity. In addition, meetings of the Party had to proceed with the strictest secrecy in order to avoid detection by the Tsar's omnipresent police.

Fourth, the medium in which to discuss revolutionary theory, with which to initiate political work among workers, and with which to train strong local revolutionary organizations was the newspaper. In *What Is To Be Done?* Lenin expounded on the absolute necessity of a strong revolutionary press. He maintained that without a newspaper, a political movement was inconceivable. He reminded his readers of the importance the regime had given to the power of the radical press by citing the vast sums of money the police had spent in the nineteenth century trying to silence it. He urged his readers to take courage from the evidence that growing numbers of workers were reading and learning from the underground press "how to live and how to die." The all-Russian language newspapers *Iskra* (The Spark), *Vpered* (Forward) and *Pravda* (Truth), served as important and effective vehicles for spreading Marxist revolutionary theory throughout the country.

Lenin's *What Is To Be Done?* altered some of Marx's major ideas. By insisting that revolutionary consciousness be brought to workers from outside their ranks, Lenin deviated from Marx's proposition that economic forces would play the leading role in the creation of the proletariat's revolutionary consciousness. But Marx was also averse to fixed formulas. He had maintained that the practical application of his philosophy would depend "everywhere and at all times on the historical conditions for the time. . . ."[7] To Lenin, late nineteenth-century history had shown convincingly that workers, when surrounded by a capitalist milieu, did not develop revolutionary consciousness. This consciousness must be brought to them by a political organization whose only *raison d'être* was revolution, whose membership was limited, and whose proceedings were secret, all characteristics requisite for survival in a repressive autocratic state. Marx and Engels, in *The Communist Manifesto*, had advocated the educational role of the party. Lenin simply built on this concept to make it work in a country fundamentally different from western European nations.

It is beyond the scope of our study to determine whether or not Marx would have approved of Lenin's ideas as expressed in *What Is To Be Done?* But there is no denying that Lenin recognized the importance of revolution in Marx's philosophy. He also realized that economic forces alone were inadequate to move history at times, and so he promoted the power of politics as a way of nudging history forward. The emphasis on political activism for changing history has become known as "political voluntarism." Henceforward, politics would replace economics in Lenin's analysis as the driving force of revolutionary change in Russia, and political voluntarism would supplant economic determinism as the principal agent of change. This contribution to Marxism was so fundamental that the ideology later became known as Marxism-Leninism.

Armed with the ideas expounded in *What Is To Be Done?*, Lenin gathered with fifty-six other delegates in Brussels on July 30, 1903 for the Second Congress of the RSDLP. Though intellectuals were in the majority, workers also were present in the group that had worked nearly two and a half years to convene the Congress. But from the opening gavel, the Congress became a shouting match over the program and structure of the Party, despite the efforts of venerable chairman G. V. Plekhanov. The noisy arguments so disturbed neighbors that on orders of the Belgian government the delegates left Brussels for London and continued their boisterous debates there.

Lenin's conduct during the London assembly left no doubt as to the importance he attached to the question of Party structure. He worked frantically to win support for the creation of the truly effective organization he had outlined in his pamphlet. Scarcely eating or sleeping, he drove himself to persuade the organization's delegates to his point of view. The efforts proved fruitless. When the Congress voted on the issue of Party structure, Lenin and his faction lost. When the question of membership for *Iskra*'s editorial board came to the floor, however, Lenin and his followers won by a narrow two-vote margin. Though his group remained a minority among Congress delegates, Lenin, on the basis of this single victory, promptly termed his faction "men of the majority," or Bolsheviks. His opposition, led by Trotsky and others, was labeled "men of the minority," Mensheviks. The Party that had been created with such promise in 1898 was moving rapidly toward an irreparable split.

When the Congress drew to a close on August 23, 1903, Lenin's popularity was in serious decline. He had lost the support of Plekhanov and Trotsky. Short of funds and discouraged by the strength of the opposition, Lenin resigned from the editorial board of *Iskra* and, at the wise urging of his wife Krupskaya, embarked for Switzerland to seek a respite from the political strife.

1905 REVOLUTION LEADS TO THE DUMA PERIOD

As Lenin settled into Swiss exile, an imperialist Russia confronted a rival imperialist power, Japan, over a weak and exploited Chinese Empire. Russia hoped that quick military victories and territorial annexations in China would glorify the homeland and appease the growing unrest in the countryside. Japan, always anxious to expand its empire, saw in the feeble Manchu Empire an easy opportunity for territorial gain. No Russian guns would stay its ambitions. The two imperialist giants battled one another for a year and a half (February 1904–September 1905) over the right to dismember China. Surprisingly, Japan emerged as an easy victor. Modernized and well prepared, it had moved quickly and effectively against the poorly organized and ill-equipped Russian armed forces.*

Early in 1905, after suffering nearly a year of shattering defeats at the hands of the Japanese, Russia was convulsed in a revolution that Lenin would later describe as a dress rehearsal for the revolutions of 1917. The opening scene was played out in St. Petersburg on the wide, snowswept square fronting the Winter Palace. There, on a Sunday afternoon in January, the troops of Tsar Nicholas II massacred hundreds of the city's workers and their families, people whose only crime was a peaceful, humble appeal for better working conditions. The identity of the person who issued the command to fire on the innocent people that "Bloody Sunday" is unknown. But history does record the significance of the occasion since it marked the first act in a yearlong revolutionary drama. The cast of characters included government officials who dealt clumsily with an unending series of strikes, and a Tsar who stubbornly resisted his alarmed ministers' advice until it was too late.

Before Nicholas reluctantly granted constitutional rights to the people, the nation and in particular the cities of St. Petersburg and Moscow suffered several bloody upheavals. The government reckoned with a sailors' rebellion on the battleship *Potemkin* as well as alarming nationalist uprisings in its Polish and Baltic provinces and in the Caucasus. Peasants engaged in looting and burning rampages, frequently attacking Jews in some of Russia's most bestial pogroms. In September, when the Russo-Japanese War drew to

---

*George F. Kennan, veteran American expert on Soviet affairs, has noted that in recent Russian history, defeat in war has led inevitably to drastic internal change. After a catastrophic defeat at the hands of western European Powers in the Crimean War, Russia emancipated its serfs. As Japan was defeating Russian forces, the Empire exploded from within and once again the Tsar was forced to implement major internal change in an effort to appease his angry people.

a close, the returning, war-weary soldiers and sailors joined in the turmoil in the cities.

These violent outbursts served merely as a prelude to the revolutionary action initiated by a Moscow printers' strike. Culminating in a general strike that has no parallel in any nation's history, the Moscow strike originated from an almost petty demand. The pay for printers' piecework did not include the typesetting of punctuation marks. When the shop workers' request for pay for setting these symbols fell on deaf ears, they walked off the job. Responding quickly, workers and professionals of every sort—small shopkeepers, transportation employees, lawyers, doctors, journalists—united in a mighty protest against the government. The Moscow strike quickly spread to St. Petersburg, where even the famed *corps de ballet* abandoned its slippers and took to the streets. Other segments of the city's population rapidly followed suit and, as in Moscow, the strike won the complete support of the work force.

Meanwhile, Lenin's and Plekhanov's factions were spending their days in endless, unproductive denunciations of the other's theoretical position. Trotsky, unable now to accept either the Bolshevik or Menshevik position, fled the humdrum life of Swiss exile and returned secretly to the Russia from which he had escaped earlier after imprisonment for illegal activities. But his return to Russia in the spring of 1905 aroused the attention of the police, and he fled across the Finnish border to safety, a time-honored practice of generations of outlawed Russians. From his vantage point just twenty miles from St. Petersburg, he waited for the opportune moment to reenter Russia.

As the general strike paralyzed the nation, Lenin eagerly seized upon any news of the tumult in Russia. He busily researched in the Geneva library to learn the techniques of street fighting. As a result, Bolsheviks within Russia received instructions from him on the use of weapons like rifles, revolvers, bombs, knives, brass knuckles, and clubs.

Lenin and Krupskaya returned to Russia in November, but it was Leon Trotsky who claimed center stage during these tense months. In October, as the general strike was tightening its grip on the country, he secretly returned from Finland to St. Petersburg and helped organize a general strike committee to lead the workers. Throughout the city, factory workers elected delegates to represent them on a workers' council or *soviet*, a body which directed strike activities. Soon a similar soviet appeared in Moscow. The soviets published daily bulletins stating the strikers' policies, distributed guns and ammunition, organized demonstrations, and set up a system of guards. The St. Petersburg Soviet, led by Trotsky (after the arrest of its first chairman), was basically a Menshevik organization, while in Moscow, Bolshevik workers dominated the council. To their discredit, the Moscow Bolsheviks put their particular goals before those of a successful strike and attempted initially to boycott the St. Petersburg Soviet.

Amidst the revolutionary turbulence, one of St. Petersburg's outstanding citizens, Paul Miliukov, united a group of the city's liberals into a new political organization, the Constitutional Democratic Party (Cadets). Miliukov and his Party gave full support to the strike.

Tsar Nicholas II, unable to quell the national upheaval, grudgingly conceded defeat and through a proclamation called the October Manifesto offered his long-suffering subjects a modicum of political freedom. His concessions were niggardly, but they represented a minute step toward constitutional democracy. The Tsar authorized the creation of a *Duma* or elected parliament, and its legislative powers were shared with an Imperial Council. But half of the Council's members were Nicholas's personal appointees, and control of the armed forces, foreign policy, and treasury remained within his hands as well.

The mere prospect of an elected parliament, however, helped end the strike and restore government control over the country. The Cadets, satisfied with the Manifesto, withdrew their support of the strike. This withdrawal, coupled with the widespread weariness of the people, left the soviets without the foundation they needed to continue their agitation. Lenin's desperate efforts to arouse interest in the soviets' call for a second general strike failed dismally. The hope of the revolutionaries waned and Russia settled into an uneasy peace. By 1906 Lenin had fled the country. After brief jail terms, members of the St. Petersburg Soviet were released; chairman Trotsky, however, received a sentence of indefinite exile to Siberia.

In retrospect, though the revolution of 1905 collapsed, the record of the revolutionaries was not without merit. For one thing, the Bolsheviks and Mensheviks, the Socialist-Revolutionaries, and, to a lesser degree the Cadets, had put their differences temporarily behind them, and under Trotsky's leadership had cooperated in the pursuit of a common goal. There was an important presage of the future, too. The idea of a workers' council, born amidst strike-ridden St. Petersburg and Moscow in 1905, would rise again in 1917 to direct and influence deeply the course of events.

Russia's promising but brief Duma Period (1906–1917) augured better things for a country that for centuries had been disastrously behind its western European neighbors. Perhaps a satisfactory answer to the old question "What is to be done?" was now within reach. True, Nicholas had stubbornly refused to work with the first two elected Dumas because their liberal views were abhorrent to a ruler firmly convinced that his autocratic powers were God-given. But after dismissing the second Duma and illegally changing election laws, Nicholas succeeded in getting the kind of conservative Duma with which he could cooperate. Thus during the years of the third (1907–12) and fourth Dumas (1912–17), the Russian ship of state sailed through relatively smooth waters, propelled by a balanced budget, an expanding railway system, and increased trade with the West. Industrial output rose and mining productivity, always an important industrial indicator, made enormous advances. International Harvester and Singer, the sewing machine manufacturer, even established offices in Russia. Prosperity also appeared on the dinner table in the form of bumper crops produced during several years of favorable weather.

Despite Nicholas's foot dragging, the Russian Empire, under the able leadership of chief minister Peter Stolypin, benefited from practical and innovative agrarian reform which, had World War I not intervened, might have changed the course of Russian history. In anticipation of opposition to his reform plan, the blunt and outspoken Stolypin built several temporary gallows for display throughout the Empire. Nicknamed "Stolypin's Neckties," they were for the immediate execution, without trial, of all terrorists who resisted the program. Stolypin's famous agrarian program offered peasants the opportunity to own their land. With the help of the Peasant Land Bank system, over 6 million peasant families became property owners. To an extent, all of Russia benefited because the new landowners took a fresh interest in cultivating the soil wisely. With nature's cooperation, grain yields increased and the future looked promising.

In 1911, while attending the opera in Kiev, Stolypin was assassinated by an agent of the secret police. At the time of his death, the minister was increasingly at odds with the Tsar and Duma conservatives. There were signs, too, of the revival of revolutionary unrest among the working class. In the early 1900s new labor laws had improved somewhat the plight of Russian workers. Now, after a lull of several years, a new wave of strikes broke out. The death of beloved novelist Leo Tolstoy in 1910 had provided St. Petersburg University students the opportunity for major street demonstrations, the first such demonstrations since 1905. But it was the famous Lena River goldminers' strike in 1912 that inaugurated a series of violent labor disputes throughout the Empire. The goldminers, subject to the harsh wilderness of Siberia, demanded an improvement in their terrible living conditions. When the request prompted no action, they went on strike. Consequently, the military intervened. During a confrontation with five thousand miners, the troops fired on the throng and killed some two hundred unarmed workers. A. A. Makharov, Stolypin's successor, failed to realize that the country would no longer tolerate the government's neglect and abuse of the workers. His comment on the Lena River massacre was inane: "so it was and so it would continue to be."[8] The Duma surprised him by calling for an investigation of the tragedy, and the ensuing report found fault with the mining company's management. The Duma's strong denunciation of the appalling conditions at the mine, however, did not assuage the anger of Russian workers. The slaughter on the Lena awakened the resentment which had lain dormant since the chaotic months of 1905.

During this same period, the Rasputin scandals surfaced. The lecherous, illiterate peasant wanderer, possessor of seemingly hypnotic powers, had for years been a favored intimate of the royal family. Tsarevich Alexis, the adored only son and heir to the Romanov throne, suffered from the "disease of princes," hemophilia. Grigory Rasputin's reputation as a holy man with exceptional healing powers had brought him to the attention of the distraught parents, who were willing to consider any means of helping Alexis. Through hypnotism or simply through his means of inspiring faith in his ability to cure, Rasputin repeatedly restored the child to health. With each successful ministration, Rasputin ingratiated himself more deeply and personally with the Romanovs, and especially with the Tsaritsa Alexandra. By 1912 even the most loyal Duma members voiced alarm at the increasing influence that this peasant charlatan was exercising over the Tsaritsa and, indirectly, over the Tsar himself. As conditions deteriorated within the Empire, the public's knowledge of Rasputin's influence over the royal family did much to exacerbate the alienation between the Tsar and his people. To those astute enough to recognize the nation's precarious situation, these events seemed to seal the doom of the Empire.

WORLD WAR I LEADS TO THE MARCH REVOLUTION* AND RULE BY PROVISIONAL GOVERNMENT AND THE PETROGRAD SOVIET

Historians have long disputed the significance of World War I as the major factor in the demise of the Russian Empire. Some scholars reason that without Russia's unfortunate and unprepared participation in the war the country might have survived Nicholas's ineptitude. Russia did have serious labor problems, but so had other nations involved in the transition from an agricultural to an industrial economy. The country was also experiencing increasing problems with national minorities within its boundaries, and Lenin could rightly repeat the phrase that the Empire was a "prison of nationalities."[9] But in an era of rampant nationalism, Russia was not alone in dealing with a problem that was not necessarily unsolvable.

To other scholars, the Duma Period, despite its promise for changes, offered too little to cope successfully with the persistent problems of Russian society. The country was in a state of decay. The most visible manifestation of this decay was Nicholas Ro-

---

*Some history books refer to this revolution as the February Revolution since, according to the old style Julian calendar, which was thirteen days behind, the revolution occurred in late February. The Gregorian or Western calendar was adopted by the Soviet government in 1918. To be consistent we are listing dates according to the Western calendar.

manov, a Tsar unfit for the leadership of a nation in crisis. With Russia's disastrous entrance into World War I in 1914, the decay spread rapidly and eventually destroyed the Empire.

Russia's participation in World War I can be recorded briefly. The nation entered the war on the side of the Allied Powers, France and England. Opposing them were the Central Powers, comprised of the German, Austrian, and Ottoman Empires. Russia's peasant soldiers fought valiantly but suffered enormous losses. In 1916 Nicholas dismissed the head of Russia's armed forces and took personal command of the troops, leaving domestic affairs to Alexandra. Under Rasputin's baneful influence, the Tsarina dismissed competent ministers and officials and replaced them with Rasputin's corrupt, inefficient sycophants.

The end of the Romanov Empire came unexpectedly, almost quietly, in a series of events known as the March Revolution. While the Tsar was encamped with his troops at Mogilev in March 1917, his subjects in Petrograd,* war-weary and frustrated by the necessity of having to queue up to buy bread and fuel in the bone-chilling cold of a Russian winter, began citywide demonstrations. The refusal of the troops to quell the disturbances marked the beginning of the end. The Duma was unable to respond to the situation and wired news of the unrest to the Tsar. But the startling news prompted no action from Nicholas. Turmoil quickly spread, and finally a Duma committee, formally attired complete with top hats, travelled to Pskov where Nicholas had been detained by the army. There, on March 15, 1917, at the respectful request of his ministers, Nicholas signed papers of abdication renouncing the throne in favor of his brother, Grand Duke Michael, who subsequently declined to serve. No Romanov would again succeed to the throne. Nicholas and his family were arrested shortly thereafter and presumably executed by the Bolsheviks in July 1918. A dynasty had collapsed, and new forces were emerging in the country's cities.

With the Tsar's abdication, leading members of the Duma formed a Provisional Government under the leadership of Prince Georgi Lvov. The Government assumed the name "Provisional"

*After the beginning of the war, St. Petersburg was renamed Petrograd, then after January 1924 Leningrad.

since it awaited the election of a Constituent Assembly. The new
ruling body included only one socialist, Alexander Kerensky. But
the socialists, Marxist and non-Marxist alike, were busy organizing workers with an energy and spirit reminiscent of the revolutionary days of 1905. As the tumult in the capital city spread and
grew more violent, the Petrograd Soviet of Workers' and Soldiers'
Deputies rose like a phoenix from the ashes of the earlier soviets
to represent and to guide the proletariat through the March Revolution. This Soviet, an unwieldy, Menshevik-dominated body of
fifteen hundred, held daily meetings in the same Winter Palace
that had become headquarters for the Provisional Government.
Approval from the Soviet was necessary before the Provisional
Government could put into effect any of its acts or orders; without this approval, no one obeyed the government's dictates. As a
result, for the eight months between March and November, a
dual, quarrelsome, and ineffective government ruled the Empire.

LENIN AND TROTSKY RETURN FROM EXILE

The existence of two governing bodies in the Petrograd Winter
Palace notwithstanding, the March Revolution was virtually
leaderless. Soon, however, two leaders would return from exile to
their homeland, ready to seize the opportunity unexpectedly
given them.

When Lenin first received word in Switzerland of the abdication of Nicholas, he responded skeptically. He attributed the
Tsar's fall to the result of a capitalist struggle, with power merely
transferred to the bourgeoisie now represented by the members of
the Provisional Government. Not until late March did he respond
to the Bolsheviks' urgent pleas for guidance amidst the chaos that
was rapidly enveloping the nation's capital. He determined to reenter Russia as quickly as possible, but enemy German territory
lay between him and the Russian border.

Lenin concocted several ludicrous schemes with which he
hoped to evade passport officials and cross into Russia. One plot
called for him and Grigory Zinoviev, neither of whom knew Swedish, to use passports identifying them as two Swedish deaf-mutes.
Krupskaya quickly put an end to this unrealistic scheme as she
reminded Lenin that he might fall asleep, see Mensheviks in his

dreams, and "start swearing and shouting, 'Scoundrels, scoundrels!' and give the whole plot away."[10] Finally, after prolonged negotiations with the German government, Lenin, Krupskaya, and thirty other emigré revolutionaries were put in a sealed railway car and shipped through Germany, Sweden, and Finland. The German government agreed to assist Lenin and his group because it hoped the emigré revolutionaries would weaken, if not destroy, the Provisional Government, which was committed to supporting the Allied cause against Germany. Ignoring the vigorous protests of some of his colleagues, who viewed his negotiations with the Germans as collaboration with a hated reactionary wartime enemy, Lenin cooperated fully. He was desperate to return to Petrograd and help usher the revolution forward from its bourgeois stage to a socialist one.

After the sealed car reached the Finnish-Russian border, the emigrés sledded a short distance over snow to the little Russian train awaiting them. Arriving at Petrograd's Finland Station in the late evening of April 16, Lenin and his group were greeted by uproarious crowds, military bands blaring the "Marseillaise," Bolshevik signs and slogans, and a mounted searchlight spraying its beams across faces in the crowd as soldiers stood at attention and presented arms. The people received Lenin as a returning hero despite his eleven-year absence. In his first address to the cheering crowds, Lenin spoke of the March Revolution as paving the way for an epoch of worldwide revolution. But he revealed the full extent of his views in a brief speech the next day before two Party meetings. The speech was published in *Pravda* on April 20, and it became known as the "April Theses." Lenin attempted to guide his Bolsheviks with major directives which called for an end to support for the imperialist war effort and for Russia's Provisional Government as well; he advocated the transfer of all power to the soviets, and the nationalization and redistribution of land; he insisted that the RSDLP modernize its program and rename itself the Communist Party; and finally he demanded that a new International be formed to replace the defunct Second International. The "April Theses" elicited the disapproval of nearly everyone in the RSDLP, Mensheviks and Bolsheviks alike. Contrary to Lenin's analysis, they argued that the bourgeois stage of economic development must expand fully before giving way to socialism, as

Marx had described. But the opposition crumbled within a few
months and most of Lenin's directives became Party policy, especially after Party members viewed with dismay the Provisional
Government's refusal to deal with the land question even as peasants were revolting against their landlords. Lenin's directive calling for the nationalization of land became attractive to both Party
members and peasants. The "April Theses" established Lenin as a
preeminent revolutionary leader, and his speech delivered the
first blow against the Provisional Government.

Besides Lenin, another leader of the first rank returned to Pet-
rograd after the March Revolution. In exile in New York City,
Leon Trotsky had been editing his radical Russian journal *Novy
Mir* (New World) and earning his living as a freelance journalist.
He had chosen to distance himself from both the Bolshevik and
Menshevik factions. But a few days after the Tsar's abdication,
Trotsky made plans to return to the country that had jailed and
exiled him for his participation in the unsuccessful revolution of
1905. With funds raised by New York friends, he embarked for
Russia on March 27, a full two weeks before Lenin's departure
from Swiss exile. British officials, however, detained him at Hali-
fax, Nova Scotia, for more than a month until the Provisional
Government requested his release and safe passage to Russia.

As Lenin and Trotsky plunged into the activities of the Petrograd Soviet, faith in the effectiveness of the Provisional Government was steadily eroding, due in large measure to its failure to
settle the agrarian question. The land issue was a crucial one for
many land-owning officials within the government and for millions of peasants who had always believed that the land was theirs
by virtue of centuries of unremitting toil. But the Provisional
Government continued to sit on its hands, and so Lenin's position
as defined in the "April Theses" attracted adherents within the
Party and among some socialist groups. He had proposed the nationalization of land, and this news excited illiterate peasants
who thought that nationalization meant that land would be taken
from landlords and put into peasant hands. By the end of May, a
majority of the representatives in the Petrograd Soviet was sympathetic to Lenin's views. And in early July, the Bolshevik Party in
Petrograd dramatically swelled its growing ranks when Trotsky
and 4,000 of his followers formally joined the Party and cast their

lot with Lenin. Trotsky also brought to the Bolsheviks his unsurpassed reputation as a revolutionary and tireless organizer. The Bolshevik Party now possessed an invincible team: Lenin, the charismatic leader and Trotsky, the brilliant organizer.

SUMMER 1917: THE JULY DAYS, LENIN'S *STATE AND REVOLUTION*, AND THE KORNILOV AFFAIR

July was significant for more than the growth of Bolshevik strength. There was a feeling among the people in Petrograd that the Bolsheviks would initiate some drastic action. Violence did occur, but it did not originate with the Bolsheviks. In early July, the Provisional Government's new Minister of War, Kerensky, announced a major offensive against the Austrian armies on the southwestern front. After a few initial victories, the Russian army met with fierce resistance after the Germans sent reinforcements. The Kerensky offensive was failing. On July 19 the Germans mounted a counteroffensive and the Russian army fled in a disorderly rout, suffering yet another crushing defeat and losing the last of its best troops.

A few days before the German counteroffensive, knowledge of Kerensky's unsuccessful offensive touched off an explosion in Petrograd known as the "July Days." Between July 16 and 19 more than four hundred people were killed or wounded. Soldiers and sailors fought bloody clashes, some defending the Provisional Government, others fighting for its destruction. Blaming the Bolsheviks for the insurrection, the Provisional Government published trumped-up evidence which called Lenin a German agent, and thus implying that the Bolsheviks had created the uprising on orders from the Germans. In defense of the Bolsheviks, Trotsky countered that the Party's role in the uprising was that of an unsuccessful peacemaker that had attempted to restrain the army's First Machine-Gun Regiment from taking to the streets at the beginning of the revolt. Most probably the Bolsheviks did disapprove of the uprising, but as events unfolded they reluctantly gave it their support. Only later did they deny participation in what had proven to be a poorly organized and ill-directed insurrection.

The July Days uprising was a disaster of major proportions for Lenin and the Party. As the Germans initiated their counteroffensive and the full extent of the failure of the Kerensky offensive became public knowledge, rumors bombarded the people of Petrograd. They believed the Provisional Government's claim that Lenin was a German spy and that Party members were betrayers of the Russian nation. Angry crowds smashed the presses of *Pravda,* and Lenin and his colleagues barely eluded the mobs that attacked the mansion where they were living. Because warrants had been issued for their arrest, Lenin, Zinoviev, and other Bolshevik leaders fled to a forest hideaway in the environs of Petrograd, then crossed the border into Finland. Throughout the city, arrest and imprisonment became the lot of all known Party members, Trotsky and Leo Kamenev (a leading Bolshevik) among them. Needless to say, Party membership plummeted because the population now equated Bolshevism with treason.

The seriousness of the situation for the Bolsheviks did not escape Lenin. In a note to Kamenev written in late July from his Finnish hideout, he asked that his comrade publish a manuscript that he had begun a year earlier in Switzerland if outraged countrymen should kill him. This essay, *The State and Revolution,* was Lenin's greatest contribution to Marxist political theory, but was never completed. During August and September, despite the embarrassing failure of the July Days and the threat to his own life, Lenin finished and polished the first six chapters, leaving unwritten the chapter on the revolutions of 1905 and 1917. Lenin, in this work on the Marxist theory of state, was providing a justification for a Bolshevik seizure of power that would be followed by a dictatorship of the proletariat.

Using extensive quotations from the works of Marx and Engels, Lenin generally reiterated their ideas on the state as an agency of repression but developed in more detail the concept of the dictatorship of the proletariat. Also, he emphasized more than Marx or Engels the violent, merciless, and protracted character of the dictatorship. After the proletariat had concentrated its forces of destruction against the bourgeois state, the workers would organize themselves into a dictatorship of the proletariat "to crush the resistance of the exploiters and to *lead* the enormous mass of the population . . . in the work of organizing a socialist economy."[12] In crushing the remaining recalcitrant capitalists, Lenin admitted that the dictatorship of the proletariat would inevitably commit "excesses on the part of *individual persons.*"[13] These excesses would be halted spontaneously by the people themselves in the same way "any crowd of civilized people, even in modern society, interferes to put a stop to a scuffle or to prevent a woman from being assaulted."[14] In any event, individual excesses would be a small price to pay if the dictatorship of the proletariat succeeded in annihilating its enemies, especially the bourgeoisie. Lenin believed that resistance to the dictatorship would never come from any quarter of society except the bourgeoisie.

After the proletariat had quashed the resistance of capitalists and the workers had begun to construct a socialist society, the dictatorship of the proletariat would not yet disappear. It would be needed to implement the goal of Marx's celebrated maxim: "From each according to his ability, to each according to his needs." The people would receive basic necessities according to their needs when they "had become so accustomed to observing the fundamental rules of social intercourse and when their labor had become so productive that they voluntarily worked *according to their ability.*"[15] Lenin further observed that no Marxist had ever promised a communist society in the near future; as for Marx and Engels, they had merely forecast its eventual arrival. A communist society could not be constructed with "the present productivity of labor and . . . *the present* ordinary run of people."[16] Lenin saw correctly that communist programs depended on a population that was community-oriented rather than self-centered. To achieve this goal, the dictatorship might be lengthy, but most assuredly it would be centralized, highly authoritative and, if need be, ruthless against its enemies.

While Lenin wrote *The State and Revolution* in his Finnish hideaway, Trotsky served a brief term in prison. The Party meanwhile lost its chief organ, *Pravda.* The future of the Bolsheviks after the July Days looked bleak and their return to respectability exceedingly doubtful.

The Provisional Government was also rapidly losing any credibility it still had among the people. In late July, Kerensky succeeded Prince Lvov as Premier and proceeded to frustrate and alienate the population due to his inability to govern a country rapidly sinking into chaos. He was unable to work successfully with liberal governmental groups and so he reluctantly sought support from the conservatives, who asserted themselves by passing laws restricting freedom of the press and assembly. The Kerensky government also indicted Lenin, in absentia, for treason.

In August the Bolsheviks, still in disgrace, slowly regrouped. Secretly they held a Party Congress in Petrograd where they elected the absent Lenin as honorary president. Lenin forwarded to them clear and specific instructions: gain control of the soviets and develop plans for an armed takeover of the Provisional Government.

The Bolsheviks involved themselves in the political scene once again, and the Petrograd workers, angry victims of a wartime economic crisis, came under the sway of Party propaganda which addressed their problems with the call: "Peace, bread, and freedom!" As mistrust and anger toward Kerensky deepened, hostility toward the Bolsheviks faded. But without the unforeseen boost obtained from the infamous Kornilov affair, it is improbable that the Party would have regained its former strength and restored its leader's prestige.

The July Days had aroused the worst fears of extreme right-wing factions, which had constantly campaigned for the Provisional Government's firm control over the army and for the elimination of socialists, especially Bolsheviks, from the political arena. These conservatives soon found a leader in General Lavr Kornilov, who had been recently appointed Commander-in-Chief of the Russian armies. Once described as a soldier with the heart of a lion and the brain of a lamb, this simple military man had risen to high command by dint of hard work and an exciting wartime escape from an Austrian prison camp. The latter feat had transformed him into a legendary figure in a nation with few military heroes. Kornilov's view of the Russian political situation was as simplistic as his guileless soldierly nature. He saw the Petrograd Soviet as the source of the government's problems. The Provisional Government, Russia's only legitimate authority, must be strengthened and the Soviet's influence weakened, destroyed if possible. In attempting to carry out this policy, General Kornilov unwittingly played an important role in hastening the fall of the Provisional Government and in strengthening the power of the Bolsheviks.

Using the German occupation of Riga, a city three hundred miles from the capital, as a flimsy excuse, Kornilov in early September ordered the Provisional Government and the Soviet to evacuate Petrograd, ostensibly in the interest of safety. When the Soviet balked at the order, he promptly called additional troops to assist him. Meanwhile, Kerensky received a message from a phony intermediary who pretended to relay orders from Kornilov. The note requested that Kerensky resign as Premier and transfer his power to Kornilov. Kerensky responded by ordering Kornilov's dismissal. The startled general, totally innocent of any machinations against Kerensky, not only refused to comply but publicly attacked the Provisional Government as a pro-German body and appealed to the people to support him in order to save the nation.

The Petrograd Soviet and the city's socialist bodies seized the moment. Organizing themselves as the Committee for Struggle Against Counterrevolution, they barricaded streets, dug trenches, strung barbed wire, and disrupted transportation and communication systems. Kornilov's forces, as they arrived in Petrograd, were stopped, isolated, and finally persuaded by the city's socialists to change allegiance. The troops' decision to desert Kornilov brought the farce to a quick and ignominious end. A few days later, the government arrested the general and restored temporary calm to the capital.

During the Kornilov crisis, Kerensky had turned to the Bolsheviks for help, supplying them with arms and even releasing Trotsky and other Party members from prison. Kerensky attempted to reorganize his government now that the conservatives in it had lost favor due to the Kornilov fiasco. Lenin's Bolsheviks, meanwhile, drove for power. They obtained for the first time at least half the seats in the Petrograd Soviet, and by October Trotsky had become the Soviet's chairman. Kerensky was isolated. He had severed his ties with the discredited Right, and he was confronted by a Left increasingly dominated by Bolsheviks..

BOLSHEVIKS AND OTHER SOCIALISTS TOPPLE THE PROVISIONAL GOVERNMENT IN THE NAME OF THE PETROGRAD SOVIET

As Bolshevik strength increased, a serious difference of opinion divided its leaders. Although they agreed on the inevitability of revolution, they quarrelled over its timing and tactics. From Finnish exile, Lenin had urged that the leadership develop plans for an armed uprising. But Trotsky, Zinoviev, and Kamenev did not agree with Lenin's push for immediate action, despite his eloquent warning that "history will not forgive us if we do not assume power now."[17]

In the end Lenin prevailed. Secretly returning to Russia he appeared at the October 23 meeting of the Party's Central Committee. After a harrowing ten-hour debate, his plan for an immediate armed takeover won acceptance. Two of Lenin's oldest comrades, Kamenev and Zinoviev, were in such strong disagreement with the proposed plan that they published a newspaper article revealing the scheme and their opposition to it. The government questioned Trotsky about the plot, but he denied its existence. At the very same time, he was using the Soviet's Revolutionary Military Committee, formed originally to protect the capital, as a Bolshevik general staff for directing the armed uprising.

In spite of the Kamenev-Zinoviev article and the rumors floating about the city, the Provisional Government took no steps to defend itself. When it finally declared the Military Committee illegal and ordered the arrest of the Bolshevik leadership, it was too late. On the night of November 6–7, the world's first successful workers' revolution took place, a revolution later known around the globe as the "October Revolution" (or November Revolution according to the Gregorian calendar). The Bolsheviks, aided by other socialists and mutinous military units, had little trouble seizing control of Petrograd. At 10 A.M. on November 7, the Military Committee formally announced the overthrow of the Provisional Government and promised to abolish landed proprietorship, to place workers in control of production, and to create a soviet government. The takeover had occurred so quietly and with so little opposition that on this same morning the city's population went about its business, unaware that the Military Committee controlled the State Bank, bridges, main thoroughfares, railway stations, and the central post office. During the night of November 7, the Military Committee occupied the Winter Palace, the seat of the Provisional Government, and jailed most of the ministers. (Kerensky had fled earlier in the day in a car provided by the United States embassy.) The Military Committee in a mere twenty-four hours commanded virtually all key points in the capital.

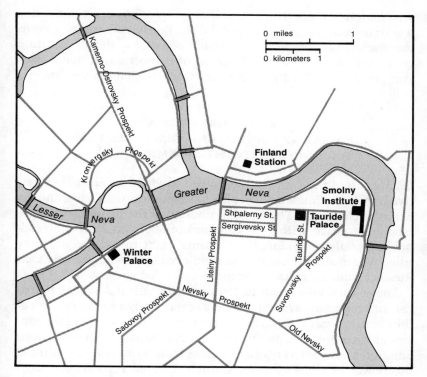

Petrograd

At the Smolny Institute, the revolution's headquarters, Lenin on the day of victory addressed the assembled delegates to the Second All-Russian Congress of Soviets and roused them with the statement, "We shall now proceed to construct the socialist order!"[18] American journalist John Reed, a Marxist and devoted admirer of Lenin, was present to record the historic statement. He described Lenin "gripping the edge of the reading stand, letting his little winking eyes travel over the crowd . . . apparently oblivious to the long-rolling ovation which lasted several minutes."[19]

Despite the energetic support of the Petrograd Soviet, Lenin and his Bolsheviks were well aware that the fate of the revolution hung by a slender, fragile thread. The Party, claiming a quarter of a million members, had to win over and establish a government

for a nation of more than 125 million people. The order of the day
was to consolidate power. Little did the Bolsheviks realize that in
the years ahead, the new state would contend with a devastating
civil war, an international blockade of its port cities, and a two-
year famine which would leave city workers near starvation.

LENIN WORKS FOR A
SOCIALIST SOCIETY AND DISSOLVES THE
CONSTITUENT ASSEMBLY

Leadership of the country was in the hands of an elected executive board, the Council of People's Commissars, which had chosen
Lenin as chairman. The Council undertook the major tasks of establishing peace with Germany and of abolishing private land-
holding while upholding the peasants' right to use the soil they
tilled. Lenin and his commissars believed somewhat naively that
Russia could immediately become a socialist society.

The council also began to dismantle the cultural, social, political, and economic systems of old Russia, though in many parts of
the country local Bolshevik soviets were still fighting to gain control of their areas. A plethora of decrees poured forth daily from
Smolny. These edicts abolished class structures, severely limited
the power of the Orthodox Church, created revolutionary tri-
bunals to replace the old legal system, established women's equality, and brought the Russian calendar in line with that of the
Western world. While the population coped with these and other
drastic changes, the food situation worsened and another sub-zero
Russian winter intensified every problem of the nascent state.

The Bolsheviks faced another problem with the pending elections for the long-promised Constituent Assembly. Since the 1870s
nearly every Russian reformer had cried out for the creation of a
freely elected Russian parliament. The Bolsheviks had been no
exception. Trotsky's slogan, "Long live the Constituent Assembly," was one of the rallying cries of the November Revolution.
But Lenin, ever the realist, feared that a nationwide election would
spell disaster for the Bolsheviks, whose supporters were primarily
the relatively small groups of urban workers. Accordingly, he attempted to delay the election, but without success. In late Novem-

ber, three weeks after the Petrograd coup d'état, more than 41 million people voted in Russia's first—and last—multiparty election. Lenin's fears were confirmed. The Socialist-Revolutionaries polled more than 17 million votes or 58 percent of the total, while the Bolsheviks claimed a modest 9.8 million or 24 percent of the vote. Trailing far behind the Socialist-Revolutionaries and Bolsheviks were the Cadets and Mensheviks with 2 and 1.4 million votes respectively. Russian voters had made their will known clearly: agrarian socialism was to take precedence over the Marxist, urban model of social change.

Before the first meeting of the Constituent Assembly, Lenin proceeded to augment Bolshevik power by muting the voices of those speaking against the dictatorship of the proletariat, which meant in essence Bolshevik leadership. He imposed a ban on newspapers that published anti-Bolshevik articles or that spread confusion by distorting facts. He established the all-Russian Commission for Suppression of Counterrevolution, which became the Party's secret police. It was known popularly as the Cheka, and was the forerunner of today's KGB. In a December 26 article in *Pravda,* Lenin served notice that preserving the Constituent Assembly was not his top priority: "Naturally, the interests of this revolution stand higher than the formal rights of the Constituent Assembly."[20] He could not place a ban on the Assembly or dispatch the Cheka to arrest its delegates since the entire country was anxiously awaiting the opening meeting. On January 18, 1918, the first and only day of the Constituent Assembly's existence, Lenin and the Bolshevik delegation arrived four hours late and sullenly took their seats among the tense and unruly gathering of the 707 elected delegates. Outside the Tauride Palace, where the meeting was taking place, crowds cheered in support of the Assembly. When the crowds became too vociferous, belligerent Red Guards (the Bolshevik militia) fired loaded rifles over the heads of the people.

Inside the palace the delegates sang the "Internationale" and elected the Socialist-Revolutionary Victor Chernov as chairman. Then pandemonium became the order of the day. The Bolsheviks interrupted every speaker with whistles, jeers, and catcalls while Lenin pretended to be asleep. Despite these disruptive tactics, Assembly delegates rejected the Bolshevik dictatorship, declared

Russia a republic, approved an armistice with Germany, called for an international socialist conference, and voted for land reform. As Chernov read the text of the newly passed land decree, a Bolshevik sailor informed the chairman that the Red Guards were tired and that the meeting must adjourn. While Chernov protested, the lights were turned off. Bolshevik soldiers and sailors forced the meeting to end and the delegates hurried off into the bitter January night. Many of them feared for their safety. The Constituent Assembly never reconvened; it was dissolved on orders from Lenin. The age-old question "What is to be done?" had now been decided by the guns of soldiers and sailors. The principle of a government *for* the people but not *by* the people has continued to be the foundation on which the Communist Party has built a superstate.

It is sometimes difficult to understand how the Bolsheviks assumed control of the government in the weeks following the November Revolution. After all, the coup d'état was executed in the name of the Petrograd Soviet, which contained numerous socialist elements besides the Bolsheviks, primarily, the Mensheviks

---

Political Power in Russia Since 1900

1900	Autocracy is headed by Tsar Nicholas II, the last emperor of the 300-year-old Romanov dynasty.
1905	Revolution leads to the October Manifesto. The monarchy continues with an Imperial Council sharing legislative powers with an elected parliament or Duma. In reality, most of Nicholas's powers remain absolute.
1917	The March Revolution leads to the abdication of Tsar Nicholas II. A dual interim government exists comprised of leading members of the Duma in the Provisional Government, and elected deputies from workers and soldiers in the Petrograd Soviet. Both bodies claim as their major goal the creation of a Constituent Assembly.
1917	The November Revolution places the Bolsheviks in power in the name of the Petrograd Soviet. A Bolshevik dictatorship exists under the guise of a soviet government. The election of the Constituent Assembly takes place.
1918	Lenin dissolves the Constituent Assembly and solidifies the power of the Bolsheviks.

and Socialist-Revolutionaries. How did the Bolsheviks gain the upper hand? At the time of the revolution, the Bolsheviks commanded more than half the seats in the Petrograd Soviet chaired by Trotsky. Additionally, the Bolsheviks functioned as an organized unit under the leadership of Lenin and the Party Central Committee. It is true that socialists other than Bolsheviks participated in the November Revolution, just as it is true that socialists other than Bolsheviks assumed a few leadership positions in the Council of People's Commissars. But at all times, Lenin and his Party controlled the decisions of the new government. This stranglehold was never more evident than when the Red Guards shut down the Constituent Assembly and sent its delegates home. Lenin's government had no need for socialists other than Bolsheviks.

CIVIL WAR AND WAR COMMUNISM ARE FOLLOWED BY THE TENTH PARTY CONGRESS AND NEW ECONOMIC PROGRAM

The tasks confronting Lenin and the Bolsheviks seemed insurmountable in the early months of 1918. Even as the Party struggled to extricate the nation from World War I, anti-Bolshevik forces within the country were rapidly coalescing, and the war-weary population was sucked into the vortex of a vicious civil war. The new state's Red Army, an offshoot of the Red Guards, faced the combined but disunited forces of those who opposed Bolshevism. The "Whites," as they were called, agreed only on their rejection of Bolshevism. They were a mixture of monarchists, Mensheviks, Socialist-Revolutionaries, and other dissatisfied elements. They fought against the unified Bolsheviks under the brilliant direction of Trotsky, the Soviet state's War Commissar.

The Bolsheviks also had to contend with an international blockade of Russian ports by the Allies, including the United States, as a reprisal for Russia's separate peace with the Central Powers. The Bolsheviks had withdrawn Russian troops from the war in March 1918 by signing the Treaty of Brest-Litovsk with Germany. This treaty stripped from Russia 1.3 million square miles of its richest and most productive land. (Russia renounced the terms of the treaty after Germany surrendered to the Allies.) The inter-

---

Russia: Bolshevik or Communist?

The Bolshevik Party emerged after the November Revolution as the main socialist group in power throughout Russia. The Party was officially renamed "Communist" in March 1918 to distinguish itself from the RSDLP and the Mensheviks. The nation today is called "communist" because its leaders are members of the Communist Party, *not* because the country has attained communism.

Russia is also characterized as "Marxist" since its leaders are self-proclaimed followers of Marx, "socialist" since the state owns the major services and means of production, and since the society is in the transitional stage before communism, and "Soviet" since the Bolsheviks led the November Revolution on behalf of the Petrograd Soviet.

---

national blockade, the loss of productive areas, and the intense civil war drained the country's already anemic economy. More important, these developments threatened the very existence of the young state.

Thus in the spring and summer of 1918, a desperate government responded with extreme economic measures termed War Communism. The government proclaimed that the radical measures represented the first steps toward the creation of a true socialist state which, under Communist Party leadership, would move confidently toward the final goal, a communist society. In reality, the measures turned the country into a huge military camp with every sector of the population falling under direct government rule. Production and distribution were thoroughly centralized. In the cities, the Bolsheviks nationalized major industries without compensation to bourgeois owners and placed them under the direction of the Supreme Economic Council. In the countryside, grain surpluses were requisitioned from the peasantry. Local Party leaders organized the poorest of the peasants to fight the *kulaks* or wealthy peasants if the latter refused to cooperate with government demands for food surplus. To make matters worse, these Committees of the Village Poor often received assistance from imported city laborers, who frequently brutalized villagers in their zeal to seize available surplus.

The resistance of kulaks and other peasants to these committees and to the requisition of grain surplus was fierce. Many villagers armed themselves against the marauding committees, often torturing and murdering government officials assigned to collect the grain. In another form of defiance, peasants deliberately cut production, growing only enough food for the needs of their immediate families. In some areas the resultant decline in productivity plummeted to 20 percent of previous levels. Russia would pay a horrifying price for this form of resistance when, in 1920, the country would begin an agonizing two-year famine.

In order to appreciate the peasants' resentment at War Communism and to understand Lenin's subsequent cancellation of these measures in 1921, we must remember the villagers' preoccupation with the land question. For centuries peasants had yearned for their own land. The Emancipation of 1861 had represented a giant step toward fulfillment of that ancient dream, but redemption payments, poor quality soil, and other restrictive factors had effectively turned that dream into a nightmare of continued poverty under a repressive regime. During the summer of 1917, as the influence of the Provisional Government waned, peasants had begun expropriating large estates spontaneously. In June and July alone, the number of estates seized by peasants rose from 577 to 1,122. After the November Revolution, when Lenin officially abolished private land ownership and assured peasants free use of the land they tilled, he was simply acknowledging a fait accompli. To peasants, Lenin's idea of state-controlled land ownership in the name of the people was meaningless. They looked upon the land and the food from that land as their own. When the dictates of War Communism forced peasants to the bitter realization that the government was claiming ownership of the surplus produced on the land, their anger knew no bounds.

In the long run, though the Red Army triumphed in the Civil War, the draconian measures of War Communism succeeded in estranging the masses from the communist government. Peasants and workers alike bitterly resented the policies of nationalization, centralization, and requisition, and they vented their anger in uprisings that no amount of police terror could suppress. But the most dangerous revolt occurred in March 1921 at the naval base on Kronstadt, an island fortress originally built by Peter the Great to protect his capital city of St. Petersburg. Formerly very loyal adherents, the Kronstadt sailors now angrily denounced the

Communist Party and its policies. Sons of peasants and workers, the Kronstadt sailors shared the country's disillusionment with the communists' indifference to the soviets. Electing their own Provisional Revolutionary Committee, they proclaimed their defiance of the government with the slogan, "Soviets without Communists!" Red Army units immediately moved in, executed thousands, and crushed the revolt. The crisis passed but Lenin and his government continued to face serious challenges. The signs of discontent were everywhere present.

Lenin acted decisively at the Tenth Party Congress, which was in progress during the Kronstadt revolt. He stifled the rising voices of opposition within his own Party. Stating that "the opposition's time has run out and that the lid's on it,"[21] he succeeded in outlawing all dissension within the membership. Any criticism of Party decisions was now termed "factionalism" and was punishable by expulsion from the ranks. A subsequent purge reduced Party membership by two hundred thousand (or roughly a third), and the new secret police organization, the GPU, replaced the Cheka and was charged with the power to arrest disobedient Party members. Besides curtailing freedom of criticism and factional groupings within the Party, Lenin outlawed non-communist political organizations like the Socialist-Revolutionary Party and the Menshevik Party. Thus by 1921, the Russian people heard but one voice and knew but one master, and that was the Communist Party.

After dealing with political opposition, Lenin addressed during the Tenth Party Congress the discontent in the countryside and in the cities. He proposed a series of economic changes, which later became known as the New Economic Program (NEP). He could silence the sailors at Kronstadt and political opponents within and without, but he could not muzzle the peasants and workers, nor did he want to do so. Lenin was particularly concerned about the peasantry since he realized that without its support, the Communist Party would have no chance of success: "We have to understand that with the peasant economy in the grip of a crisis, we can survive only by appealing to the peasants to help town and countryside."[22] NEP would receive peasant support, although some socialist objectives would be sacrificed in the process.

The new policies promptly ended War Communism, especially

the despised requisition of food surplus. It was replaced with a tax in kind set at a fixed percentage. In other words, peasants gave to the government a fixed proportion—rather than the entirety—of the surplus they produced. This fixed percentage encouraged them to increase their share of the surplus, which they could then sell, barter, or do with as they wished. Further concessions permitted peasants to lease land and to hire labor. NEP basically returned to peasants the right to control the products of their labor. NEP's limited economic freedom also extended to merchants. Though the state retained ownership and management of major enterprises such as banks and railroads, merchants were free once again to manage their shops, to hire labor, and to carry on trade with other merchants. Under NEP factory workers were permitted to create trade unions and possessed the right to strike!

The Western world immediately concluded that the young state was abandoning socialist programs for the greener fields of capitalism. True, Lenin had reinstated individual direction and incentive in production, but he had not restored by and large the right to own private property or the means of production. The state, in the name of the people, still retained legal ownership of the land, although peasants were able to regard land holdings as their own; the state continued to own and to control the major enterprises, which employed over 84 percent of the industrial workers. The creation of NEP did not mean that Lenin was embracing Western capitalism, but this "state capitalism," as it was called, did introduce capitalist incentives into the economy. As a consequence, NEP encouraged individualism more than the desired collectivist attitude.

THE COMINTERN STRIVES FOR WORLD REVOLUTION

As Russia started on the road to economic recovery, it did not neglect its foreign policy goals. Under the leadership of Foreign Affairs Commissar Georgi Chicherin, it quickly realized an important short-range goal: the resumption of trade relations and the establishment of diplomatic ties with the world community. The long-range goal of the state, the spread of socialist and communist ideology throughout the world, presented a more difficult problem. Marx had explained that the proletarian revolution must be international, and Lenin hoped the workers' revolution in Russia would ignite similar revolutions in other countries. The Soviet state desperately needed economic and military aid from other nations, especially highly industrialized ones. But other workers' revolutions did not occur despite the turmoil in several European nations at the close of World War I. As a consequence, in March 1919 Lenin invited communist parties throughout the world to join him in Moscow, now the capital of the Soviet state, to establish an international communist organization. The new organization took the name "Third International," since in the latter part of the nineteenth century two other international workingmen's organizations had been formed to unite the proletariat in the face of capitalism but had failed in their mission. Lenin's organization, also known as the Communist International (or Comintern for short) went far beyond this goal. When formally established in 1920, it boldly presented its aims:

> [The Comintern] strives to win over the majority of the working class and the broad strata of the property-less peasantry, fights for the establishment of the world dictatorship of the proletariat, for the establishment of a World Union of Socialist Soviet Republics, for the complete abolition of classes and for the achievement of socialism—the first stage of communist society.[23]

From its inception the Comintern, supposedly a broad international organization, fell under the dominance of the Soviet Communist Party. Lenin and later Stalin used the Comintern as a powerful vehicle for the spread of Russian influence and as a forceful adjunct to Soviet foreign policy. In 1943, when Stalin dissolved the Comintern as a goodwill gesture to the Allies during World War II, the fraternal bonds among communist parties throughout the world had become so strong that the need for an external organization appeared superfluous.

LENIN HAS SECOND THOUGHTS

Until his first stroke in 1922, Lenin was the unquestioned leader of the victorious communist regime. His extraordinary leadership had kept strong-willed and sometimes antipathetic personalities working cooperatively. But he had also aroused hatred among some Russian radicals. In August 1918 Lenin suffered near-fatal injuries when Dora Kaplan, a Socialist-Revolutionary, shot him in an assassination attempt. Though he came close to death, he soon recovered and plunged back into the demanding life of national leader. By 1921, however, Lenin's health showed signs of serious deterioration, and his nerves were in such a state that even a ringing telephone jarred him. On May 26, 1922, a frantic phone call from his sister Maria brought doctors, including physician brother Dmitri, to the leader's bedside at Gorki: the diagnosis, a stroke; the damage, partial paralysis of the body's right side. When his family tried to reassure and to comfort him with optimistic predictions about his recovery, he silenced them with the starkly honest statement: "No, this is the first bell."[24] Lenin's cool recognition that death was near did not break his fighting spirit. Summoning his will, he struggled to regain the strength needed to continue his work. But the next "bell," a second, more serious stroke in December, left him incapacitated and unable to work for more than a few minutes each day.

Lenin's meager writings in December 1922 and in the early months of 1923 reveal an anguished man, deeply troubled by the nature of the state he had helped create. In the workers' state so passionately described by Lenin in his earlier works, the people through elected councils would themselves serve as both legislators and executors of the nation's will. The soviets would be the instruments of a truly democratic government. But the new nation had not evolved as Lenin had envisioned. Party bureaucrats stood aloof from the proletariat and peasantry. The ruling *apparatchiki*, or the Party bureaucracy, had developed into a dictatorship *over* or, at best, *on behalf of* the masses. In his last dictated article, "Better Fewer, But Better," Lenin even proposed to have the papers and documents of the highest-ranking Party committee, the Politburo, examined by a lower committee responsible for accountability. The committee would supervise the Politburo to ensure that Party leaders remained responsive to the needs of the people instead of cultivating personal power. The article so horrified members of the Politburo that they thought of suppressing its publication in *Pravda*. "Better Fewer, But Better" eventually reached the pages of the Party newspaper, but it received no further consideration.

Another worry that greatly preoccupied the ailing Lenin was the

problem of choosing a successor. Lenin's "Testament" or will and
its paragraph-length codicil clearly revealed the leader's anxiety
that his successor might be the able but overconfident and overly-
bureaucratic Trotsky, or, worse yet in Lenin's view, an already
too-powerful Joseph Stalin, whose crude and dictatorial ways had
earned the leader's strong disapproval.

Lenin did not live to solve the two problems which had so
troubled him during the closing years of his life. On March 9,
1923, he suffered a third stroke. After this he taught himself to
write with his left hand and he became well enough to travel from
Gorki to his Moscow office. But on the morning of January 21,
1924, a high fever, followed by a loss of consciousness, marked the
end. At 6:30 in the evening, with Krupskaya keeping vigil at his
bedside, the country's premier revolutionary and founding father
quietly relinquished his hold on life, making way for a new leader
and a new generation of communists.

Summary and Comment

Karl Marx was tantalizingly ambivalent about the possibilities for
"the social regeneration" of Russia. In the closing years of his life,
Marx showed a very clear interest in the revolutionary potential
of the Russian Empire. He learned the Russian language and had
planned to focus on Russia in the second part of *Capital*. When
asked if agrarian Russia would have to evolve through full capitalist development, he declared that his schema applied only to
Western capitalist societies. He suggested that the primitive communal economy prevalent in Russia might take a non-capitalist
route to socialism. Just a year before his death, Marx wrote "If the
[Russian] revolution comes at an opportune moment, if it concen-
trates all its forces to ensure the free development of the rural
commune, this commune will soon develop into an element that
regenerates Russian society and guarantees superiority over countries enslaved by the capitalist regime."[25] Unlike many of his followers, Marx left open the possibility of a Russian socialist state
based not on the oppressed worker, but rather on the peasant
millions.

Lenin, however, was not overly concerned by the fact that Rus-

sia was an agrarian society in the initial stages of capitalist development. He declared that revolutions were made by revolutionaries, not by economic forces. Capitalism in the late nineteenth
century was not developing as Marx had predicted. Capitalists had
accommodated trade unions and had paid higher wages to mollify
workers who, as a result, were showing no signs of a revolutionary
consciousness. Thus Lenin introduced a fundamental change in
Marxist theory. He placed more importance on politics, rather
than economics, as the agent of change. Moreover, he developed
effective political strategies to lead a successful revolution and to
remain in power after the revolution.

What were Lenin's political strategies? He insisted on a highly
organized, selective, and secretive political party of full time professionals for leading the revolution. Once in power, the party
would rule as a dictatorship, nationalize and centralize the economy, and employ police terror to control the population.

On one point, however, Karl Marx was absolutely correct: the
good life described in his communist society required a strong industrial and agricultural base to support it. Every Soviet leader
after Lenin would devote his talent and energy to creating an economic base, which, according to Marx, should have been there in
the first place.

Further Reading

Lenin committed his life and writings to adapting Marxist thought
to an agrarian Russia and to realizing a proletarian revolution.
He succeeded so dramatically at each challenge that Marxism in
the Soviet Union became known after his death as Marxism-
Leninism. Today, students should read Lenin's works to learn
about his political thought and revolutionary tactics.

BY LENIN

Lenin, V. I. *Collected Works.* Moscow: Progress Publishers, 1964.
     The *Works* consists of forty-five volumes and a one-volume
     index.
Tucker, Robert C., ed. *The Lenin Anthology.* New York: W. W.

Norton, 1975. The anthology focuses on Lenin as revolutionary and includes more than sixty selections and letters.

The following works are fundamental for an understanding of Lenin's complex revolutionary theories.

Lenin, V. I. *What is to be Done?* New York: International Publishers, 1969. The 1902 work argues for the necessity of a party of professional revolutionaries for seizing power.

————. *Imperialism, the Highest Stage of Capitalism.* New York: International Publishers, 1939. The 1916 work supplies Marxism with a cogent theory of international economic relations as they functioned in the early decades of the twentieth century.

————. *The State and Revolution.* New York: International Publishers, 1943. The 1917 work, Lenin's most important contribution to Marxist political theory, defends the seizure of power and the establishment of a militant dictatorship.

————. *Left-Wing Communism, An Infantile Disorder.* New York: International Publishers, 1940. The 1920 pamphlet is Lenin's response to Machiavelli's *Prince*. It is a popular distillation of revolutionary strategy and tactics and can lay claim to the title "Lenin's masterpiece."

ON LENIN

Conquest, Robert. *V. I. Lenin.* New York: Viking, 1972. The author presents "a picture of Lenin, the political animal, in action and thought."

Fischer, Louis. *The Life of Lenin.* New York: Harper and Row, 1964. The author is an anti-communist liberal and an expert on the USSR. The book emphasizes Lenin's personal and political struggles in the creation of the first socialist state.

Payne, Robert. *The Life and Death of Lenin.* New York: Simon and Schuster, 1964. This thorough biography analyzes many of Lenin's writings and places them in a historical context.

ON THE LENIN ERA

Reed, John. *Ten Days That Shook the World*. New York: Random House, 1960. The book is the best account of the November Revolution, and perhaps the best account of any revolution.

Ulam, Adam B. *The Bolsheviks: The Intellectual and Political History of the Triumph of Communism in Russia*. New York: Collier, 1965. The book is a detailed and engrossing account of Lenin and his times beginning in 1825 with the Decembrists and concluding with Lenin's death in 1924. Ulam is one of the foremost scholars of Soviet history.

Wolfe, Bertram D. *Three Who Made a Revolution*. New York: Dial, 1964. This is the classic study of the lives of Lenin, Trotsky, and Stalin in the formative years of Russian Marxism.

REFERENCE TOOL

Carr, E. H. *The Bolshevik Revolution, 1917–1923*, 3 volumes. London: Macmillan, 1950–53. These volumes discuss the political institutions, the economics, and the international impact of the Soviet government under Lenin.

"We are going full steam ahead toward socialism through industrialization, leaving our century-old 'racial' background behind. We are becoming a land of metals, a land of automobiles, a land of tractors, and when we set the USSR on an automobile and the muzhik on a tractor, let the noble capitalists, so proud of their 'civilization,' attempt to catch up. We shall see then which countries can be labelled as backwards and which as advanced."

—Joseph Stalin

3

THE SECOND GENERATION OF COMMUNISTS: JOSEPH VISSARIONOVICH STALIN, SOCIAL ARCHITECT

Five days after Lenin's death, Joseph Stalin delivered a funeral oration that resembled a litany to a saint:

> Departing from us, Comrade Lenin enjoined us to guard and strengthen the dictatorship of the proletariat. We vow to you, Comrade Lenin, that we shall spare no effort to fulfill this behest, too, with honour![1]

Stalin never concealed his admiration, even hero-worship of the Party leader. Legend has it that Joseph Djugashvili chose the pseudonym Stalin—man of steel—because the name sounded like Lenin. Despite his attempts to emulate the charismatic leader, Stalin differed radically from Lenin in character, personality, and the role he would play in the construction of a socialist state. Lenin, the revolutionary, had brought the Bolsheviks to power in the November Revolution and had solidified their position by shutting down the Constituent Assembly. But six years later, Soviet society was far from socialist; indeed NEP had introduced capitalist incentives into the economy. Socialism, the intermediate stage between Marx's capitalist and communist societies, had yet to be integrated into the daily lives of the Soviet people. The awesome task of realizing socialism would fall to Joseph Stalin. His noted biographer, Isaac Deutscher, has described him with these words:

> . . . an ordinary, prosaic, fairly sober man . . . a man who established himself in the role of super-judge and super-architect. . . .[2]

79

Stalin: From Seminarian to Communist

Joseph Djugashvili was born to peasant parents on December 21, 1879, in Gori, Georgia. Joseph's father worked as a shoemaker and later as a laborer in a shoe factory. He took it for granted that his sole surviving child would earn a livelihood in the same way. However, the boy's devoted mother set much higher goals for this son around whom her entire world revolved. She knew he was intellectually gifted. He had distinguished himself as the outstanding student at the Orthodox school in Gori. Perhaps through the pursuit of a priestly vocation, Joseph would not only give glory to God and church but would also find an escape from the poverty that plagued their lives. She persisted in this dream despite the sullen resistance of her husband, who around 1890 died in a drunken brawl. In 1894 Joseph not only graduated at the top of his class, an honor not ordinarily claimed by students of his humble origin, but by virtue of excellent entrance examination scores he was accepted, expenses paid, at the Tiflis Orthodox Theological Seminary. Years later, Stalin would often repeat the remark his mother made to him in 1936, shortly before her death: "What a pity you never became a priest!"[3]

Ironically, the young man's seminary years in Tiflis were pivotal ones in his metamorphosis from a son of the church to a son of the revolution. In the harsh and authoritarian atmosphere of the seminary, Stalin and other young students learned much more than what was offered in the formal curriculum. Georgia, a restless Caucasus Mountains dependency that had been conquered by Tsar Alexander II in the 1860s, was obstreperous, deeply nationalistic, and non-Russian. The school was a hotbed of Georgian revolutionary fervor. Nationalistic students were in constant rebellion against the seminary faculty which, in its determination to Russify the students, forbade the young men to read or speak their native tongue, calling it a "language of dogs." In the long run, however, this oppressive measure benefited Stalin, since it compelled him to master the Russian language. When his Russian article "Marxism and the National Question" was published in 1913, it brought him to the attention of Lenin, who commented favorably on it.

Periodic searches of the students' rooms often resulted in the discovery of Populist and Marxist revolutionary literature. Expulsions were frequent, and for periods of time the seminary closed down to carry out systematic searches of the rooms. But the school's intrusive regime did not deter the students' pursuit of forbidden reading. One of Stalin's fellow seminarians later described the clandestine activity in this way:

> Secretly, during classes, services, and sermons, we read 'our' books. The Bible was open on the desk, but on our laps we held Darwin, Marx, Plekhanov or Lenin.[4]

In 1899 Stalin was expelled from the seminary because, according to school records, he had failed to appear for final examinations. His own version of the departure from school was more colorful. In answer to a Party questionnaire issued in 1931 he wrote: "Kicked out of an Orthodox theological seminary for [possessing] Marxist propaganda."[5]

Stalin never completed what would have been the equivalent of a high school education. But it would be a mistake to consider him an uneducated man. The seminary curriculum, despite the exclusion of much philosophy and social science, gave him a good grounding in mathematics, history, and literature. It also included Russian, Greek, and Latin, in addition to the theology and scripture courses typical of a religious school.

While still a student Stalin became a member and then leader of one of the many secret socialist and Marxist study circles that flourished under the noses of seminary authorities and the Tiflis police. He eventually joined the Social Democrats and assumed responsibility for direction of a workers' study circle in which he taught Marxist dogma. After his expulsion from school, Stalin worked as a clerk at the Tiflis Geophysical Observatory, and there he continued to teach Marxism to workers.

The ex-seminarian's first arrest occurred in 1902 in Batum, the town to which he had moved when intraparty clashes among Georgian Social Democrats had made him an unpopular figure in Tiflis. In Batum, where unrest among oil refinery workers was rampant, he found a fertile field in which to sow Marxist revolutionary ideas. His efforts resulted in his police arrest along with other Social Democrat activists. During this first imprisonment, the historic split between Bolsheviks and Mensheviks was occurring in London. Stalin remained loyal to Lenin, a man known to him only through books and articles. After serving an eighteen-month prison term, the "man of steel" spent an added three years in Siberian exile.

Sometime between 1906 and 1907 Stalin married a Georgian peasant girl who devoted herself entirely to his welfare, and who bore his child. She prayed that he would abandon the profession of revolutionary. Her death in 1910 left in Stalin's heart a void that was never filled. He once remarked to a friend: "She died and with her died my last warm feelings for people."[6]

Between 1902 and the November Revolution of 1917, Stalin spent more than half his time, about nine years total, in Tsarist prisons or in internal exile. When not jailed or exiled, he often helped organize bank robberies to secure money for Party activities. Satisfied to work behind the scenes, Stalin acquired a reputation for daring and dogged perseverance, as evidenced by his seven escapes from exile and by his determination to remain on Russian soil when other revolutionaries, Lenin and Trotsky included, sought refuge in foreign countries. The years from 1902 to 1917 must surely have hardened the character of the country's future social architect.

After the March Revolution, Stalin returned from Siberian exile before Lenin and Trotsky arrived, and he assumed a leadership role among the Bolsheviks. An orthodox Marxist, he viewed the Provisional Government as a bourgeois institution, and therefore to be tolerated until Russia could develop into a mature capitalist society. Only then could the Bolsheviks overthrow the government in the violent revolution predicted by Marx and Engels in *The Communist Manifesto.* At the time, he and other Party leaders at home urged cooperation between the Bolsheviks and the Provisional Government. But Lenin, upon his arrival in Russia, bitterly attacked the idea of cooperation. His call for an immediate seizure of power in the name of the proletariat appeared preposterous to most Bolsheviks. Stalin, though, had always admired the unmitigated militancy of Lenin's writings and quickly swung into line with Lenin's radical position. Consequently, Stalin grew steadily in stature among the Bolsheviks. In July, when Lenin was absent from Petrograd, Stalin delivered the Central Committee report at the Sixth Bolshevik Party Congress, an honor ordinarily reserved for Lenin.

Working in Lenin's shadow, Stalin collaborated closely with the Bolshevik leadership. Party and government assignments followed rapidly, and Stalin gathered to himself an increasing number of important offices. In 1917 alone he served as a member of the Bolshevik General Staff, the Central Committee Presidium, and the Politburo. After the November Revolution he added to his responsibilities the posts of Commissar of Nationalities and Commissar of the Army. By 1922 his responsibilities also included the directorship of the Workers' and Peasants' Inspectorate and membership on the government's organization bureau. Most important, he had also become the General Secretary of the Party, a position from which he would one day control both Party and nation. A man seemingly without charisma or leadership ability, Stalin had quietly and unobtrusively mastered the instruments of power with which he would drive his nation mercilessly into the twentieth century.

The Construction of Socialism and Destruction of Lenin's Party

USSR SOLVES SOME PROBLEMS AND CREATES NEW ONES

By the mid 1920s the Soviet state had seen the resolution of a number of problems which at one time or another had challenged Lenin and the Party. Power firmly rested now in the hands of the Communist Party. The Red Army by the end of 1920 had triumphed in the Civil War, which had claimed in combat, hunger, disease, and terror some nine million people. NEP was enabling the nation to recover from the devastation of three calamities: World War I, the Civil War, and War Communism. The program was also easing tensions between the Party and peasants, who were obligated to the state as taxpayers rather than as the victims of surplus requisitions. In the cities, workers were benefiting from improved housing, hospitals, and convalescent centers, though they were still enduring rationing and unemployment. On the international scene, the Soviet state had signed a diplomatic and economic treaty with the Weimar Republic of Germany in 1922 (the Rapallo Treaty), and two years later it had been recognized *de jure* by all the great powers except the United States, which did not resume formal diplomatic relations with the country until 1933. But in three other areas—the relations of the non-Russian nationalities to the new state, the power and composition of the Communist party, and the pursuit of the Marxist vision of a socialist society—the young nation had created new problems by virtually contradicting in theory and in practice the promises and aspirations voiced in the November Revolution.

Referring to the old Tsarist Empire as a "prison of nationalities," Lenin had consistently upheld the right of minorities to self-determination, including separation from the old Empire, though he sometimes limited the beneficiaries of this right to the proletarians of each nationality. On November 15, 1917, a week after the socialist takeover, Lenin and the Council of People's Commissars acted on behalf of the nationalities in the Russian Empire by issuing "The Declaration of the Rights of the Peoples of Russia." The document set forth four principles: 1) the equality and sovereignty of the peoples of Russia; 2) the right to self-determination, including separation; 3) the abolition of special privileges enjoyed by Great Russians and of restrictions on nationalities; 4) the free development of minorities.[7] Within a month of the Declaration, the Ukraine, Finland, Estonia, Latvia, and Lithuania declared their independence from Russia and a few months later Georgia, Armenia, and Azerbaijan followed. Alarmed at this wholesale abandonment of the socialist cause, Lenin dispatched Red Army units to these areas. Between 1918 and 1920 the Communist Party managed to create a few Soviet Socialist Republics on the periphery of Russia, while within the Russian Soviet Federated Socialist Republic (RSFSR) it recognized several autonomous republics and a number of autonomous regions. In 1922 the Republics formed a new political federation called the Union of Soviet Socialist Republics (USSR). But the promise of self-determination for minorities, when tested, was hollow rhetoric.

USSR Today

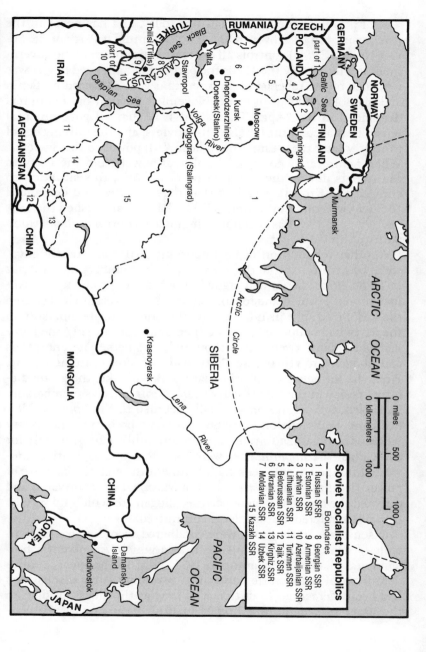

Soviet Socialist Republics

– – – Boundaries

1 Russian SFSR	8 Georgian SSR
2 Estonian SSR	9 Armenian SSR
3 Latvian SSR	10 Azerbaijanian SSR
4 Lithuanian SSR	11 Turkmen SSR
5 Belorussian SSR	12 Tajik SSR
6 Ukrainian SSR	13 Kirghiz SSR
7 Moldavian SSR	14 Uzbek SSR
	15 Kazakh SSR

0 miles 500 1000
0 kilometers 500 1000

Real power in the USSR does not today, and has never in the past, resided in the government. The Communist Party of the Soviet Union (CPSU) controls all aspects of the country; the government is a facade. By the 1920s the party's unchallenged power was evidence of the reversal of an important goal advanced by Lenin and his Bolsheviks prior to the November Revolution. Lenin had demanded in his "April Theses" in 1917 that all governmental power be placed in the hands of the soviets, and the rallying cry of the Party later that summer had been "All power to the Soviets." When Lenin failed to transfer political power from the Party to the soviets during the initial years of his rule, this situation so enraged the Kronstadt sailors that they revolted and demanded "Soviets without Communists." The Party that crushed the sailors' revolt in 1921 has still not relinquished control of the nation's political life.

Another repudiation of an important goal consistently advocated by Lenin involved the matter of Party membership. In *What Is To Be Done?* Lenin had argued for a Party of professional revolutionaries. His demand for limited Party membership had caused the RSDLP to split in 1903. But by the mid 1920s membership in the Party had ballooned to more than a million; in 1917 the Party had only about twenty-five thousand members. The enormous and sudden growth of the Party had two concomitant effects. First, the influence of the old guard of Bolsheviks, the group dictating policy in the Party's early years, diminished as membership increased. Second, power gradually accrued to the *apparatchiki*, full-time, high-echelon Party bureaucrats who became necessary to keep the organization functioning smoothly. Unfortunately for the CPSU, the *apparatchiki* were too often unimaginative, provincial-minded people seeking fulfillment through the exercise of power. To these people, the ideas of Marx, which motivated and directed the old guard, were petrified slogans to which lip service could be rendered, but not lives committed.

Discussions in the Party were conducted according to the principle of democratic centralism, an idea which underwent a fundamental change in meaning in 1921. Prior to that year, Lenin's definition of democratic centralism regarding Party discussions had been: "*Freedom to criticize, so long as this does not disturb the unity of a definite action.*"[8] In 1917 discussions, even contrary opinions held by Party members, contributed to the growth and dynamism of the Party. When Kamenev and Zinoviev voted against the November seizure of power by the Bolsheviks and other socialists, and worse yet, when they published Bolshevik plans for the armed takeover, neither one was liquidated or expelled from the Party. Democratic centralism was a vital principle with which to govern the Party. But after the ban on internal opposition at the Tenth Party Congress in 1921, democratic centralism came to mean that information, rather than discussion, streamed upward from the ranks while discipline flowed downward from the leadership.

By the mid-1920s, the Soviet Union was a far cry from Marx's vision of a socialist society. The dictatorship of the proletariat, Marx maintained, would direct production and distribution in a highly industrialized, classless, and international society. But the communists had developed a dictatorship on behalf of the proletariat in only one country, and a poor agrarian nation at that! To avoid economic collapse the Party had introduced NEP, which reinstated capitalism on a limited scale in the cities and almost without restriction in the countryside. Classes emerged more distinctly as the economy gained new life. Stalin would inherit a nation drifting away from Marx's vision of socialism, increasingly ruled by the fist of the party leader and his *apparatchiki* and troubled internally by dissatisfied nationalities.

STALIN RISES TO POWER AND
ANNOUNCES A NEW POLICY:
SOCIALISM IN ONE COUNTRY

In the early 1920s, Stalin seemed an unlikely candidate to succeed such a great revolutionary and charismatic leader as Lenin. The man from Georgia held important and powerful positions in the Party and government, but the Party veterans viewed him condescendingly as a mere bureaucrat, competent and efficient but no more. Some senior communists even regarded him as intellectually undistinguished and personally unambitious. Stalin probably would have faded as a Party luminary by the mid-1920s despite his positions of power had it not been for the death of Lenin.

In a brief memorandum dictated December 24–25, 1922, Lenin,

having already suffered two strokes, called the party's attention to
what he saw as a struggle for leadership between Trotsky and Stalin, a struggle that might ultimately divide the Party in two. In this
document, later known as his Testament, Lenin complimented
Trotsky as the most capable man on the Central Committee,
though he frowned upon the man's "excessive self-assurance
and . . . excessive preoccupation with the purely administrative
side of the work."[9] Lenin was even less kind to Stalin, questioning
whether the General Secretary, who had accumulated unlimited
authority, would "always be capable of using that authority with
sufficient caution."[10] About a week after the transcription of this
testament, the ailing Lenin learned that Stalin had treated Krupskaya discourteously. Flushed with anger, Lenin dictated a brief
codicil to his Testament: "Stalin is too rude and this defect . . .
becomes intolerable in a General Secretary. That is why I suggest
that the comrades think about a way of removing Stalin from that
post. . . ."[11] Lenin was not yet done with Stalin. From his sickbed
in early March 1923, he made plans for a major campaign to de-
mote Stalin. A third stroke, however, permanently debilitated the
party leader until his death ten months later. Had Lenin recovered
from the stroke and lived perhaps a year longer, Stalin probably
would have fallen. As it was, Stalin, through political machinations, succeeded in suppressing the publication of the Testament.
Since Lenin had also critically assessed Trotsky, Zinoviev, Kamenev, and other leading communists in the same document, no one
was eager to see the Testament in print.

Stalin retained his powerful Party positions, and in the latter
half of 1923, exactly as Lenin had predicted, struggled with Trotsky
for leadership of the CPSU. Stalin joined with longtime communists Zinoviev and Kamenev to form a *troika* that opposed Trotsky, his strongest rival for Party leader. The General Secretary
moved quickly to consolidate his power. He strengthened his support by enlarging the Central Committee and filling those positions with his own men. Stalin also seized every opportunity to
associate himself with the name of Lenin. In April he presented a
series of lectures entitled *The Foundations of Leninism* which he
dedicated to the Lenin Enrollment, the name given to the nearly
quarter of a million new Party members and followers of the
General Secretary. A new journal, *Bolshevik*, popularized Stalin's

interpretation of Leninism. By the middle of 1924, Stalin's position was becoming invulnerable as evidenced by his criticism of Zinoviev and Kamenev, whom he now charged with doctrinal mistakes.

Trotsky's undoing had already begun in May 1924 at the Thirteenth Party Congress, where he declared unwittingly "My Party right or wrong,"[12] and thereby publicly approved the changes initiated by the General Secretary since Lenin's death. After the Congress Trotsky's bright political star rapidly faded. Within a short time he was expelled from the Politburo, from the Central Committee and, in November 1927, from the Party itself. Finally, fourteen months later, the Party ordered his deportation from the Soviet Union. Lenin's one-time heir apparent settled eventually in Mexico where, in 1940, a Stalinist agent wielding a pick ax murdered him. Similar fates befell Zinoviev and Kamenev, who were executed during the 1936 purges.

The struggle for power was hidden behind policy debates. Since 1921 the party had discussed few controversial issues, but now Lenin's formula of democratic centralism announced at the Tenth Party Congress would, for a few years, be suspended. No aspect of domestic or foreign policy was sacrosanct from discussion. Was the pace of industrialization satisfactory? Should the kulaks be favored or taxed out of existence? Should NEP be continued? Was a bureaucracy overtaking the party? Should socialism be constructed in the Soviet Union alone or must the Soviet people await international revolution before socialism could be achieved? Of the many issues discussed during this period, the question of creating socialism in the USSR (as opposed to the establishment of international socialism) was most important since it affected other policy decisions as well.

As late as April 1924 some Politburo members doubted the viability of constructing socialism in one country. They advocated international socialism as realized through permanent revolution, a view first advanced summarily by Karl Marx and later expanded and defended by Trotsky. According to this principle, the proletarian revolution would occur successively in different countries rather than simultaneously. To Trotsky and other Party members, permanent revolution meant that the November Revolution of 1917 represented merely a stage in the permanent inter-

national struggle against capitalism; it was not an end in itself.
In *The Foundations of Leninism* Stalin agreed with Trotsky's
principle:

> For this [socialism in the USSR] the victory of the revolution in at
> least several countries is needed. Therefore, the development and
> support of revolution in other countries is an essential task of the
> victorious revolution.[13]

Eight months later, in December 1924, Stalin reversed his position. In "The October Revolution and the Tactics of the Russian
Communists" he maintained that "the victory of socialism in
one country, even if that country is less developed in the capitalist sense . . . is quite possible and probable."[14] The new doctrine had no historical or philosophical justification. The General
Secretary would often resort to this method when announcing
shifts in policy. With the support of leading communists such as
Nikolai Bukharin and Mikhail Tomsky, Stalin made "Socialism
in One Country" the new Party line, and he relegated international socialism to a position of secondary importance. But
once their cooperation was no longer needed, Bukharin and
Tomsky were demoted. Tomsky would later commit suicide and
Bukharin would be executed by the end of the 1930s.

Stalin believed that "Socialism in One Country" represented a
realistic goal for the USSR. The country had survived without
Western aid since the November Revolution. In addition, the Soviet Union possessed sufficient natural resources, manpower, and
skills to create by itself a strong socialist society, which in turn
would serve as a model and provide assistance to the proletariat in
other countries.

To construct socialism, the USSR had to first build a strong
economic base. Marx had warned that without a highly developed
industrial economy, the proletarian revolution would merely
spread poverty among workers. Since industrialization had only
recently arrived in Russia, the economic foundation for socialism
was lacking. It must be constructed, and Stalin and the Party
would see to the task.

"Socialism in One Country" was Stalin's most important contribution to Marxist-Leninist theory. Though the policy appeared

to be unprecedented, it advanced some ideas and tendencies already articulated by Lenin. Stalin's predecessor, for example, had stressed the role of political voluntarism in communist ideology. Under Stalin the Party would exercise a much greater role in transforming society than Lenin had ever imagined. Stalin commented on the importance of the political will in a 1926 publication, *Concerning Questions of Leninism:* ". . . in the proletarian revolution the seizure of power is only the *beginning,* and power is used as a lever for transforming the old economy and organizing the new one."[15] Political voluntarism, not Marx's economic determinism, would continue to explain why the social fabric of the USSR was changing.

Another justification for Stalin's new policy was the perception of capitalist encirclement and the attendant belief in the expansionist and bellicose character of capitalist societies. It was Lenin who had explained that capitalism in the era of imperialism survived periodic economic crises by finding new sources of raw materials and untapped markets; the expansion of capitalism into other countries often occurred violently through military intervention. Stalin accepted Lenin's theory of the inevitability of war between socialist and capitalist countries. He believed that the Soviet Union, encircled by Japan and the capitalist countries of western Europe, remained in constant danger. He articulated this fear in *Concerning Questions of Leninism:*

> It should not be forgotten that for the time being the revolution has been victorious in only one country. It should not be forgotten that as long as capitalist encirclement exists the danger of intervention, with all the consequences resulting from this danger, will also exist.[16]

Capitalist encirclement added urgency to the already important task of constructing socialism in the USSR. Socialism would not only represent a major step toward the attainment of communism, the penultimate goal of the historical process, but it would also strengthen the USSR in the event of capitalist aggression. Marx's notion of the dissolution of the state suddenly became inappropriate for the Soviet Union. During a period of capitalist encirclement, the state and its defensive agencies like the army and police required strengthening, not elimination. Logically, this one change in theory necessarily precipitated other fundamental ideological changes. How did Stalin defend these changes in communist ideology? In one of his last publications, *Marxism and Linguistics*, penned in 1950, he wrote in a manner reminiscent of Marx's "Theses on Feuerbach." Concerning changes in communist ideology, Stalin explained:

> [Marxism is not] a collection of dogmas which 'never' change, regardless of the changes in the condition of development of society. . . . Marxism as a science cannot stand still; it develops and perfects itself . . . consequently, its separate formulas and deductions cannot but change in the course of time, cannot but be replaced by new formulas and deductions corresponding to the new historical tasks. Marxism does not recognize any immutable deductions and formulas, applicable to all epochs and periods.[17]

No Marxist had described better than Stalin the flexibility of communist ideology!

STALIN ENGINEERS A SECOND REVOLUTION

The dogged determination of the Soviet people in the face of agonizing suffering and deprivation as they struggled to create a socialist society almost defies description. Stalin himself called the period from 1928 to 1932 "a revolution from above," and historians have labelled it "a war against the nation," "the second revolution," and "Russia's Iron Age." However characterized, the cataclysmic events set in motion by Stalin in the late 1920s cruelly and forcibly changed the lives of millions of people and thrust the Soviet Union into the forefront of international leadership.

As late as 1927 there was no indication that the USSR would embark on a program of rapid industrialization and collectivization. True, the Party in December 1926 had demanded that the country change its economic base from an agrarian to an industrial one. And true, a year later, the Party at its Fifteenth Congress had ordered the State Planning Commission to detail a five year plan for the economic development of the nation. But during this period Stalin was advocating gradualness and caution in domestic affairs, and he was still supportive of NEP.

When Lenin and the Party had introduced NEP in the early 1920s, they viewed the economic measures as no more than temporary since NEP marked a retreat from the goal of transforming the USSR into a powerful socialist nation. In 1921 the order of the day had been survival, and NEP in the early years had appeased the masses and stimulated growth in industry and agriculture. But after 1925 NEP had revealed serious shortcomings. Twenty-five million peasant households, most of them poorly equipped and using primitive methods of farming, could barely produce enough food to feed their families. Moreover, the eight hundred thousand kulaks, industrious peasants who were capable of producing a food surplus, deliberately curtailed production. They refused to produce grain beyond their immediate needs because the state had fixed prices too low for them to make a satisfactory profit. In 1927 poor weather conditions and the kulaks' failure to produce surplus grain left the country two million tons short of the minimum amount of grain needed for the population. The USSR could not feed itself, and it could not export grain. Without agricultural exports it could not generate the required capital to purchase from Western countries the heavy equipment for industrialization. "Socialism in One Country" was in jeopardy. A dire situation necessitated drastic measures, and in 1927, at its Fifteenth Congress, the Party resolved to take the offensive against kulaks. It imposed limits on the leasing of land and the hiring of labor by kulaks. It also advanced voluntary collectivization (the pooling of land and resources) as a way to facilitate economic planning, to increase grain yields, and to introduce socialism in agriculture. These new domestic policies indicated that Stalin was moving warily on the peasant question since collectivization was voluntary instead of mandatory and since he restricted the power of kulaks through economic measures rather than eliminating the kulaks themselves. This show of temperance on Stalin's part lasted only a few months. When grain deliveries again fell short in early 1928, the General Secretary threw caution to the wind. He sent search parties into the rural areas to confiscate grain from kulaks, and encouraged Committees of the Village Poor to denounce hoarders.

Throughout 1928 and 1929 the policies of voluntary collectivization and requisition from kulaks proved unsuccessful. As late as October 1929 only 4 percent of peasant households had

joined collectives, and the requisition of food had initiated a class
battle akin to civil war. At the end of the year Stalin unleashed
the full apparatus of the state against kulaks. He called on Party
members to pass "from the policy of *restricting* the exploiting
proclivities of the kulaks to the policy of *eliminating* the kulaks
as a class."[18] The directive encouraged open warfare against all
peasants who could be identified loosely as kulaks. Party members, city workers, and police and army units joined together to
liquidate the most recalcitrant kulaks and to dispatch the others
to a barren existence in Siberia or to the archipelago of labor
camps scattered throughout the country. The poor and landless
peasants also joined the fight by attacking, looting, and destroying kulak homes and possessions. The kulaks, in desperation,
often burnt their crops and slaughtered their herds and flocks
rather than allow the product of their labor to be seized by a government stripping them of all they valued. For Stalin the war
against kulaks fulfilled the double purpose of eliminating a dangerous opponent to collectivization and of serving notice to the
rest of the peasant population that failure to cooperate with the
new agricultural programs would be met with brutal force.

Besides crushing the kulak class, warfare in the countryside
forced millions of peasants to collectivize. The peasants who preferred to hold on to their land were branded as kulaks and treated
accordingly by Party members and poor peasants. Where friendly
persuasion had failed, terror yielded dramatic results. By March
1930, only a few months after Stalin's directive against kulaks,
peasant households in collectives had risen to an astronomical
58 percent. Even Stalin was concerned about the bloodshed that
had accompanied the organization of collectives. Thus he softened
the restrictions of the collective system. He permitted households
to withdraw from collectives with no penalty, though this allowance lasted only a few months. Other relaxations were more
enduring. Peasants were permitted to retain their homes for family use, and to keep their cattle, poultry, and small farm implements. Most important, each peasant household could cultivate a
small garden plot about one acre in size. The produce from these
"kitchen gardens" could be sold and the profit retained by the en-
terprising farmer. The slackening of restrictions in conjunction
with a new Party drive brought millions of peasants into the

collectives. In 1933 the total of collectivized households rose to 65 percent, and in 1936 it surpassed 90 percent.

Some peasants worked in agricultural institutions other than collective farms (kolkhozes). The government employed thousands of peasants in machine tractor stations (MTSs), which owned and operated heavy machinery for the plowing, seeding, cultivating, and harvesting on collectives. Other peasants spent their work days on state farms (sovkhozes), large five-thousand-acre "factories in the field" owned by the government and managed by its supervisors. Sovkhoz farmers worked on a hourly basis like most factory employees. Kolkhozes, machine tractor stations, and sovkhozes virtually socialized the agricultural sector of the nation. The only vestige of private property was the household garden plot.

Socialist organization did not lead automatically to abundant agricultural production, however. The destruction wrought by despairing kulaks had reached formidable proportions. By the end of 1932 the USSR had lost approximately half its horses, cattle, hogs, and two-thirds of its sheep and goats. When Stalin released these figures he made no mention of the loss of kulaks and other peasants, an indication of the value he placed on human life. This secrecy also served to hide from the West the awful magnitude of the human destruction. The significant drop in the number of draft animals and the death and uprooting of millions of peasants so adversely affected agricultural production that the USSR produced considerably less food in 1932 than in 1928, though the monetary value of the food had increased slightly.

The downtrend in real agricultural production between 1928 and 1932 shifted the entire burden for the economy onto the shoulders of the urban workers. A prime reason for collectivization had been to increase crop yields by replacing the un-mechanized, individually managed peasant farms with a centrally planned, highly mechanized agricultural system worked by a collectivized peasantry. Rejecting the idea of foreign loans or investments, Stalin depended instead on increased crop yields to feed the population and to turn food surplus into capital for purchasing the heavy machinery needed for industrialization. This need was especially acute between 1928 and 1932, the years of the First Five Year Plan.

Soviet Agriculture

Before the First Five Year Plan

Household farms: in 1928 25 million peasant households worked on small farms (less than thirty acres) using obsolete equipment and methods of cultivation.

After the First Five Year Plan

Sovkhozes or state farms: The large 5,000 (or more) acre factories in the field are owned by the state and farmed by peasants who are paid wages. In 1932 there were over 4,000 state farms, a threefold increase in the number of *sovkhozes* existing prior to 1928.

Kolkhozes or collective farms: Peasants combine their land, labor, and capital voluntarily, and they share in the net proceeds of cooperatives according to the quantity and quality of the work they do. In 1932 there were 50,000 *kolkhozes* as compared to 2,000 in 1928.

Machine Tractor Stations: Owned and operated by the state, machine tractor stations performed the heavy work on collective farms such as plowing, seeding, and harvesting. They were created in 1929, and by 1935 there were more than 4,000 of them servicing the *kolkhozes*. In 1958 they were disbanded and sold their assets to collective farms.

Private peasant plots: Households belonging to collectives have been allowed by law since 1935 to cultivate a small garden plot—about one acre. The plots are comparatively more productive than any other agricultural institution in the USSR; they regularly yield a surplus which is sold on the open market to supply important supplementary income for peasants.

In 1928, in the name of the Party he now dominated, Stalin assumed responsibility for the country's escape from backwardness. The blueprint for the escape took the form of a grandiose five year plan which enumerated stupendous production goals in agriculture and industry. Stalin announced that beginning October 1, 1928, the country would raise gross output in five years by more than 200 percent. Heavy industry would triple its output while light industry products and agricultural goods would double. To support the efforts toward the realization of the five year goals, electrical power would increase by more than 400 percent! By any measure the goals of the plan were extraordinary and, as events would prove, quixotic.

The country's emergence from agricultural and industrial back-wardness touched strong emotions in the hearts of Soviet workers. Many citizens responded energetically, as reported by a young American, John Scott, who chose to work for five years in the Soviet Union as a skilled electrician. According to Scott, many young Soviet workers were enthusiastic about socialist construction, and they suffered every hardship willingly since at the end of the sweat and pain would lie the promised land. One laborer voiced this optimistic prediction:

> But then, after all, look at what we're doing. In a few years now we'll be ahead of everybody industrially. We'll all have automobiles and there won't be any differentiation between kulaks and anybody else.[19]

Other workers resisted the inhuman pace dictated by the all-dominant plan, as evidenced by this diatribe against local leaders:

> You well-fed devils have sucked the juices out of us enough. You hypocritical wall-eyes are pulling the wool over our eyes. For twelve years already you have driveled and agitated and stuffed our heads. Before you shouted that the factory owners exploited us, but the factory owners did not force us to work in 4 shifts, and there was enough of everything in the shops. Now we work in 4 shifts. Where before 4 men worked, now only one works. You are bloodsuckers, and that's not all, you still want to draw blood out of our veins. If you go to a shop now and want to buy something, the shops are empty; there are no shoes, no clothing; there is nothing the worker needs.[20]

The plan aroused extreme emotions in workers, either boundless enthusiasm or remorseless hatred. No one remained unaffected.

Rapid industrialization ushered in new problems for the urban areas. The need for an increased labor force resulted in a significant influx of peasants into the cities. Many of these first-time workers were young and unskilled, and a million and a half of them were women inexperienced in industrial labor. The ensuing demand for food, housing, and consumer goods quickly turned a difficult situation into an intolerable one. When workers were unable to find shelter, they migrated from job to job, to the great distress of plant managers who had impossible production quotas to fulfill. The government, in an effort to stabilize the labor pool and facilitate the work of the police, reintroduced the internal passport system reminiscent of Tsarist days. What Lenin had called "a document of barbarism" once again became a part of daily life for Soviet citizens. New arrivals in a city had to register at the local police station within twenty-four hours. Without proper registration papers, workers and peasants alike were in violation of the law and subject to severe punishment.

In an attempt to increase an already feverish pace toward industrialization, the Sixteenth Party Congress held in 1930 adopted the slogan "The Five Year Plan in Four Years." Critics argued that the rate of industrialization was too rapid, but Stalin answered them unequivocally:

> We are fifty or a hundred years behind the advanced countries. We must make good this distance in ten years. Either we do it, or we shall go under.[21]

On December 31, 1932 the First Five Year Plan officially ended. The final gains fell considerably short of projected goals, but with the exception of agriculture nearly every industry showed sizable increases in production. The output of coal had improved by 80 percent, steel by almost 50 percent, oil and iron by nearly 100 percent. The amount of electrical power produced had risen by more than two and a half times, and consumer goods by more than 60 percent.

Unfortunately, the quality of the products was uneven, and the statistics on the quantities produced were unreliable. The plan required factory managers to achieve dazzling results with a work force lacking skills or experience and oftentimes undernourished for the long work hours demanded of it. To avoid reprimand or punishment by Party leaders, many managers resorted to lies, deceit, and the production of poor quality goods that were often useless once they left the assembly lines. For example, a manager, in an effort to reach or even surpass an assigned quota, might produce shirts without pockets or buttons; to meet the deadline for the completion of a locomotive, another manager might turn

First Five Year Plan			
	1927–28 *(actual)*	*1932–33* *(goal)*	*1932* *(actual)*
Heavy Industries			
Coal (million tons)	35.4	75	64.3
Oil (million tons)	11.7	22	21.4
Pig iron (million tons)	3.3	10	6.2
Steel (million tons)	4.0	10.4	5.9
Electricity (billion kilowatts)	5.05	22	13.4
Light Industries			
Consumer goods (roubles in billions)	12.3	25.1	20.2
Wool cloth (million meters)	97	270	93.3
Agriculture			
Gross agricultural production (roubles in billions)	13.1	25.8	16.6

Source: Alec Nove, *An Economic History of the U.S.S.R.* (Baltimore: Penguin, 1969), p. 192.

out a machine with wheels so defective as to make the engine utterly unfit for service. In one documented case a locomotive rolled out of the factory with seventy defects even after being overhauled!

Despite the inaccurate reporting and shoddy quality, production increases during the First Five Year Plan baffled the imagination. While the USSR was raising production, Western nations were floundering in a prolonged economic depression. Just as astounding, the Soviet Union was industrializing without any economic assistance from the agricultural sector, where production totals were decreasing yearly. Stalin and the Party accomplished this economic miracle by severely limiting consumer goods and by ruthlessly accumulating and reinvesting capital in industry.

When the plan was completed, the USSR ranked among the world's emerging industrial powers.

The Second Five Year Plan, covering the years 1933 to 1937, again emphasized heavy industry, but unlike its predecessor the second plan set more realistic goals and underscored quality in production. Stalin had utilized effectively the five year plans to control and expand the economy. In November 1936 the General Secretary announced over radio to the nation:

> Our Soviet society has already, in the main, succeeded in achieving socialism; it has created a socialist system, i.e., it has brought about what Marxists in other words call the first, or lower, phase of communism.[22]

PURGES DECIMATE THE PARTY AND TERRORIZE EVERY SECTOR OF THE NATION

Collectivization and industrialization transformed the economic base of the USSR, but the purges of the middle and late 1930s bled the heart and spirit of the nation. By the end of the decade, of the Politburo members alive during Lenin's rule, only Stalin and Trotsky remained, and the exiled Trotsky would be assassinated in the summer of 1940. Nearly three-quarters of the Central Committee members elected in 1934 did not survive the decade, and more than half of the delegates to the 1934 Party Congress were arrested for antirevolutionary activities. The purges did not spare ordinary Soviet citizens either. Under official Party orders, the secret police apprehended a percentage of the population in every district of the nation. At least eight million, perhaps more, were arrested, tortured, and sentenced to hard labor in the gulags stretching across the desolate Siberian landscape. The purges liquidated long-standing Party members and terrorized the people of the Soviet Union into sullen submission.

The periodic purge, introduced in 1921 at the Tenth Party Congress, was meant to rid the Party of members suspected of being greedy for power or privilege. The early purges usually included hearings at local-level courts, which reprimanded or dismissed culprits from the Party. The purges of the middle and late 1930s, in stark contrast, involved trials and convictions of vast numbers of Party members, armed forces personnel, and other citizens. They provided one of the bloodiest chapters in the history of a people whose past has included the savagery of the Mongol invasions and the reign of Ivan the Terrible.

Stalin's views on purging Party members were never hidden from the Soviet people. In an important discussion of the Party in *The Foundations of Leninism* the General Secretary proclaimed: "*The Party becomes strong by purging itself of opportunist elements.*"[23] This statement was consistent with the view of the Tenth Party Congress on purges. But Stalin's definition of "opportunist elements" was vague and allowed for an almost all-inclusive category of potential offenders. He included among opportunist elements "reformists, social-imperialists and social-chauvinists, social-patriots and social-pacifists."[24] Anyone could qualify as an opportunist element, and, as time would show, the purged CPSU members would most frequently be people who in some way had opposed or criticized the leader. In the same article Stalin admitted his intolerance for competing ideological positions within the Party:

> The theory of 'defeating' opportunist elements by ideological struggle within the Party . . . is a rotten and dangerous theory, which threatens to condemn the Party to paralysis and chronic infirmity.[25]

The warning to fellow Party members and to the Soviet people was clear: the General Secretary would permit no deviation from the Party line. In the 1930s, Stalin made good on his promise by virtually destroying the principle of open policy discussion articulated by Lenin in 1917.

The great Stalinist purges were preceded by what might be termed "rehearsals," trials of Party members and other people during the late 1920s and early 1930s. These innocent victims defended themselves unsuccessfully against charges of counter-revolution and sabotage. Their punishments ranged from long prison terms to exile. The trials represented, in one sense, Stalin's ruthless response to the widespread opposition to the Five Year Plan and collectivization. Disagreement with his policies and methods of carrying them out had arisen from every quarter of

the country. Intense objections to Stalin's methods were even
voiced in the leader's home. Nadzheda Alliluyeva, diligent Party
member and Stalin's second wife since 1919, disagreed with her
husband about his ironfisted treatment of peasants. One November evening in 1932, after her husband had addressed her rudely in
front of guests, Nadzheda took her own life. She had despaired at
the increasing violence of her husband's leadership, and she could
find no solution but suicide.

Opposition came from within the Party as well. The authorized
Party history published during the Khrushchev era revealed the
existence of an anti-Stalinist group in the mid 1930s. According to
the official source, old guard Party members at the Seventeenth
Party Congress in early 1934 contemplated decisive action against
Stalin.

> Many Congress delegates, particularly those who were familiar with
> Lenin's testament, held that it was time to transfer Stalin from the
> office of General Secretary to some other post.[26]

They hoped the new position would assuage Stalin's vanity and
effectively remove him from the seat of power. The transfer never
took place, and historians have been unable to uncover the specif-
ics of the intended action or the delegates' reasons for failing to act.

When the old guard Bolsheviks did not act, they lost a final
opportunity to fight free of Stalin's vicelike grip. The vital organization described by Lenin in *What Is To Be Done?* was doomed.
Trotsky's dire prediction concerning the Party had now become
reality:

> The organization of the Party takes the place of the Party itself; the
> Central Committee takes the place of the organization; and finally
> the dictator takes the place of the Central Committee.[27]

Though peasants, urban workers, and long-time Party members
railed privately at Stalin's leadership, delegates at the Seventeenth Party Congress, dubbed the "Congress of Victors," heaped
upon the General Secretary an unending tribute of praise. They
lauded him as "the outstanding genius of the era," the "leader of
the working classes everywhere," the "field marshal of the pro-

letarian forces, the best of the best."[28] In a numbing excess of
adulation the delegates voted "to accept as Party law all the proposals and considerations of Comrade Stalin's speech."[29] At the
conclusion of the Congress the idea of purges and mass trials
seemed unthinkable, even fantastic.

Ten months later, on December 1, 1934, a bullet shattered the
jubilant mood of the Seventeenth Congress. Leningrad Party
leader Serge Kirov died at the hand of a disillusioned Party comrade named Leonid Nikolaev. The same day Stalin issued the following directive:

1. Investigative agencies are directed to speed up the cases of
those accused of the preparation or execution of acts of terror.

2. Judicial organs are directed not to hold up the execution of
death sentences pertaining to crimes of this category . . .

3. The organs of the Commissariat of Internal Affairs are directed to execute the death sentences against criminals of the
above-mentioned category immediately after the passage of
sentences.[30]

This directive set the stage for the great Stalinist purges. Kirov's
assassin and thirteen alleged accomplices were tried in camera
and executed later that same month. During the interrogations,
the accused had implicated numerous Party members, many of
them former critics and opponents of Stalin. Ultimately, the trail
of denunciations and innuendos led to Zinoviev, Kamenev, and
fourteen other old guard communists. In August 1936 the group
was tried publicly for plotting Kirov's death and for organizing a
terrorist center under the direction of Trotsky. The nation and the
world press followed this first show trial in astonishment as the
sixteen defendants were found guilty, sentenced to death, and immediately executed.

Other show trials followed quickly. In January 1937 seventeen
high-ranking communists "confessed" to sabotage and conni-
vance with Germany and Japan to destroy the USSR. Later in June
the trials felled many of the highest ranking officers of the armed
forces. The accusation was espionage on behalf of Germany and
Japan. The final major spectacle occurred in March 1938 when

Victims of Purges

Communist Party

	Total Membership before Purges (Early 1930s)	Purge Victims
Politburo	9	5 (including Kirov)
Central Committee (members and candidates)	139	98 (executions)
Seventeenth Party Congress Delegates	1966	1108 (executions, imprisonments, or arrests)
CPSU	1,874,488	c. 300,000 (executions, imprisonments, arrests, or expulsions from Party)

Armed Forces

	Total Membership before purges (Early 1930s)	Purge Victims (executions, imprisonments, or arrests)
Marshals	5	3
Army Commanders	15	13
Corps Commanders	58	30
Divisional Commanders	195	110
Regimental Commanders	406	211
Officer corps	70,000	35,000

NOTE: The figures concerning purge victims are more suspect than the usual Soviet figures because they come from secondary sources or personal accounts of disenchanted Soviet citizens.

Sources: Basil Dmytryshyn, *USSR, A Concise History,* Fourth Edition (New York: Charles Scribner's Sons, 1984), pp. 183–84, 536; Merle Fainsod, *How Russia Is Ruled* (Cambridge: Harvard University Press, 1965), p. 440.

Bukharin and twenty other top Party members succumbed to charges of sabotage, espionage, and conspiracy to kill leaders of the Soviet Union. Between show trials, the state imprisoned or executed for assorted treasonous activities millions of lesser known Party members, military officers, and ordinary Soviet citizens. The archipelago of labor camps teemed with Stalin's real and imagined enemies.

A year after the last show trial, at the Eighteenth Party Congress, the General Secretary made this announcement: "We shall have no further need of resorting to the method of mass purges."[31] He spoke the truth. The Party was now broken physically and psychologically. The leadership of the armed forces now belonged to a younger, less experienced generation that recognized Stalin as its undisputed leader. The sensational, sometimes luridly publicized purges shattered the spirit of the Soviet people, and convinced a horrified nation that in the midst of enemies at home and abroad, only Stalin stood between the USSR and those who would destroy it.

DIALECTICAL MATERIALISM GROUNDS STALIN'S VIEW OF THE WORLD

Marxists have consistently, though not in the same way, grounded their view of the world in materialism, which provides an important philosophical perspective from which to understand the decision-making process of Soviet leaders and those of other Marxist nations. In a 1938 work, *History of the Communist Party of the Soviet Union (Bolsheviks), Short Course,* Stalin wrote an article, "Dialectical and Historical Materialism," purporting to present communism's philosophical world view. Many communists considered the essay to be the finest summary of Marxism's *Weltanschauung.*

Stalin was not a philosopher. His forte was the area of practical politics. "Dialectical and Historical Materialism" contributed nothing original to the Marxist conception of materialism, but it offered a clear, succinct account of communism's world view. Stalin analyzed Marxist philosophical materialism under three points, one of which dealt directly with matter as the essence of the world, while the other two items addressed epistemological concerns such as the reality of ideas and the extent of the knowable. Stalin believed that ideas were mirror images of physical objects—in other words, ideas reflected or copied objects; also, there were no limits to what could be known—the mysteries of today were the discoveries of tomorrow.

In commenting on the nature of the world Stalin stated:

> . . . that the world was by its very nature *material*, that the multifold phenomena of the world constituted different forms of matter in motion, that interconnection and interdependence of phenomena, as established by the dialectical method, were a law of the development of moving matter, and that the world developed in accordance with the laws of movement of matter . . .[32]

To Stalin and other communists, matter was not the only property of objects. The dialectic constantly changed the forms of matter through internal contradiction. For example, when steam meets ice a new entity—water—emerges. The dialectic also placed objects in a continuum of change where every object was related to and dependent on other objects. For example, the material aspect of water is two atoms of hydrogen and one atom of oxygen, but this definition of water is meaningless in isolation. Between temperatures of 32 and 212 degrees Fahrenheit, the atoms assume a liquid form; above the boiling point they turn into vapor and below the freezing mark they become ice. The matter in water is always related to other physical elements, in this case atmospheric temperature, and only when water participates in an interconnected whole does it become something, i.e. liquid, vapor, or ice. Dialectical materialism according to Stalin explained the universe as being material, dynamic, and interconnected.

Change and development in the universe occurred continuously, beginning with slight imperceptible quantitative changes but then erupting abruptly into fundamental qualitative changes. As water receives more heat, it changes only slightly; but at the boiling point the liquid becomes transformed qualitatively—it becomes vapor. Human beings, too, are material objects which have resulted from sudden qualitative changes. To communists the dialectic is active even today in nature and history. The next significant qualitative leap in human history will occur when capitalist countries are transformed into communist societies, thus completing the qualitative change introduced in human history in 1917 with the occurrence of the November Revolution.

Marx of course had never adumbrated a natural philosophy. He had limited his study of materialism to human history. The philosopher responsible for extending Marx's materialist conception of history to the natural world was Friedrich Engels. Indeed Stalin quoted Engels extensively in the section of his essay on materialism. And the thinker who coined the phrase "dialectical materialism" was Lenin's Marxist mentor, Plekhanov.

Dialectical materialism, when functioning as the philosophy of a communist dictator, carried with it significant ramifications which the early Marxists could not have prefigured. If objects are material, and if ideas are reflections of material objects, then ideas can be changed by surrounding people with different objects. In Stalin's words, "whatever was his manner of life, such was his manner of thought."[33] It was possible, according to the theory of dialectical materialism, to influence and perhaps to control the thoughts—hence the development—of human beings. The "copy" theory of knowledge and, more seriously, the implied "putty" theory of human nature was a crude and simplistic extension of Marx's economic determinism. But Stalin and the party proceeded to create a socialist environment around the Soviet people. Through the Five Year Plans Stalin hoped to construct a socialist economy in the Soviet Union with which to create new socialist human beings. Leaving nothing to chance, the General Secretary directed the Party to manage other facets of life in the nation, including education, art, music, literature, radio, and newspapers. The goal was not to punish people by restricting their choices but to remold them by permeating their existence with socialist material objects.

According to Stalin, if people spurned socialist material objects, they not only threatened the creation of socialism, but by their actions they became material objects capable of influencing other people in a way deemed erroneous. Much like cancers threatening the life of an organism, resisters and betrayers of the Party became human malignancies endangering the life of the nascent socialist society. For the USSR to survive and prosper, these human cancers had to be eradicated, exactly as Stalin had done to kulaks during collectivization and to treasonous Party members during the 1930s.

According to the philosophy of dialectical and historical materialism, human beings possessed value and dignity as a *group* of people striving to construct a communist society. The group took precedence over the individual. Though this collectivist view did not necessitate the murder of human beings, it provided a rationale which permitted the elimination of some individuals for the good of the group. Stalin's purges take on a different light when viewed against this backdrop of dialectical and historical materialism.

A New Era for the USSR: World War II and the Rise to World Power

THE SOVIET UNION DEFEATS THE GERMAN ARMIES AND SUFFERS ENORMOUS LOSSES

The 1930s witnessed the metamorphosis of the USSR from a weak, agrarian, underdeveloped state to an industrialized, collectivized, socialist giant. The 1940s would mark the growth of the Soviet Union into a world power. But the new era would dawn disastrously with a German invasion of the homeland and a bloody, protracted patriotic war to reestablish hegemony over Soviet territory.

The seeds of World War II were sowed at the conclusion of the First World War with the Versailles Treaty, signed shortly after the Armistice of November 1918. From its inception, the Treaty had no chance for success. Because of its harsh treatment of the Germans, its failure to solve the nationalities problem in Europe, and its inability to establish a strong, defensive European alliance system, the treaty merely gave the world a twenty-year truce before hostilities resurfaced. During these two decades, the people of Germany and Italy in particular were resentful of the Versailles settlements and succumbed to the lure of leaders and programs that promised employment of demobilized veterans and recovery of national pride. The underlying message of these post-World

War I programs was simple and direct: redress the Versailles injustices.

Meanwhile, in the young Soviet state, the Communist Party was battling for its very life in a ferocious civil war, and a decade later it struggled against recalcitrant peasants to attain socialism. In the realm of international relations the USSR worked hard through the undertakings of Foreign Affairs Commissar Chicherin and his successor Maxim Litvinov to win acceptance in the family of nations. The efforts of Litvinov proved successful when, under the threat of rising Nazi militarism, the Soviet Union joined the League of Nations in 1934 and entered into an alliance with France in 1935.

Adolf Hitler's military buildup, a flagrant violation of the Versailles Treaty, greatly worried Stalin. When the Führer annexed Austria and part of Czechoslovakia in 1938, the Soviet leader turned to Western nations for their support in halting Germany's eastward encroachment. But England and France were unwilling to challenge the advance, a fact clearly demonstrated by the fateful meeting in Munich on Sept. 30, 1938. Neville Chamberlain and Edouard Daladier, representing Great Britain and France respectively, bought a temporary peace with the Nazis by accepting Hitler's annexation of the German-speaking area of Czechoslovakia. Though Stalin was officially the ally of France at this time, he played no part in the negotiations that appeased Hitler and betrayed the democratic Czech republic.

The Munich meeting taught Stalin that the USSR stood alone. It could expect no help from Western democracies, since they were obviously averse to confronting an aggressive, rejuvenated Germany. Hitler was making no secret of his determination to gain *Lebensraum* (living space) for the overcrowded German people by expanding eastward. The Nazi leader had earlier ratified with the Japanese the anti-Comintern Pact, which soon broadened to include Fascist Italy and Spain, thus increasing Stalin's sense of complete isolation.

The General Secretary's solution to this beleaguering situation stunned a world not slow to absorb its threatening significance. Through emissaries, Stalin and Hitler signed a mutual nonaggression pact. Often described as an unholy alliance, the Nazi-Soviet pact was ratified on August 23, 1939. The secret protocol of

the treaty permitted the Germans to invade western Poland while
their ally, the Soviet Union, was allowed to take control of eastern Poland and to overrun Finland and the Baltic states. As events
would soon prove, the pact was no more than a temporary ar-
rangement based on the needs of both leaders. Hitler hoped the
alliance would silence Stalin while the Nazi war machine rolled
over Europe, and Stalin was buying more time to strengthen his
western defenses against the inevitability of German attack. The
Nazi-Soviet Pact would be ruthlessly violated within two years,
but meanwhile it partitioned much of Europe between either
Nazi or Soviet rule—at least on paper.

The plans for the dismemberment of Europe did not remain for
long in the briefing room. The ink was barely dry on the pact
when on September 1, 1939, Nazi troops invaded Poland. France
and England, finally facing up to the inevitable, responded two
days later with a declaration of war against the Third Reich. The
Second World War had become a reality. The German war machine's triumphant subjugation of much of Europe between 1939
and 1941 included weak, young states like Poland and Czechoslovakia, born after the First World War, as well as continental powers like the Third French Republic. Great Britain remained a sovereign nation, but it was hard pressed and stood almost alone
against a seemingly unbeatable Nazi military machine. The
United States, sympathetic to the plight of the invaded democracies but determined to remain neutral, did no more than revise
its Neutrality Act to favor Britain's wartime needs. It continued to
resist Winston Churchill's urgent pleas for American involvement in a struggle that threatened the future of democracy
throughout the world.

In 1940 the uneasy alliance between Hitler and Stalin was beginning to wear thin. Quarrels over territorial gains and concern
over the political and military growth of the other made a clash
inevitable. Hitler seized the initiative with a stunning invasion of
the Soviet Union in the early hours of June 22, 1941. He hurled
against the USSR over three million experienced troops along a
two-thousand mile front extending from the Ukraine into Finland. The Führer launched his "Operation Barbarossa" at this
time because the Soviet Union was still recovering from serious
losses incurred the previous year in the war against Finland. Dur-

ing the "Winter War" of 1939–40, the Finns' tenacious defense against a Soviet invasion cost the Red Army a million soldiers before the small nation was defeated. The USSR would now experience even greater losses as hundreds of thousands of Red Army men fell in the first weeks of fighting. Hitler's prediction that Slavs would one day become slaves to their Aryan superiors seemed on the verge of fulfillment.

The circular issued to Party and government organizations by the Council of People's Commissars and the CPSU Central Committee on June 28, 1941, described the nation's plight in language reminiscent of Hitler's arrogant prophecy concerning the future of the Slavic race. Detailing the movement of German troops through Lithuania and Belorussia, the circular warned: "[Now is] being decided the question of life and death of the Soviet state, whether the nations of the Soviet Union live free or become slaves."[34] But why were there no words from Stalin during the first terrible week of the invasion? Why was it the subdued and halting voice of Viacheslav Molotov that announced to the nation on the day following the attack that Germany had invaded the homeland? And why, when the British Ambassador arrived on June 28 to make final an alliance with the Soviet Union, was he received by Molotov and allowed to depart from the country without any communication with Stalin?

When German troops first crossed into Soviet territory, Stalin was asleep in his villa outside Moscow. He was awakened by a 4:00 A.M. phone call from General Georgi Zhukov, who related news of the attack. Within a few hours, Stalin was informed by a Foreign Office report that Germany had issued a formal declaration of war. The General Secretary's worst fears had become grim reality. Yet no government or Party official, not even the highest-ranking officers of the general staff, dared to state the appalling truth that Stalin alone was responsible for the nation's unreadiness to withstand the Nazi assault. During the 1930s Stalin had made himself the sole authority in every sector of the rapidly expanding government and Party bureaucracy. Engineers, agronomists, weapons technicians, and the general staff stood silent and subservient before his unchallenged power. Stalin's involvement extended to highly technical matters such as bomb designs and infantry rifles. When Hitler demonstrated an increasingly ar-

rogant and menacing attitude toward his Soviet ally, and when
Nazi troops amassed along the Soviet border, Stalin doggedly ignored the obvious, and his general staff feared to correct him.
Even after receiving news of the Nazi invasion, Stalin at first
ordered that his troops not return fire! As the Führer's troops advanced unrelentingly, Stalin cracked under the pressure, suffering
a nervous breakdown which left him temporarily incapable of issuing commands or participating in meetings.

For a week and a half, the country heard nothing from the man
who for more than a decade had ruled the Soviet Union with
an iron fist. The uneasy silence was broken on July 3 when Stalin, speaking in a low, soft monotone, stopping frequently and
breathing heavily, appealed to the citizens of the USSR to rally
around the Party of Lenin and to pursue in surrendered areas a
scorched-earth policy. "In case of a forced retreat of Red Army
units," he advised, "all rolling stock must be evacuated, the enemy must not be left a single engine, a single railway car, not a
single pound of grain or gallon of fuel."[35] The General Secretary
had resumed leadership of the war-torn nation.

The struggle between Nazi Germany and the USSR was only
one area of conflict in a six-year global war which raged on land
and sea, engulfing entire continents in a maelstrom of destruction. But in the vortex of World War II, the Nazi-Soviet clash displayed an intensity all its own. For six months after the June 22
offensive, the Germans knifed progressively deeper into the Soviet homeland in the hope of capturing Leningrad, Moscow, and
the Ukraine. Their drive might have been successful and the Soviet Union might have fallen if it had not been for several unre-
lated events. First, the Soviet forces recovered from the initial
trauma of the invasion and offered increased resistance to the ad-
vancing armies. Second, the German campaign in the Balkans
temporarily diverted forces away from its eastern front. Finally,
near the end of July the attacking forces suffered a fatal five-week
delay as Hitler and his generals quarreled over the direction of the
invasion. When the German High Command finally targeted
Moscow as the primary objective of the invasion, summer was already fading into fall, and the Führer's forces would soon confront
the USSR's most formidable features: space, mud, and climate. In
past centuries the nation had more than once been saved from
subjugation by what Bertram D. Wolfe has aptly termed "General

Distance (with his aides, General Mud and General Winter) and his age-old strategy of the 'scorched earth.'"[36] Long travels over vast distances without food or fuel, an early and severe winter, and interminable miles of mud eventually played havoc with the Führer's finest regiments. Like Napoleon nearly a century and a half earlier, Hitler grossly underestimated the courage and steadfastness of the enemy as well as the expanse and harsh climate of the Soviet homeland.

In early December, as the overextended German war machine ground to a halt, a Soviet winter offensive was underway. Casualties were enormous, but Stalin's forces achieved the important goal of preventing Nazi armies from resting or regrouping. Nevertheless, the exhausted Germans resumed the offensive in the summer of 1942, with the objective of seizing the Caucasus oilfields and Stalingrad. The Germans reached Stalingrad in September and then endured a military stalemate for four months before a Soviet counteroffensive ousted them from the city limits. The Soviet counteroffensive was successful because Hitler, fearful that a defeat at Stalingrad would cost him enormous prestige, forbade his commander to cease the assault. Had Field Marshal Friedrich von Paulus been allowed to retreat in time, the Sixth Army might not have been doomed, and its defeat on January 30, 1943, would not have gone down in history as the greatest a German army had ever suffered. Stalingrad became a turning point in the war. Hitler's troops launched another offensive in July 1943 but it was not enough. Soviet forces continued to gain momentum as they recaptured control of their homeland and moved inexorably toward Berlin, forcing in collaboration with the other Allies the unconditional surrender of the Third Reich on May 7, 1945.

The year 1943 was significant for more than the beginning of the victorious Soviet drive toward Berlin. In December, Stalin, Churchill, and Franklin D. Roosevelt met at Teheran for a summit meeting to plan the reshaping of the European continent when it became increasingly obvious that the Nazi regime was crumbling. At Teheran, then later at Yalta and Potsdam,* Stalin outmaneuvered his wartime allies, often playing one against the

---

*At Potsdam, Harry S Truman replaced Roosevelt, and Clement Attlee succeeded Churchill.

other as he laid the groundwork for future Soviet domination of
eastern Europe. One of Stalin's most significant diplomatic coups
was his collaboration with President Roosevelt in vetoing Churchill's plans for the establishment of an Allied second front in the
Balkans and northern Italy and later for the creation of a postwar
federation of Danubian states. Instead, the second front originated in northern France, leaving Stalin free to extend and make
permanent the Soviet presence in eastern Europe.

STALIN DRIVES POSTWAR RECONSTRUCTION

To the postwar Soviet population the figure of Stalin stood out in
high relief. The General Secretary was the indomitable, all-wise,
larger-than-life hero who had engineered the Soviet triumph in
the Great Patriotic War, as World War II was and still is known in
the USSR. In the closing years of the leader's life, this cult of personality assumed awesome proportions. Posters lauded the General Secretary as "All-Wise Leader and Teacher." According to a
popular journal he was the "Luminous Star" who had brought
"unlimited happiness to the Soviet people." Party comrades
would not be outdone by the citizenry in the outpouring of ac-
colades for the leader. Nikita Khrushchev began a letter to Stalin
with this salutation: "Dear Father, Genius Teacher, Savior of the
Fatherland." Lavrenti Beria, head of the secret police, found these
words appropriate to describe Stalin: "Genius combined with
simplicity and modesty, with extraordinary personal charm, with
consideration and paternal concern for all."[37]

The real heroes of the Great Patriotic War, however, were the
Soviet people. During four terrible years they had overcome almost insurmountable obstacles, and they had driven the Nazis
from Leningrad, from Moscow, from Stalingrad, and finally from
every inch of Soviet soil. They had added new truth to the age-
old saying, "Only the Russians can conquer Russia." Stalin himself in a burst of praise at the end of the war had paid homage to
the courage, resolution, and legendary resistance of the Soviet
population:

> Our Government made not a few errors. We experienced at mo-
> ments a desperate situation in 1941–42, when our Army was re-

treating, abandoning our own villages and towns. . . . A different people could have said to our Government: 'You have failed. . . . We shall install another government which will conclude peace with Germany and assure us a quiet life.' The Russian people, however, did not take this path . . . it made sacrifices to ensure the rout of Germany.[38]

But Soviet citizens had paid a terrible price for victory. Official military casualties numbered over 7 million, and civilian losses were probably twice that number—a total of over 20 million Soviet deaths. Material destruction was no less staggering. Soviet figures listed the decimation of 1,700 cities, 70,000 villages, 98,000 collective farms, 84,000 schools, 71 million horses and other livestock, and a majority of Russia's bridges, hospitals, and libraries. In all, the USSR had lost approximately one-ninth of its population and one-quarter of its property in the battle against the Nazis.

At war's end the USSR faced one of the most colossal rebuilding challenges in history. And the architect in charge was almost sixty-six years old. But before channeling his energy into the reconstruction of Soviet society, Stalin, through his secret police, dealt harshly with returning "enemies," about five million soldiers, POWs, slave laborers, and refugees whose only crime was that they spent part of the war outside of the USSR. The General Secretary had vowed not to repeat Russia's experience after the Napoleonic Wars. In 1812, as Russian soldiers returned home from their victory over Napoleon's Grande Armée, they brought back with them the radical ideas that fomented the Decembrist Revolution of 1825. Therefore, new repatriates, some of whom had spent much of the war among the German enemy, were viewed by an irrationally suspicious Stalin as a contaminated, potentially treasonous element and hence a danger to the Soviet population. Not taking any chances, the General Secretary had all returnees quarantined as soon as they set foot in the USSR. Some were shot on the spot, and others were sent to Siberian labor camps.

Stalin's suspicions extended to Soviet citizens who had lived in German-occupied zones. These people had exhibited dangerous attitudes by engaging in private farming. It was imperative, judged Stalin, to reconvert them to socialist ideals by reestablishing collective farms. As always, the CPSU assumed responsibility for the socialist reconversion drive, which had appeared as a priority as early as 1944 in the Party newspaper *Pravda:*

> During the occupation, the German invaders tried by every method to poison the consciousness of Soviet men and women. . . . It is the duty of Party organizations to stimulate tirelessly the political activity of the workers. . . . Particular attention must be paid to the question of implanting in the population a socialist attitude . . . overcoming the private-property, anti-collective farm, and antistate tendencies planted by the German occupants.[39]

The CPSU after World War II no longer resembled the Party of earlier decades. Due to enormous membership drives between 1940 and 1947, the CPSU enrollment skyrocketed from 3.4 to 6.3 million members. The Party had the membership to implement Stalin's directives, but it was not the Party that had achieved the remarkable goals of the 1920s and 1930s. Most older members had vanished in the purges or in the war, and the few who remained exerted little influence. The leadership of the Party now came from the new enrollees, and they were not an inspired lot. Milovan Djilas, noted Yugoslav communist, coined the phrase "new class" for these communists whose primary interest was wielding power by shuffling paperwork. New class members also saw that with Party membership came numerous social amenities such as the opportunity to purchase meat, butter, shoes, and shirts from special Party stores while the Soviet masses queued for hours in front of state stores. In the West, class structure had resulted from the inevitable development of capitalism, while in the USSR, Party privilege was fabricating it.

With the secret police in charge of processing returnees after the war and with Party organizations reconverting the Soviet people in formerly occupied areas, the General Secretary could now commence with the economic reconstruction of a war-torn society. Everyone was eager to rebuild Soviet society, though people believed that the backbreaking pace of socialist construction in the 1930s was behind them. The USSR had won the war, and the United States and Great Britain, two bulwarks of capitalism, were among its allies. There was much work to be accomplished, but the immediate future of the country looked promising. People were hopeful that the long-promised good life was finally within their reach.

Stalin burst this bubble of optimism in February 1946 when he decreed that the industrialization and collectivization programs of the 1930s had to be continued and even accelerated. The Party would engineer "a new, mighty, upward surge in the economy, which would make possible an increased level of industrialization, to a point twice the pre-war level. . . . This will take at least three Five Year Plans, if not more. But it can be done, and we must do it!"[40] The Soviet people, exhausted from the war years, would shoulder the burden of becoming a world power. There would be no time to savor victory, and there would be no lessening of the frantic pace of the prewar five year plans.

The Fourth Five Year Plan (1946–50) appeared as grandiose in its goals and backbreaking in its demands as the First Five Year Plan of 1928–32. No other leader could have demanded—and received—such toil and sacrifice from his people. The new plan would rebuild the war-torn country. Furthermore, it would restore and then surpass the prewar production levels in agriculture and heavy industry and raise the cultural and material life of the people, resulting in the Soviet dominance of the world in scientific development. The plan would initiate a process of transforming the USSR into a world power strong enough to repel every kind of foreign encroachment. The Soviet people had vanquished the Nazis, but the victory against world capitalism had yet to be achieved. The plan would guarantee that the Soviet people would never hear again the steps of invading armies.

As the Fourth Five Year Plan went into action, urban workers responded positively to Stalin's plea for dedication, determination, and sacrifice. They labored to the limits of exhaustion on inadequate diets to meet the elevated goals of the plan. And their efforts produced spectacular results. At the conclusion of the plan, high priority items such as steel, coal, and oil had surpassed their assigned production quotas, though lower priority items such as wool fabrics and household goods lagged somewhat behind. The iron will of Stalin, coupled with the indomitable courage and indefatigable energy of the urban population, had produced another economic miracle.

The results in agriculture, however, did not match the successes in industry. Several factors accounted for low productivity in the countryside. The war had wrought widespread devastation which extended not only to the population and landscape but to farming implements and animals as well. For example, the Soviet Union had lost seven million horses and seventeen million head of cattle in the war. The shortage of horses and cattle adversely affected agriculture since numerous peasants depended on draft animals for power. A second factor contributing to low productivity was the very low priority assigned to agriculture by the architects of the Fourth Five Year Plan. The investment in agriculture was one-sixth of the capital put into industry, or about the same amount allocated to transportation. Despite war damage and insufficient capital allocations, agriculture might have recorded a notable increase in production had the peasants enthusiastically supported postwar farm programs. But the peasantry felt frustrated and oppressed, and erupted in revolts reminiscent of those in the early 1930s.

One of the first programs enacted by Stalin reclaimed for *kolkhoz*es the land that peasants had taken for themselves. During the war, many peasants had added to their garden plots by stealing land from the *kolkhoz*es, and some peasants had even parceled out collective lands among themselves. By September 1947 the government had reclaimed fourteen million acres from the private holdings of the peasantry.

No doubt the support for collectivization among peasants had waned during the war. If the Party hoped to mold peasants into socialist human beings, it needed to exercise more effective administrative control in the countryside. In an attempt to establish this control, the Party increased the size of *kolkhoz*es; 250,000 collectives were consolidated into fewer than 100,000 *kolkhoz*es. The larger collective farms also profited from greater mechanization and divison of labor; in theory they should have been more productive. But peasant dissatisfaction with the collective system offset any technological advantages that accrued from amalgamation.

Other programs created enormous hardship for peasants. For example, the government required every household to deliver 200 liters of milk to the state each year. But less than half of the peasant households owned cows! Also, the currency reform of 1947

The Fourth Five Year Plan

	1940	1945	1950 (goal)	1950 (actual)
Heavy Industries				
Coal (million tons)	165.9	149.3	250	261.1
Oil (million tons)	31.1	19.4	35.4	37.9
Pig iron (million tons)	14.9	8.8	19.5	19.2
Steel (million tons)	18.3	12.3	25.4	27.3
Electricity (billion kilowatts)	48.3	43.2	82	91.2
Light Industries				
Consumer goods (index)	100	59	—	123
Wool fabrics (million meters)	119.7	53.6	159	155.2
Agriculture				
Grain harvest (million tons)	95.6	47.3	—	81.2

Source: Alec Nove, *An Economic History of the U.S.S.R.* (Baltimore: Penguin, 1969), p. 293.

effectively wiped out the savings that some peasants had accumulated during the war. The reform required the entire population to exchange cash for new currency at the rate of ten rubles to one, but did not adjust correspondingly taxes and other fixed obligations to the government. If, for example, a peasant household had saved the equivalent of $1,000, it was required to exchange that amount for $100 in the new currency and to pay taxes that remained fixed at the pre-exchange level. In spite of these burdens so destructive to peasant morale, agriculture managed a slow recovery, approaching its prewar level by the end of the Fourth Five Year Plan.

By 1950 the USSR was emerging as a world power. In economic

and political influence it had surpassed the faltering British Empire and a weakened France. Its erstwhile enemy in the Far East, Japan, had signed away its empire as the price for peace with the Allies. The communist countries and parties around the globe looked to the Soviet Union for leadership.* To all these nations and their people, Stalin was synonymous with authority in the USSR and communist leadership throughout the world. Despite this prominence, or perhaps because of it, mystery and intrigue surrounded the last years of the leader's life.

INTRIGUE FILLS STALIN'S LAST YEARS

Beginning in 1948 the purge crept back into the lives of the Soviet hierarchy. After the death of Stalin's right-hand man and heir apparent, Andrei Zhdanov, a massive purge decimated the Leningrad Party organization. Thousands died in this bloodbath that supposedly rescued Leningrad from a plot to surrender the city to the British. As in 1934 after the murder of Kirov, rumors implicated Stalin both in the death of Zhdanov and in the design of the subsequent purge. Stalin's satraps feared that he was moving against any of his would-be successors.

In 1952, after a thirteen-year interim, the CPSU leader unexpectedly summoned a Nineteenth Party Congress. The events at the Congress revealed Stalin's strategy of attacking the growing power of those in the chase to succeed him. In his first move, he assigned the reading of important reports to two different persons. Georgi Malenkov, a party *apparatchik* who was widely believed to be Stalin's designated successor, read the Central Committee's main report. A relative newcomer, Nikita Khrushchev, was entrusted with the presentation of new Party rules. This ceremonial procedure of seemingly minor importance had major implications for Malenkov. By selecting two people to read these reports, Stalin may have intended to cloud the succession issue and diffuse whatever power his second in command may have accrued. In a second move, at an open Central Committee meeting, Stalin ad-

---

*Though Stalin had dissolved the Comintern in 1943 he created in 1947 an international communist organization called the Cominform (Communist Information Bureau).

ministered a bitter tongue-lashing to two long-standing Politburo members, Anastas Mikoyan and Molotov. Finally, in an attempt to weaken the power of veteran Bolsheviks in the Politburo and Secretariat, the ever-shrewd Stalin doubled the membership in each committee. This move benefited Leonid Brezhnev, who took his place as a member of the newly enlarged Secretariat. Stalin's moves virtually checked the power of contending Party members. Undoubtedly the General Secretary recalled his own role in the power struggle that embroiled Politburo members while Lenin, mute and helpless, lay dying.

While the intrigue within the Party continued, an era of calamity commenced for Soviet Jews. The period between 1948 and 1953 has been aptly described as the Black Years for Soviet Jewry. The assault on Soviet Jews was in retaliation for the murder in January 1948 of Solomon Mikhoels, a noted Yiddish actor whom Stalin had handpicked during the war to drum up support for the USSR in Western countries. Following Mikhoels's death, a murder ordered by Stalin, hundreds of Jewish intellectuals succumbed to arrest, imprisonment, or execution. The Black Years also witnessed the closing of virtually all Jewish theaters, newspapers, and synagogues.

This anti-Semitic drive climaxed in January 1953 with the arrest of nine doctors, seven of whom were Jews, from the Kremlin Medical Service. According to the lurid accusations, the doctors had deliberately undermined the health of Stalin and Soviet military leaders and were responsible for the premature deaths of Zhdanov and other high-ranking officials. Furthermore, they were supposedly operating as spies and terrorists within the country. Flaunting the forced confessions before the Party hierarchy, Stalin berated the leadership for its failure to recognize the dangers threatening the state: "You are blind like young kittens; what will happen without me? The country will perish because you do not know how to recognize enemies."[41] These "enemies" were never executed because Stalin died before he could carry this new purge to its violent conclusion.

After the Great Patriotic War it appeared that Stalin might live indefinitely. Instead of showing signs of exhaustion after the war, he had thrust himself enthusiastically into the task of rebuilding the country. But on March 1, 1953, he suffered a severe stroke which left him incapacitated. His personal physician could not treat him since he had been detained in prison as a member of the Doctors' Plot. His inner circle of aides probably could have helped, but they did not dare to touch him; such was the fear the General Secretary had inspired in his entourage. Indeed, the leader's demise may have been hastened by the failure of those around him to call for immediate medical assistance. On the morning of the stroke, the security men who noticed that Stalin had failed to stir at his usual hour refused to approach their charge without a summons. When Politburo members arrived later in the day they looked at the paralyzed and speechless victim and decided to return home. It might be dangerous to view the great leader in this unseemly state! Of the doctors who eventually gathered around the bedside, the leading specialist hesitated to touch the prostrate leader. Might the apparent emergency be just another twist in the nefarious Doctors' Plot? The suspicion, mistrust, and fear that Stalin had sowed among those closest to him now deprived him of the aid and comfort he might otherwise have had as his life came to a close on the evening of March 5, 1953.

Stalin's death meant that the last social architect of the USSR had departed. The General Secretary had designated no successor. A new generation of businessmen would take up the reins of power and administer this vast country of fifteen republics and more than one hundred nationalities.

Summary and Comment

The ideological language used by Joseph Stalin differed little from the words employed by Karl Marx almost a hundred years earlier. They both wrote about the communist party, industrialization, and socialist society. They both spoke of the same goal: a communist society in which vital goods and social services would be bountiful and within the reach of everyone. But Marx had claimed that the development of societies would proceed according to economic laws. He believed that communist society would be the outcome of a gradual, predictable process of economic development. He stressed economic determinism. On the other hand,

Stalin had inherited from Lenin a Soviet Union which was in the first stages of industrialization and which was surrounded by the highly developed industrial societies of western Europe and Japan. He knew that communist programs could not exist without industrialization, and that industrial societies were the powerful ones in the community of nations. As a result, he accelerated the industrialization of the Soviet Union in a series of five year plans, and he did so with the backing of a compliant Party and secret police, which bullied and terrorized the people into accepting a centralized and nationalized economy. Farmers worked on collective and state farms, and urban workers labored in factories owned and directed by the state; all were obedient to the directives of the Party leadership in Moscow. What should have occurred naturally, according to the economic forces Marx had analyzed, appeared rapidly because of the iron will of Stalin and the Party. Political voluntarism, not economic determinism, created socialism in one country. Marx and Stalin employed a similar vocabulary, but the two men emphasized different processes with their words.

This political will, as exercised by Stalin, was incredibly powerful. Its legacy is still apparent in today's Soviet Union. In one generation, despite a devastating world war, the Soviet Union raised overall production fourfold and heavy industrial production ninefold. Military spending increased by twenty-six times, and these funds assured the nation greater security from foreign invasion than ever before. The socialist edifice, however, had been erected at the cost of enormous suffering. Stalin had built his socialist society on the skeletons of his people, just as Peter the Great in the eighteenth century had constructed St. Petersburg on the bones of the Russian people.

Further Reading

No one has argued seriously that Stalin was a first-rate thinker. His writings were either practical pieces devoted to issues of the day or summaries of ideas basic to Marxism. But he wrote simply and clearly and demonstrated a command of the ideological nuances of Marxism.

BY STALIN

Stalin, J. V. *Works.* Moscow: Foreign Languages, 1953–55. The thirteen volumes include writings up to the mid-1930s. The series is incomplete and has remained that way since Khrushchev exposed Stalin's crimes in 1956.

Franklin, Bruce, ed. *The Essential Stalin: Major Theoretical Writings, 1905–52.* Garden City: Doubleday, 1972. The book contains a helpful thirty-eight page introduction which puts Stalin's theories and actions in a historical context.

The following two works became classics of Marxist thought during the author's lifetime.

Stalin, Joseph V. *Foundations of Leninism.* New York: International Publishers, 1939. A collection of lectures delivered in April 1924, the book presents the fundamental tenets of Leninism, or as Stalin called it, Marxism in the era of imperialism and the dictatorship of the proletariat.

————. *Dialectical and Historical Materialism.* New York: International Publishers, 1940. The work originally appeared as a chapter in the 1938 book, *History of the Communist Party of the Soviet Union (Bolsheviks);* it is the finest summary of the principles of dialectical and historical materialism in existence.

ON STALIN

Deutscher, Isaac. *Stalin, A Political Biography.* Second Edition. New York: Oxford University Press, 1967. This is the classic biography of Stalin.

Tucker, Robert C. *Stalin As Revolutionary, 1879–1929.* New York: W. W. Norton, 1973. In addition to being a biography, the book is a study in the formation of a dictator.

Ulam, Adam B. *Stalin, the Man and His Era.* New York: Viking, 1973. The book examines Stalin's life against a backdrop of world events.

ON THE STALIN ERA

Conquest, Robert. *The Great Terror: Stalin's Purges of the Thirties.* London: Macmillan, 1968. The highly documented book on the purges attributes ultimate responsibility for the executions of Soviet citizens to Stalin.

Medvedev, Roy A. *Let History Judge: The Origins and Consequences of Stalinism.* Trans. Colleen Taylor. New York: Alfred A. Knopf, 1971. Written by a dissident Soviet Marxist, the book presents a sustained and comprehensive critique of the genesis, development, and triumph of Stalinism.

"Marxist theory helped us to win power and consolidate it. Having done this we must help the people to eat well, dress well, and live well. You cannot put theory into your soup or Marxism into your clothes. If, after forty years of socialism, a person cannot have a glass of milk or a pair of shoes, he will not believe socialism is a good thing, no matter what you tell him."

—Nikita Khrushchev

4

THE THIRD GENERATION OF COMMUNISTS: NIKITA SERGEYEVICH KHRUSHCHEV, BUSINESSMAN

When Nikita Khrushchev emerged as de facto leader of the Soviet Union in the fall of 1953, numerous Party officials viewed him as innocuous and bereft of the ambition necessary for leadership and power. Some even regarded the First Secretary* as a pygmy when compared to the giant, Stalin. Khrushchev himself remarked: "If you put fifteen of us [Presidium members] end to end it would not make Stalin."[1] But this Party leader belonged to a new generation of communists. Instead of the stark simplicity of Stalin's uniform, Khrushchev sported a white shirt, silk tie, and three-button worsted suit. In place of the incessant speeches on collectivization and the need for heavy industry for constructing socialism, Khrushchev spoke of consumer products for the long-suffering and hard-working Soviet people. The Stalinist design for socialist society had given way to the demand for better and plentiful goods and services.

Not a timid Marxist, Khrushchev boldly broke with the country's Stalinist past. But he was unable to introduce communism in the Soviet Union—he never brought the country to the promised land of milk and honey. In 1964 this businessman who wanted the good life for his people received the dubious distinction of being the first Soviet leader to suffer dismissal from office. Despite this disgrace, Khrushchev merits a respectable place in the history of the USSR, though the CPSU hierarchy would not and does not admit it. Edward Crankshaw, in his biography of Khrushchev, aptly characterized this leader's role:

---

*After Stalin's death the leader of the Party assumed the title of First Secretary; not until 1966 did "General Secretary" return to common usage.

He brought the Soviet Union through the great change . . . secured
the peace and laid the foundations for prosperity.[2]

Khrushchev: From Peasant and Miner to Moscow Chief

Nikita Khrushchev was born on April 17, 1894 in the small peasant village of Kalinovka, Kursk, near the Ukraine. For the Khrushchev family, the emancipation of serfs in 1861 had brought nothing but a continuation of the harsh living conditions under which
they had ground out a miserable existence. Typically, peasant
families lived in *izba*s, small one room cottages with mud or
wooden walls. *Izba*s also sheltered small animals belonging to
the family. Peasants ate meat infrequently, and they often exhausted their grain supply by Christmas after which a diet of
pickled cabbage and cucumbers meant the difference between
starvation and survival. One Russian doctor reported that peasants ate so little food that even the everpresent Russian influenza
had difficulty thriving in *izba*s.[3] With diseases like diphtheria, ty-
phus, and syphilis contributing to the tenuousness of peasant life,
Nikita was lucky to survive childhood.

Like other Kalinovka boys the young Khrushchev engaged in
farm work at an early age. He kept watch over the animals of the
village and later herded livestock for the local landlord, a woman
who farmed 5,000 hectares. These jobs ingrained in him an
affinity for the soil which remained with him throughout his life.
Between the ages of seven and twelve, Nikita managed to obtain
two years of schooling where he learned some scripture, elemen-
tary math, and basic reading and writing skills. Nothing in his
crude beginnings prefigured the leader Khrushchev would one day
become. Indeed he might have remained tied to the countryside
had his father not foresaken peasant life for the mine pits.

Each autumn after the harvest, the elder Khrushchev made his
way to the Donbas coal mines in the Ukraine to work with thousands of other transplanted peasants. These seasonal laborers
dreamed of earning enough money to sustain their families
through another harsh Russian winter and to buy a horse, without which no peasant could hope to become prosperous. Around
1908 the father moved his family to a mine settlement near the

industrial center of Yuzovka in the Donbas, which was at the time the most important industrial region in the Empire. As hard as he tried, he never accumulated enough money to purchase the horse that would have improved the family's livelihood.

A shrewd fifteen year old, Nikita displayed sufficient talent to rise from the coal pits and become an apprentice fitter. As a semi-skilled laborer, he worked in several factories, nearly all of them foreign owned. While Lenin schemed of revolution from his European exile, and while the youthful Stalin was making his escape from Siberian exile, the teenaged Khrushchev experienced the grim life of the proletariat. His experiences with foreign capitalists permanently shaped his outlook on life, as he later explained:

> I worked at a factory owned by Germans, at coal pits owned by Frenchmen, and at a chemical plant owned by Belgians. There I discovered something about capitalists. They are all alike, whatever their nationality. All they wanted from me was the most work for the least money that kept me alive. So I became a communist, and all my conscious life I have worked with my whole heart and all my energy for my Party.[4]

Khrushchev's path to the Party was not that direct. He did not become a Party member until 1918, well after the great November Revolution.

It is not unusual for Soviet hagiographers to fashion stories that reveal the virtuous evolution of leading citizens like Khrushchev from rebellious worker to dedicated revolutionary. If the truth be told, however, Khrushchev ascended the workers' ranks as a skilled laborer; at the outbreak of World War I he was even exempt from the army because he qualified as an indispensable worker. After the Tsar abdicated in 1917, the twenty-three year old Khrushchev earned a place in the local soviet, though his interest appeared to be self-serving since the soviet was created, among other reasons, to protect miners against the mine owners. Only in the spring of 1918 did Khrushchev join the Communist Party. In effect, this pragmatic worker had simply transferred his allegiance to the ruling power.

In his first Party assignment in the autumn of 1918, Khrushchev became a military commissar and reported to a Red Army unit fighting north of the Donbas. His responsibility was to organize Party cells in the front lines of the Red Army and to indoctrinate illiterate peasant soldiers with a sense of purpose amidst the savagery of the Civil War. Because Khrushchev showed promise as a political organizer, the Party released him from the Army near the end of the war and dispatched him to the Yuzovka mines to serve as assistant manager of a mine and secretary of the mine's party cell.

Khrushchev created his reputation as a dedicated Party official during this period. The nascent Soviet state was in chaos as the vicious Civil War drew to a close. There was massive unemployment, and armed bands (including groups of war-orphaned children) ravaged the countryside in search of food. Peasants often survived by eating grass and bark, and, in extreme cases, the corpses of neighbors. People fortunate enough to work were paid irregularly by the state, and there were few consumer goods available to purchase in any case. Amidst this turmoil Khrushchev and other Party officials forced the people to work by whatever means were available. Khrushchev cajoled, bullied, and when necessary resorted to Lenin's dreaded secret police, the Cheka, to get the workers into the mines. He succeeded admirably, restoring the mines of Yuzovka to full production within a few years.

Khrushchev did not remain long at the Yuzovka mines. His wife of six years died of hunger and exhaustion in the great famine of 1921–22, and the Party reassigned the widower to the Donets Mining Technical School to receive a formal education. The Party hungered for men like Khrushchev, men who had a genuine rapport with workers as well as the brashness to crush them when necessary, men with a talent for the practical task of building an industrial state under the most adverse conditions. At the technical school, Khrushchev received his first formal introduction to Marxism, and its tenets struck a responsive chord, as he later commented:

When I listened to lectures on political economy and the lecturer spoke about the wage system under capitalism, about the exploitation of the workers, it seemed to me that Karl Marx had been at the mine where my father and I worked.[5]

But Khrushchev's knowledge of Marxist ideology never advanced beyond the rudimentary. If theoretical principles were not corroborated by experience, they remained beyond the grasp of this communist who lacked a speculative mind. Khrushchev was a leader and an organizer, and at the technical school he plied those skills as local Party secretary with as much devotion as he gave to his academic work.

After graduation in 1925, Khrushchev assumed the post of party secretary of a sprawling, four hundred square mile industrial area near Yuzovka (later renamed Stalino). The assignment meant that Khrushchev had won a position in Stalin's apparatus. He was now a full-time Party functionary, an *apparatchik*. Clearly, the man from the workers' ranks belonged to a new generation of communists. He had never identified himself with a revolutionary pseudonym like Lenin or Trotsky, and he had never designed blueprints for the socialist transformation of society like the grand architect Stalin. Khrushchev functioned like a businessman, and the industrial production in his region was his main concern.

In carrying out the duties of his new position Khrushchev displayed a trait that was to become characteristic of his public image. He canvassed his territory with an energy uncommon among other Party members, who preferred the soft sofas and warm offices of Party headquarters. Supported by his second wife, Nina, whom he had married in 1924, the talented administrator received a series of quick promotions in the Ukrainian Communist Party. When Lazar Kaganovich, head of the Ukrainian Party, moved to Moscow, he brought Khrushchev with him. Kaganovich assumed leadership of the Moscow Party organization, and in 1932 he elevated his hard-working functionary to second in command. Khrushchev had captured the attention of Kaganovich because he had energetically implemented Party directives and because he shared no revolutionary past with old guard Bolsheviks. Fortunately for Khrushchev, his knowledge of Marxism was minimal. Therefore, Khrushchev could easily perform his job without raising ideological questions. His Stalinist superiors, who were averse to the questioning of Party orders by purists, welcomed this trait.

After several interim appointments, which included First Secretary of the Moscow region, Khrushchev was assigned to the Ukraine in 1938. During his twelve-year stay, the First Secretary of the Ukrainian Party treated the people so viciously that he acquired the title "Scourge of the Ukraine." He directed a thorough purge of dissident elements within the Ukrainian Party, and he accompanied the Soviet troops in order to supervise personally the expansion of Ukrainian territory into eastern Poland after the 1939 Nazi-Soviet pact left Stalin free to destroy Polish independence. Following World War II Khrushchev remained on the job to direct Ukrainian postwar reconstruction. The First Secretary cut a large figure in the Ukraine. Despite running the risk of displeasing an increasingly arbitrary and suspicious Stalin, Khrushchev encouraged his own cult of the individual to develop. Ironically, a few years later in 1956, he would attack and disparage Stalin's excesses and personality cult.

In 1949 Khrushchev was summoned to Moscow to become Secretary of the Central Committee and First Secretary of the Moscow region. CPSU leaders were rewarding their man in the Ukraine for a job well done. But the Moscow to which Khrushchev returned was different from the one he had left in 1938. Stalin in particular was far from the virile leader who had systematically crushed opposition within the Party. The General Secretary was an ailing curmudgeon, arbitrary in his actions and mistrustful of all who surrounded him. Malenkov managed the CPSU, and Lavrenti Beria functioned cautiously as head of the secret police; Beria retained his position only because he fawned on Stalin. When Khrushchev joined this twosome, he initially profited from his long absence from Moscow and the Party's power struggles. His name was untainted by Party intrigue and the frenzied economic programs of the postwar USSR. Shrewdly recognizing the advantage of his position, he stealthily insinuated himself into Party politics, first as head of several unsuccessful agricultural reforms and then as Party organizer who suddenly became a counterweight to Malenkov. At Stalin's last Party Congress, the Nineteenth in 1952, Khrushchev and Malenkov presented the formal reports, and the rivalry between the two was revealed to the public.

The De-Stalinization of the Soviet Union

KHRUSHCHEV RISES TO POWER

Though Stalin died on March 5, 1953, a struggle for succession may have been underway earlier in the year during the infamous Doctors' Plot. According to some historians, Stalin would have implicated not only physicians but also old Politburo members, particularly Malenkov and Beria, since they stood in line for the title of First Secretary. But Stalin's unexpected demise cancelled proceedings against the doctors and forever clouded his intentions.

Less than a week after Stalin's death, Malenkov lost his position as the front runner in the race for Party leader. He had committed a serious political *faux pas*. In his eagerness to take command, he had rashly published in *Pravda* a picture of himself in the company of Stalin and Mao Zedong. The photo, taken in 1950, had been altered to eliminate the figures of several Soviet and Chinese officials, leaving only the three. Reaction of the Party leadership was swift. Within a few days Malenkov "requested" to be relieved of his duties as Party First Secretary, though he remained an important government figure until 1957.

When Malenkov's responsibilities reverted to Khrushchev, the former Ukrainian Party chief advanced a giant step closer to leadership of the USSR. For the moment, however, he shared power with two other men as the nation moved into a brief period of three-man rule, a troika, with Khrushchev acting as Party boss and spokesman, Malenkov heading the government bureaucracy, and Beria in command of the powerful secret police. But Beria, who had masterminded Stalin's reign of terror after World War II, was now marked for elimination by the Party, which feared that with the backing of his secret police, he could easily create a dictatorship. In June, just three months after Stalin's death, Beria was arrested on the fabricated charge that he had been a British agent since 1919. Tried in absentia and without counsel, he was found guilty and shot.

Prior to Beria's arrest, the government had exonerated the physicians arrested in the Doctors' Plot and had promised swift punishment of those members of the secret police who had tortured the unfortunate men. The indictment of Beria's men and the clearing of the doctors' names marked the beginning of the Party's actions to break the power of the secret police and to dissociate itself from the crimes of the Stalin years. In February 1956 the break with the Stalin era occurred abruptly and in a sensational manner when Khrushchev, the official First Secretary, delivered a secret speech at the Twentieth Party Congress.

SECRET SPEECH EXPOSES STALIN'S DEEDS

On the night of February 24–25, near the end of the Twentieth Party Congress, Khrushchev recalled more than fourteen hundred high-ranking Party officials from their hotel rooms to Congress headquarters in the Kremlin for a secret session. Beginning just before midnight and continuing for an unbelievable four hours, the First Secretary delivered a 20,000 word address, known as the "secret speech" or "de-Stalinization speech." Not published in the USSR, the secret speech was, in the estimation of some observers, "perhaps the most important document ever to have come from the communist movement."[6]

The speech was a vitriolic denunciation of Stalin, the man to whom all those present had for years paid obsequious homage. Khrushchev attacked the General Secretary's actions as those of a ruthless and bloody tyrant, responsible for the brutal purges of the 1930s. He castigated him for the country's early defeats in World War II, and he condemned him for developing a cult of the individual.

A close examination of the carefully phrased speech reveals interesting limits beyond which Khrushchev's eloquent tongue seldom strayed. His words made eminently clear that Stalin's conduct did not become seriously reprehensible until 1934, when the mysterious events surrounding the Kirov assassination inaugurated the violent purges:

> After the criminal murder of S[erge] M. Kirov, mass repressions and brutal acts of violation of socialist legality began.[7]

He went on to remind his stunned audience that early in 1934, not too many months before Kirov's assassination, the Seventeenth

Party Congress had celebrated the Party's success in building socialism. The people who later fell victim to Stalin's terror were the same ones who had attended the congress, the very people who had worked tirelessly to construct socialism in the USSR. Khrushchev formulated the question certainly on the minds of his numbed listeners: "How then can we believe that such people could prove to be 'two-faced' and had joined the camps of the enemies of socialism. . . ?"[8]

Khrushchev also excoriated Stalin for the enormous losses suffered by Soviet forces during the early years of World War II. Stalin had always maintained that the setbacks experienced by the Soviet army were the result of the Nazi surprise attack. In truth, Khrushchev explained, warnings about the German offensive had come from Winston Churchill and from "our own military and diplomatic sources."[9] When the Nazi soldiers marched on Soviet soil and fired on Soviet troops, Stalin further issued the order "that the German fire was not to be returned."[10] Unwittingly and singlehandedly, the General Secretary had helped German armies to win easy victories on the eastern front.

The erroneous decisions that led to the slaughter of thousands of Soviet soldiers in the early months of World War II and the malevolent scheming that caused the death and torture of innocent Party members in the purges of the 1930s occurred because too much power had accrued in the hands of one person. In Khrushchev's words, there had developed around the General Secretary a "cult of the individual."[11] Stalin had encouraged the proliferation of Stalin prizes, of towns and streets named after him, and of statues bearing his likeness. Even the national anthem did not have one word about the CPSU but instead included sentences like: "Stalin brought us up in loyalty to the people. He inspired us to great toil and acts."[12] Stalin had been transformed "into a superman possessing supernatural characteristics akin to those of a god."[13] The problem with such a deification, Khrushchev continued, was that "such a man supposedly knows everything, sees everything, thinks for everyone, can do anything, is infallible in his behavior."[14] Khrushchev could not have formulated a better description of an absolute dictator and the problems often accompanying dictatorships.

The secret speech, however, did not stigmatize Stalin's accomplishments before 1934. Indeed Khrushchev underscored Stalin's contributions in the November Revolution, the Civil War, and the construction of socialism in the USSR.

Rumors of the speech filtered through the Moscow Party structure within twenty-four hours, and in a few days a printed version of the talk was read at special Party meetings throughout the country. The secret speech found its way abroad, and in June 1956 it was published in its entirety by the State Department of the United States.

At home in the Soviet Union some young citizens who heard rumors of the speech demonstrated vociferously against it. In Tiflis, for example, where Stalin had attended the seminary and joined the local Social Democratic Party, students rioted at the news of the defamation of their greatest countryman. Closer to Moscow, two assassination plots attempted unsuccessfully to shorten Khrushchev's life. But the reaction of Party members and others who heard of the speech was not uniformly violent. To most, the speech provided an opportunity to raise some nagging questions. Why had Stalin been allowed to torture and execute innocent Party officials? Why had Khrushchev and other CPSU leaders constantly adulated Stalin if he had possessed feet of clay? How had the Soviet system permitted such tyranny? No one better formulated the issues unearthed by the secret speech than the Italian communist leader, Palmiro Togliatti:

> Previously all the good was due to the superhuman qualities of one man; now all the evil is attributed to his equally exceptional and shocking defects. . . . The real problems are skipped over—how and why Soviet society . . . could and did depart from the self-chosen path of democracy and legality to the point of degeneration.[15]

The questions raised by Togliatti probably found their way into the inner circles of the CPSU, but they remained unanswered. How could Khrushchev divulge details about the purges without implicating himself and other Presidium members, the very people who had executed Stalin's orders? Subordinates may condemn former employers' actions, but never to the point of exposing their own active role in carrying out the orders they now repudiate.

The zenith of Khrushchev's political career, it could be said, lasted four hours—the time it took to deliver the de-Stalinization speech. The stunning exposé irreparably weakened Khrushchev's effectiveness as leader of the USSR and of the world communist movement. Until his forced retirement in 1964, Khrushchev would lack the kind of firm control over the socialist bloc nations that had characterized Stalin's rule. He would now find himself reacting to international events rather than instigating them. For both Stalin and Khrushchev, the secret speech fundamentally altered the way in which history would record them. In Stalin's case, the speech revealed the enormity of his crimes, while in Khrushchev's case, it lessened the esteem for his leadership.

SECRET SPEECH ENCOURAGES POLYCENTRISM IN EASTERN EUROPE

After 1943, when Soviet troops began their relentless rollback of Nazi armies, driving them first from Soviet soil and then from eastern and central Europe, they began to exert a control over these territories that, to a great extent, continues to this day. Historians and political scientists of this era used the term "satellite" to describe the relationship of these countries to Moscow. They viewed the USSR as a socialist "sun" around which the occupied states revolved and from which they took direction as members of the socialist bloc. But when Nikita Khrushchev stepped down from the dais on that fateful February evening, he unwittingly initiated a chain of events that would weaken the satellite pattern and give rise to "polycentrism" among the eastern European countries. The new concept of "many centers" of socialism emphasized the equality and independence of each member state. Instead of docile states accepting directives from the CPSU Politburo, these former puppet states began to exhibit a restlessness and a spirit of independence that would become a cause of serious concern to the Soviet Party hierarchy. To understand this splintering of the formerly monolithic communist rule it is necessary to review events after World War II.

World War II was a watershed in the extension of communism. Before the war the USSR and the Mongolian People's Republic*

---

*With Soviet assistance, a communist regime assumed control of Outer Mongolia in 1921. The Soviet Union so effectively integrated Mongolia within its sphere of influence that the country has functioned somewhat like a republic of the USSR.

were the only two communist countries in the world. A few years
after the war, by 1950, one-third of the world's population lived
under communism. This phenomenal growth of communist rule
has led historian Michael Kort to conclude:

> Whatever its faults or failures, Soviet foreign policy after World
> War II was dynamic, even revolutionary.[16]

Of course, the predominant spread of communist rule occurred
in Asia, not Europe, and the Soviet Union could not claim credit
for Mao Zedong's success in mainland China. In October 1949
Mao Zedong led communist rebels to power and declared the
People's Republic of China.* With this one stroke, a quarter of
the world's population had fallen under communist rule. But the
Soviet Union could claim credit for bringing communism to
North Korea, since Stalin ordered the invasion and occupation of
the country in August 1945.

In eastern Europe the spread of communist power commenced
with the infamous Nazi-Soviet pact of 1939. Under the terms of
the pact the USSR received permission from the Nazis to overrun Estonia, Latvia, Lithuania, eastern Poland, Bessarabia, and
Bukovina. British and American negotiators during the war initially objected to the Soviet Union's claim over these lands, but
Stalin outwitted his rivals at the negotiating table and annexed
the territories. This annexation added to the USSR more than 20
million inhabitants and about 185,000 square miles. The extension of Soviet influence over the remainder of eastern Europe
proved more difficult and time consuming. While World War II
was still raging on the European continent, Stalin had encouraged
the organization in the USSR of communist-led National Liberation Committees for each of the eastern European states. Then,
as the Red Army helped extirpate Nazi might from these countries, small, armed Soviet contingents remained behind to main-

---

*The communist takeover in China, which occurred without Soviet assistance,
did not please Stalin. In fact the General Secretary tried at one point to restrain
Mao by requesting that he cooperate with archenemy Chiang Kai-shek, leader of
the country's nationalist party. The problem for Stalin was that Mao controlled his
own party and army, and that he operated independently of the Soviet leader and
the CPSU.

tain order and, more significantly, to assist communist takeovers. In most eastern European states the Red Army backed the demands of the National Liberation Committees. Opponents were branded as Fascists and treated accordingly—with arrest, trial, and execution.

Communist Rule in 1950

I. *First Communist Country*
   Union of Soviet Socialist Republics

II. *Some Communist Countries Created With Support and Direction From Moscow*

Bulgaria	Mongolia
Czechoslovakia	North Korea
East Germany	Poland
Hungary	Rumania

III. *Some Communist Countries Created by Revolutions From Within*
   Albania
   China
   Yugoslavia

Note: During the next thirty-five years the spread of communist rule would slow considerably. In the second category of communist countries the major addition was Afghanistan; Cuba and Vietnam joined the third group.

The muscle of the Red Army proved critical at this juncture in eastern European history. As each country won its liberation from Germany, provisional governments filled the political vacuum. The Red Army used intimidation and force to guarantee that members of the pro-Soviet National Liberation Committees assumed prominent positions in the new governments. Committee members invariably seized the governments' ministries of Information, Defense, Justice, Agriculture, and Interior. The last ministry was most important since it administered the police. Control of these ministries enabled the communists to curtail and gradually eliminate opposition groups in the governments. In this way, the Soviet Union extended its influence over Bulgaria, Czechoslovakia, East Germany, Hungary, Poland, and Rumania.

Two other eastern European nations, Yugoslavia and Albania,

followed socialist paths dictated by their own independent communist party leaders, Tito and Enver Hoxha, respectively. Hoxha assumed leadership of the new communist government in Albania immediately after the war, and remained in power until his death in 1985. He remained a steadfast supporter of the Soviet Union until 1966, when he turned his back on Soviet leadership and transferred his loyalty to China's Mao Zedong. Until this break, however, Albania voluntarily included itself in the eastern European bloc dominated by Moscow. But the country implemented policies devised in its capital Tirana, not Moscow, and it exercised political independence from both the Soviet satellite states and the USSR.

The postwar Yugoslav story is different from the tale of Albania or the satellite states. The hero of the resistance against the Nazis, Joseph Broz, popularly known as Tito, came to power after winning nationwide elections. Initially he functioned as a pro-Soviet communist, like Hoxha in Albania. Stalin, however, wanted more than loyalty from Tito; he insisted on the Soviet domination of Yugoslavia. Tito resisted and the perfervid nationalist Yugoslavs supported him. He vetoed the creation of joint Soviet-Yugoslav companies, rebuked the exaggerated claims of Soviet military assistance during the war, and blocked the infiltration of Soviet intelligence agents into the Yugoslav army, the Yugoslav Communist Party, and the secret police. Every move Stalin initiated, Tito negated.

Soviet-Yugoslav enmity remained a family affair until 1948, when Stalin expelled Yugoslavia from the Cominform and followed up the expulsion with punishing political and economic sanctions. Armed skirmishes even occurred along the Yugoslav border. Tito never capitulated. He steered the country on an independent socialist course, developing a separate foreign policy and a native ideology stressing decentralization. This first crack in the monolithic communist edifice occurred during Stalin's lifetime, long before Khrushchev's secret speech. Stalin checked any further spread of this "Titoism" by instituting a series of purges which effectively silenced communist nationalists in other satellite states.

The USSR realized an enormous advantage in maintaining a communist bloc in eastern Europe. Together the eight nations

Contemporary Eastern Europe

contained more than one hundred million inhabitants, and their combined national income equalled 40 percent of the income of the USSR. These nations supplied the Soviet Union with cheap raw materials and ready markets for manufactured goods. Just as important, they shielded the USSR from a bourgeois western Europe, thereby enhancing as never before in its history the defensive posture of the Soviet Union's western border.

A problem with the master-slave relation, if the eastern Europe-USSR relationship can be depicted as such, is that the master seldom acknowledges the interests of the slave. What Stalin and the CPSU wanted for eastern Europe rarely coincided with the interests of the people, especially in Poland and Hungary, where puppet regimes constantly suppressed seething nationalist feelings and unintentionally encouraged a burgeoning hatred of all things Soviet. Newspapers and periodicals carried photographs of aroused citizens toppling statues of Stalin, the leader they had been taught to venerate. The beginning of a new era for these former satellites was inaugurated by national uprisings in Poland and Hungary.

Poland exploded first. In late June 1956 disgruntled workers fought police, and dozens of people died in the melee. Intellectuals and Polish communists seized the moment to demand a relaxation of controls, which they received from the pro-Moscow communist government. This initial capitulation to nationalist feelings was consequently interpreted by the Soviets as a first step toward the weakening of their hegemony in Poland. This development greatly alarmed Khrushchev, who feared the end of Soviet influence in the country and the termination of a valuable economic relationship. Khrushchev and other high-ranking CPSU officials reacted immediately. They flew to Warsaw in late October—uninvited—and placed Soviet troops in the country on alert. After intense negotiations, the Soviet delegation reluctantly acknowledged that recent changes in the country would not undermine its communist rule. Khrushchev further agreed to withdraw Soviet troops from Polish soil and to allow the nation to make some autonomous decisions regarding its implementation of socialism.

In Hungary, where the hallmark of the pro-Soviet communist government was brutality, the people vented their frustration and anger in a full-scale revolution in late October, the timing of which was undoubtedly encouraged by developments in Poland. The revolt drew much support from the army, which enabled a

revisionist member of the Hungarian Communist Party to organize a coalition government. The new leaders promptly withdrew
Hungary from the Warsaw Pact, an alliance created in 1955 to coordinate the communist armies of Eastern Europe and the USSR.
(The Warsaw Pact was Khrushchev's answer to the North Atlantic
Treaty Organization, the alliance unifying the command of the
armies of Western Europe and the United States.) In the Kremlin's
view, the gravity of the Hungarian situation far surpassed the one
in Poland or even Yugoslavia. These two countries had at least
practiced communist rule without consulting non-communist
parties, and Poland had remained a member of the Warsaw Pact.
(Yugoslavia did not sign the document.) Now, Hungary had withdrawn from a major agreement tying it to Moscow, and it had admitted non-communist members to its coalition government.
These incidents meant heresy, and Khrushchev wasted no time in
acting decisively.

The new Hungarian government had ruled for no more than a
few days when Khrushchev ordered Soviet forces to invade the
country and crush the revolution. The Hungarians fought superior numbers and arms for several days, but the struggle was hopeless from the beginning. What force can rocks exert against tanks?
To restore a friendly government, Soviet forces killed nearly 3,000
Hungarians and wounded another 13,000. Some 200,000 Hungarians left the country, choosing self-imposed exile in the West
rather than the oppression of a Soviet-dominated state.

In 1957, in an attempt to regain for the USSR its absolute authority over the communist world, Khrushchev persuaded some
eastern European communist parties to sign the Moscow Declaration. The signatories, including Mao, merely affirmed Moscow's
position as leader of the communist world. The occasion was the
capital's celebration of the fortieth anniversary of the November
Revolution. The signing of the Declaration was more ceremonial
than it was substantive. The First Secretary could not turn back
the clock to the late 1940s when the newly created communist
countries did not question Moscow. His de-Stalinization speech
had launched a new course for communist nations. Many of them
were demanding—and would continue to demand—that they be
allowed to determine for themselves the best path to communism.

KHRUSHCHEV PLANS THE ECONOMY AND FIGHTS
TO STAY IN POWER

The sensational nature of the de-Stalinization speech and the rampant reactions to it in eastern Europe and parts of the Soviet Union dwarfed the other talks and resolutions of the Twentieth Party Congress, some of which were far more important to Western nations than Khrushchev's speech. In the important opening address to the Congress, Khrushchev outlined a new foreign policy which discounted the certainty of war between capitalist and communist countries. "There is no fatal inevitability of war," he proclaimed.[17] In its place, he presented a foreign policy better suited to short-term Soviet goals: peaceful coexistence.

> And this [peaceful coexistence] is logical, since there is no other way out in the present situation. Indeed, there are only two ways: either peaceful coexistence, or the most devastating war in history.[18]

To back his words on peaceful coexistence with action, the CPSU boss would dissolve the Cominform in April 1956.

What prompted the First Secretary to propose this new ideological change? Khrushchev believed that the proletarian movement in many parts of the world could gain "a firm majority in Parliament, and convert it from an organ of bourgeois democracy into an instrument of genuinely popular will."[19] Violent revolution would be necessary in those few countries where capitalism commanded a powerful police and military apparatus. History was not static. It was constantly on the move, and historical change demanded ideological adjustment. This point Khrushchev clearly comprehended: "Since [the November Revolution] radical changes have taken place in the historical situation that allows an approach to this question from another angle."[20] The radical change in history was the spread of popularly elected governments, and thus the new angle was peaceful coexistence.

Always a practical man, Khrushchev understood that peaceful coexistence could significantly improve domestic programs. With war between communist and capitalist societies no longer inevitable, the USSR could channel some funds usually earmarked for defense into economic ventures. Indeed the Party leader pried substantial sums from defense by suspending above-ground nuclear testing and by reducing Soviet forces between 1955 and 1958 by more than two million men.

Peaceful coexistence did not imply that the USSR had abandoned its goal of world domination. Khrushchev never lost faith in the final victory of communism, but now the battle would be waged in the factories and farms of the Soviet Union. The standard of living in the USSR, he hoped, would be elevated above that in the West, and the world would witness for itself the superiority of communism as an economic system. In the end, the Soviet Union would convert the nations of the world by the example of its economic successes. Khrushchev boldly proclaimed, " . . . with good housing, with a better and more abundant life, with good schools, we will win all the peoples for socialism and communism."[21]

The journey to the promised land would require discipline and hard work from Soviet citizens, but the CPSU would no longer terrorize workers into achieving elevated production goals. Khrushchev was selling a vision of abundance, and he hoped the dream would be sufficient to spur the population to work intensely. Khrushchev also hoped that the secret speech had dissociated the present CPSU from the Party of the Stalinist era. Stalin's Party spread fear; Khrushchev's Party sought trust. With a new aura surrounding the CPSU and with peaceful coexistence underway, Khrushchev could devise plans to boost the economy. Ultimately, he hoped that de-Stalinization and peaceful coexistence would help to put more food on the tables of the Soviet people.

Early in 1957 Khrushchev presented his first stunningly innovative program, addressing of all things the economic bureaucracy. He announced the decentralization of this bureaucracy in order to facilitate the attainment of elevated economic goals. To solve perennial industrial and agricultural problems, the decision makers, reasoned Khrushchev, must be directly involved in production instead of sitting behind desks in Moscow. Economic problems in the Ukraine, for example, would be better addressed by government officials living in the Ukraine and working not only in offices but alongside workers and managers. Khrushchev

proposed the creation of about one hundred Regional Economic
Councils, which would plan and coordinate all industry and agriculture in their respective regions. Only military armament, electricity, and chemical production would remain under the direct
supervision of Moscow. Before the Economic Councils began
their operation in May 1957, the Party encouraged massive discussion of the unprecedented reorganization. By Khrushchev's count,
forty million people participated in over a half million meetings.
The exchanges at these meetings were at times heated since the
reorganization would displace thousands of government officials
who, in their new assignments in the hinterland, would miss the
amenities they had enjoyed in Moscow.

After the Economic Councils were established, Khrushchev's
enthusiasm, if not his common sense, appeared boundless. He declared that production of milk, dairy products, and meat would
soon reach spectacular heights. In three years the USSR would by-
pass the United States in each of these areas. The forecast meant
that meat production, for example, would triple from the 1956
production level of 6.6 million tons to 21 million tons. This pro-
jection and others like it brightened the propaganda speeches that
extolled the economic advantages of the Soviet socialist system.
Unfortunately, the numbers were pie in the sky, totally alienated
from reality. Before the First Secretary could implement strategies to reach these elevated goals, he became embroiled in a battle
for his political life.

To Presidium* members like Malenkov, Molotov, and former
Ukrainian Party boss Kaganovich, Khrushchev had outdone himself. His petulence and grandiloquent projections had become intolerable. These high-ranking Party officials also used the Polish
and Hungarian revolts to discredit the First Secretary, who was
building a powerful Party base by appointing his own people to
the Regional Economic Councils. At a Presidium meeting in June
1957 the Party elite voted seven to four in favor of Khrushchev's
immediate resignation as First Secretary. Khrushchev, though,
refused to honor the Presidium vote, and retaliated by calling a
special meeting of the Central Committee. Many members of

---

*"Presidium" was the new name of the Politburo between 1952 and 1966.

the Central Committee owed their position to the Party leader. At the meeting he skillfully defended his actions and outmaneuvered the anti-Party group, as his opponents became known. Because the Presidium was accountable to the Central Committee, the latter vote blocked the attempted ouster of Khrushchev. In early July *Pravda* announced the expulsion of Molotov, Malenkov, Kaganovich, and one other Presidium member from the Central Committee.

With his opponents removed from power, Khrushchev could mold the CPSU in his image. He filled the four vacated Presidium positions with his own men, and he increased full membership from eleven to fifteen, adding four more of his supporters. The Central Committee ballooned from 220 to 330 full members. Party rank and file also expanded. Between 1956 and 1961 full membership in the Party soared from 6.8 to 8.9 million, despite the loss of 200,000 members deemed unsound for various reasons. At the turn of the decade the CPSU clearly bore Khrushchev's stamp, and it was ready to do his bidding, or so it seemed.

UTOPIAN PRODUCTION GOALS AND ASSORTED FIASCOS BRING KHRUSHCHEV DOWN

In September 1957 Khrushchev announced that the flagging Sixth Five Year Plan (1956–60) would be scuttled in midstream and replaced by the more modest Seven Year Plan in 1959. To numerous Western economists, the goals of the new plan appeared realistic. Heavy industries such as oil, pig iron, and steel would almost double production by 1965. The plan also designated as a priority greater production of consumer goods like housing and wool fabrics. The latter was projected to increase by almost five times, while the aggregate total of housing at the end of the seven years would be nine times larger than the sum for 1958. With the launching of *Sputnik I*, the earth's first artificial satellite, in October 1957, and with the goals of the plan seemingly within reach, Khrushchev displayed an inordinate amount of enthusiasm as he let the world know that the USSR would soon eclipse Western nations in economic production. He boasted that the USSR at the end of the plan would achieve the highest gross and per capita ag-

The Seven Year Plan			
	1958	1965 (goal)	1965 (actual)
Heavy Industries			
Coal (million tons)	493	600–612	578
Oil (million tons)	113	230–240	242.9
Pig iron (million tons)	39.6	65–70	66.2
Steel (million tons)	54.9	86–91	91
Electricity (billion kilowatts)	235	500–520	507
Light Industries			
Consumer goods (index)	100	162–165	160
Wool fabrics (million square meters)	303	1,485	365
Housing (million square meters)	71.2	650–660*	79.2
Agriculture			
Grain harvest (million tons)	134.7	164–180	121.1

*Total for 7 years, 1959–65

Source: Alec Nove, *An Economic History of the U.S.S.R.* (Baltimore: Penguin, 1969), p. 355.

ricultural output of any country in the world, and it would possess an industrial growth rate five times that of the United States. These achievements would bury the capitalist countries and would be realized in the shortest workweek in the world, forty-two hours by 1960 and thirty-five hours in the near future. The results of the Seven Year Plan would undeniably place the USSR on the road to full communism.

What happened? Heavy industries met or surpassed their goals, and the production of many consumer durables registered sizable advances. But after Khrushchev had elevated expectations, numerous Party personnel looked not so much at the successes of the plan as at its failures, and the plan did record some serious shortfalls. The items doing poorly did so throughout the duration of the plan, and they were the highly visible commodities of shelter, clothing, and food. For example, production levels of wool fabrics, housing, and grain remained virtually the same after seven years, and grain harvests in 1963 and 1965 were actually lower than in 1958 due to adverse weather. The fact that engineers were pumping millions of tons of crude oil from the Volga-Urals fields created little excitement, but shortages of flour triggered disillusionment in the Soviet people.

The First Secretary also bore the brunt of increasing resentment from the CPSU hierarchy for the performance of the Regional Economic Councils, which had introduced more, not less, inefficiency and confusion in economic planning. Where one center had previously controlled industrial and agricultural planning there were now a hundred such centers, sometimes competing against one another and oftentimes evincing little concern for the raw material needs of other regions. The Economic Councils had diffused power but had not decentralized the Soviet economy, and thus the problems associated with a centralized economy remained. These problems were legion. For example, if Moscow had decided on a certain tonnage goal for steel production, workers produced a heavy steel to meet their assigned quota more easily, even though the steel was too heavy for use by customers. Khrushchev himself complained once about some impractical, heavy chandeliers produced to fulfill a projected tonnage quota. Centralized decision making was incapable of handling the myriad smaller decisions that had to inevitably transpire between customer and manufacturer. The First Secretary had recognized this problem and he had attempted to address it with his Regional Economic Councils, albeit unsuccessfully.

Undaunted by the failure of the Economic Councils and by the sputtering progress of some plan items, Khrushchev had the temerity to permit *The Program of the Communist Party of the Soviet Union (Draft),* 1961, to close with the statement so characteristic of him: "the present generation of Soviet people shall live under communism!"[22] The *Program* went so far as to set the date

(1980) at which time the people would enjoy free municipal housing, free urban transport, and free health care and medicines.

In the early 1960s it became apparent that Khrushchev's grandiose plans for economic development were chimerical. The Economic Councils had failed; vital goods like grain and housing were showing little or no increase in production, and projections of a reduced work week, free municipal housing, and imminent communism appearerd preposterous. Ironically, this practical businessman had scored his most dramatic successes not on earth but in the heavens with the launching of *Sputnik I* in 1957 and with the first manned orbital flight around the earth in 1961. But the space program did not raise the material life of the people, who were demanding more housing, clothing, and bread.

Khrushchev's stock among the Party hierarchy in the early 1960s was plummeting due not only to problems in the domestic sector but also because of foreign policy fiascos. In 1950, the USSR and China had signed a treaty of friendship and alliance that had sent capital and technicians to China. The treaty was noteworthy because it formed a bond with Mao Zedong, who had secured power in China without Soviet assistance, and because the Chinese traditionally were distrustful of "foreign devils," including the Russians. Unfortunately, the warm relations between the two nations would cool by the end of the decade. Khrushchev constantly disdained Chinese interpretations of Marxism-Leninism, and worse, he mounted verbal attacks against Mao himself, the ideological spokesman of communist China. Differences between the two communist leaders sharpened in 1960 when high-ranking Chinese Communist Party member Deng Xiaoping, attending a secret conference in Moscow, accused Khrushchev of betraying the ideals of the November Revolution and suggested that China would replace the Soviet Union as leader of the world communist movement. Khrushchev responded by withdrawing all financial and technical aid from the People's Republic of China. In effect he severed Sino-Soviet relations.

Another embarrassing debacle for the First Secretary's foreign policy occurred in 1962 when he placed missiles in communist Cuba. The United States President, John F. Kennedy, viewed the missiles as a potential threat to American security. He acted swiftly by imposing a quarantine on Cuba and demanding that the USSR withdraw its surface-to-surface missiles from Cuban soil. Khrushchev did not wish to risk nuclear war and capitulated. To make matters worse, the worldwide coverage of the incident damaged Khrushchev's reputation abroad.

Criticism at home, however, was not limited to these policy fiascos. There was also the question of his personal leadership style. Khrushchev was a rambunctious and petulant leader, often acting on impulse and, in the estimation of peers, irrationally. At the United Nations in 1960, he lost control of his "enthusiasm" during a speech and pounded his fist several times on the table, and on another occasion he removed a shoe and banged on the table with it. When economic production in the early 1960s was sagging, he concocted far-fetched schemes to remedy the problem. For example, he relocated the Ministry of Agriculture to a state farm some sixty miles away from its original headquarters in Moscow. Staff members of all levels were required to spend a portion of their time in the fields. Within a year, more than three-quarters of the staff tendered resignation notices!

By October 1964 Party leaders had had enough of the disorganization, empty economic promises, and foreign policy disasters. They could no longer tolerate the rotund, gruff man with the flamboyant, unpredictable style of leadership. While Khrushchev was vacationing at his villa on the Georgian coast of the Black Sea, the Presidium made final preparations for a coup. They secured support from the secret police and army, and they briefed the Central Committee to prevent the First Secretary from demanding that a Central Committee vote corroborate a Presidium decision for resignation, as he had done in 1957.

On October 13 Khrushchev received an urgent request to attend a Presidium meeting in Moscow. When he arrived, Party leaders took turns arraigning him. Khrushchev defended himself by explaining that he had secured peace and provided the foundation for future prosperity. Was it not true that the citizens of the USSR lived more secure and more comfortable existences than at the time of Stalin's death? The claim was accurate, but the Party elite believed that another man could better lead the Soviet Union to the promised land. The Presidium voted unanimously—and the vote was supported by the Central Committee—to demand the First Secretary's resignation from all official posts. Khrushchev succumbed. Perhaps the greatest testimony to the radical change effected by this fiery representative of the third generation of communists was his dismissal by vote rather than by execution. He died in retirement in 1971.

Summary and Comment

Marx claimed that industrialization was necessary to support communist economic programs. How could a society provide abundant vital goods like clothing and food unless machines were facilitating production? Stalin, through his five year plans, had supplied the industrial foundation Marx had demanded. The heavy machines had been created, and the electrical lines had been strung. The industrial base was in place, and the Soviet people were expecting the machines to produce long-awaited consumer goods. Khrushchev was correct in portraying communism's promise in mid-century as a glass of milk and a pair of shoes. He had sensed accurately that the USSR needed businessmen who would deliver the goods and services to make daily life easier and more comfortable. Khrushchev had the correct vision, but he could not get the job done.

To meet the challenge of attaining full communism, Khrushchev had to address two of Stalin's legacies: police terror and economic centralization. A population constantly in fear of arrest or being observed by informants would not apply itself energetically to produce abundant goods, nor would it be capable of enjoying those goods. In order to move closer to communism, Khrushchev had to halt the wave of police terror. He accomplished this task. He supported the arrest and execution of Beria, chief of the secret police, and he exposed to the Party the cult of the individual that had led to crimes and excesses on Stalin's part after 1934. But he may have admitted too much, because the de-Stalinization speech encouraged Poland and Hungary to turn away from Moscow and concentrate on the development of their own socialism. Khrushchev reacted swiftly, but his actions did not please the

Party Presidium, which attempted to unseat him in 1957. He survived this crisis, consolidated his power, and addressed the second Stalinist legacy, centralization.

Stalin's five year plans had consistently emphasized heavy industry at the expense of consumer goods. The centralization developed and directed in Moscow had worked well for heavy industry, which required generous capital investment, abundant raw materials, and sophisticated technical skills. The government was the ideal institution to marshal resources for the production of iron, steel, and electricity. But centralization had not worked as well in the production of consumer goods, where manufacturers and consumers had to constantly interact with one another. It might take years before a bureaucrat in Moscow learned that the chandeliers made in Tbilisi were so heavy that they were falling from the ceilings. A less centralized economy, one in which the consumer reported the deficiency immediately to the chandelier maker, would permit the problem to be corrected promptly. Khrushchev understood the problems created by centralization, and he hoped his Regional Economic Councils would solve them. But they merely multiplied the confusion and waste instead of eliminating them. Thus Khrushchev was unable to deliver the consumer goods which his people demanded. He stands as a transitional figure, as a leader able to see and articulate national needs, yet unable to find the means to fulfill them.

Further Reading

There is a wealth of material available on the life of Khrushchev, a man not loath to talk and write about himself. His era, though brief, held the world's attention through his prodigious efforts to move his nation forward and by his stunning revelations about the Stalin years. This era was also characterized by a cultural "thaw." The most articulate writer of this period was Alexander Solzhenitsyn, whose harrowing chronicles of the Soviet gulag system received a brief period of official approval and public attention during Khrushchev's reign. Khrushchev himself, however, authored no works of ideological or philosophical merit..

ON KHRUSHCHEV AND HIS ERA

Breslauer, George W. *Khrushchev and Brezhnev as Leaders: Building Authority in Soviet Politics.* London: George Allen and Unwin, 1982. This scholarly work explores the development of the authority of the two leaders through the appeal of their policies.

Crankshaw, Edward. *Khrushchev, A Career.* New York: Viking, 1966. The book is easy to read and covers the leader's life from birth to that fateful day in October 1964 when the Presidium unseated him.

Dmytryshyn, Basil. *USSR, A Concise History.* Fourth Edition. New York: Charles Scribner's Sons, 1984. The 700-page work covers the USSR from the turn of the twentieth century to 1984, but almost half of the book contains appendices of helpful tables and important documents such as the full text of Khrushchev's de-Stalinization speech.

Fejtö, François. *A History of the People's Democracies: Eastern Europe Since Stalin.* Trans. Daniel Weissbort. New York: Praeger, 1969. The scholarly discussion is organized topically and covers trends in several countries simultaneously.

Frankland, Mark. *Khrushchev.* New York: Stein and Day, 1966. This essay is written for the non-specialist.

Khrushchev, Nikita. *Khrushchev Remembers.* Trans. and ed. Strobe Talbott. Boston: Little, Brown & Co. 1970. The memoir is interesting but its contribution to Khrushchev scholarship is minimal.

Medvedev, Roy A., and Zhores A. Medvedev. *Khrushchev: The Years in Power.* Trans. Andrew R. Durkin. New York: Columbia University Press, 1976. The notes and research materials for this book were confiscated by the KGB in 1971. The work analyzes Khrushchev's policies from the perspective of two dissident Soviet Marxists.

Solzhenitsyn, Alexandr I. *The Gulag Archipelago.* 3 volumes. Trans. Thomas P. Whitney (volumes one and two) and Harry Willetts (volume three). New York: Harper and Row, 1973–78. The 1,930 pages cover the gulag system between 1918 and 1956.

————. *One Day in the Life of Ivan Denisovich.* Trans. Max Hayward and Ronald Hingley. New York: Praeger, 1963. The brief novel caused a sensation in the Soviet Union when it first appeared in *Novy Mir* on November 20, 1962. It chronicles a twenty-four hour period in the life of a prisoner in Stalin's gulag.

"A good Bolshevik is one who unmasks shortcomings and bravely smashes all that is old and outdated to pave the way for progress."

—Leonid Brezhnev

5

THE THIRD GENERATION OF COMMUNISTS: LEONID ILYICH BREZHNEV, BUSINESSMAN

The Kremlinologists, those Western observers who monitor and interpret Party policy, who forecast that Khrushchev's fall would clear the way for radical policy changes, were quickly disappointed. Leonid Brezhnev was Khrushchev's protégé and heir apparent. It is true that Brezhnev had been instrumental in Khrushchev's ouster. But the new leader and his colleagues had objected to what they saw as the former First Secretary's subjectivism, authoritarianism, and mad improvisations. Khrushchev's basic promise to deliver more consumer goods and services was upheld. In this sense, "Khrushchevism" continued without Khrushchev.

The contrast in personality between Khrushchev and Brezhnev was striking. The unpredictability and at times bizarre conduct of Khrushchev was matched by the opposite extreme of Brezhnev's pragmatic and calculating manner. A story Brezhnev recounted to President Richard Nixon in 1972 revealed as much about the Soviet leader as it did about peasant life:

Once there was a Russian peasant who was traveling on foot to an isolated village. He knew the direction but not the distance. As he passed through a birch forest he chanced upon a wizened old woodsman whom he asked how far away the village was. The old man shrugged and said: 'I do not know.' The peasant sighed, shifted his bundle from one shoulder to the other and strode on. Suddenly the woodsman shouted out: 'Fifteen minutes down the road.' Perplexed, the peasant wheeled around and asked: 'Why didn't you say so at once?' The old man replied calmly: 'First I had to see what size steps you take.'[1]

Like the old man, Brezhnev examined national problems deliberately and without fanfare, and he supplied solutions garnered from decades of experience. Undramatic leadership ought not to be confused with ineffective or weak leadership. Brezhnev ruled the USSR for eighteen years, longer than Lenin and Khrushchev combined. A Western diplomat once described him in this way: "[He was] a soviet-style manager-politician-executive, the efficient organization man, a communist in a gray flannel suit."[2] Brezhnev was a consummate third-generation communist.

Brezhnev: From Engineer to Heir Apparent

Leonid Brezhnev was born on December 19, 1906 in Kamenskoye (now Dneprodzerzhinsk), a town of about 20,000 people located in the center of the Ukrainian metallurgical industry. Leonid, the oldest of three children, represented the fifth generation of steelworkers in the family. He would probably carry on the family tradition, but his mother Natalya had greater ambitions for her son. She hoped her son would become an engineer and live in the part of town inhabited by workshop bosses, foremen, and other highly paid factory members. An education, she believed, would get him there. Natalya saved every available kopeck to pay for her son's tuition and for the tutor who would prepare him for the entrance exam.

Little is known about Brezhnev's preschool years. His father worked inordinately long hours in a steel mill, and the mother controlled the household. A robust, strong-willed woman, Natalya exerted a powerful influence on her son. She succeeded in pushing him toward a better life when in 1915 young Leonid earned admittance to the preparatory class at the boys' high school. The Brezhnevs paid part of the tuition, and the remainder was waived since the boy had scored exceptionally high on the entrance exam.

High school rigorously challenged a steelworker's son. With forty-four other students in his class, Leonid embarked on a traditional course of study: languages, science, history, mathematics, geography, and art. After the November Revolution and the ensuing Civil War, the curriculum in Leonid's school may have changed, but the challenge remained the same. Leonid seldom did better than average work, though he was doggedly persistent. He graduated with a class of about a dozen students in the summer of 1921. The remaining thirty or more students had fallen victim either to the curriculum or to the most turbulent and bloody period in the country's history.

While Brezhnev attended high school, the Russian Empire collapsed after a series of wars and political upheavals. During the Civil War, Ukrainians experienced unimaginable turmoil and suffering. Within three years they witnessed the rise and fall of governments by Ukrainian nationalists, communists, anticommunist White Army leaders, and for a few months Austrian and German troops. Each change of government was accompanied by large-scale reprisals and random butchery. Throughout all the violence and devastation in the Ukraine, the older Brezhnev remained employed when work was available, and the determined Natalya did what was necessary to keep the family together. The Brezhnevs had acquired the habit of survival.

Kamenskoye became economically depressed after the Civil War, and so the Brezhnevs left for Kursk, the town of their ancestors in western Russia. In Kursk the father found work, and the two younger children entered school. Leonid now made the first important political decision of his life. The sixteen year old joined the junior Communist Party organization, the Komsomol.* He knew little about communist ideology, but he was pragmatic enough to realize that the Party organization was the means to a good job or admission to a higher education institution. The young Brezhnev's instincts proved correct when the Party selected him for a four-year course in land surveying at the Kursk Land Tecknikum. During his final year at the school he met Viktoria Petrovna, the woman who would be his lifelong companion and supporter, and by whom he would have two children.

Leonid Brezhnev by the late 1920s had married, begun a family, earned a technical education, and belonged to the proper political organization. He was admitted to the Party in 1929 as a candidate member.**

---

*Young people from fourteen to twenty-seven years old could join and still may join this important feeder organization of the Party.

**CPSU members serve as candidate members without voting privileges for at least one year before they may apply for full membership.

Brezhnev's future in the Party looked bright until his matriculation at the prestigious Moscow Agricultural Academy. Students
at the academy were handpicked to become part of a new tech-
nocratic elite in agriculture. Any ambitious twenty-four year old
would have seized the opportunity to live in Moscow—the center
of power—and to study at the Agricultural Academy, the gateway
to future power and prestige. But Brezhnev dropped out of school
in 1930, probably because he found himself on the wrong side of a
political issue with an administrator at the school. He returned to
the city of his youth, Kamenskoye, to work in metallurgy and to
be with his mother and father, who had resettled there in 1927. To
Party officials, this move had truncated a promising political
career.

In Kamenskoye, now a bustling metropolis of 100,000, Brezhnev
displayed seemingly boundless energy and dedication. He worked
in the factory by day and at night attended the local metallurgical
institute, from which he graduated in 1935. He also served at the
institute as Party secretary in charge of the political leadership of
six hundred students. After serving in the army for the minimum
compulsory period of one year, he expected to work in the factory
upon his return home. But local Party leaders had other plans.
They made him director of the Institute, which had expanded
into a multitrade technical college. This appointment accelerated
the engineer's spectacular rise through Party ranks, an ascension
that gained even more momentum after Khrushchev assumed
leadership of the Ukrainian Communist Party in 1938.

After a series of quick promotions, Brezhnev became Secretary
of Propaganda for the entire Dneprodzerzhinsk (formerly Kamenskoye) region in 1939. The promotion made him the fifth leading
apparatchik in the most important industrial region in the
Ukraine. It also marked him as a Khrushchev protégé. Numerous
qualities in the thirty-two year old had caught Khrushchev's eye.
Brezhnev was Russian in ancestry as well as outlook, but he had
been reared in the Ukraine—he knew the area and its people well.
He was a trained engineer, an enthusiastic supporter of Stalin,
and his police record, as well as those of his friends and relatives,
was clean. Brezhnev represented the kind of Party member
Khrushchev needed to crush Ukrainian nationalist feelings and to
sovietize the area. As a consequence, the First Secretary protected
the engineer and carried him up the Ukrainian Party ladder. From

this moment, Brezhnev's career advanced or declined with the fortunes of Khrushchev.

In the early 1950s Brezhnev reached the upper echelon of Party leadership. He became Party Secretary of Moldavia, one of the USSR's fifteen republics, and he was elected to the CPSU Central Committee and appointed to the Party Presidium and Secretariat. In the last year of Khrushchev's rule, it was obvious that Brezhnev had climbed to the position of heir apparent.

Why would Brezhnev risk a secure future as a Party leader to plot the removal of the man who had been responsible for his stellar rise in the Party? During the 1960s dissatisfaction with Khrushchev was widespread. Brezhnev and other Presidium members criticized among themselves the First Secretary's unpredictable emotional outbursts such as the United Nations shoe-banging incident, and they berated his foreign policy debacles, in particular the severence of relations between the USSR and China. By 1964 their patience had run out. When Khrushchev did not retire on his seventieth birthday as he had earlier indicated to some foreign dignitaries, the Party decided that it was time for action. The coup was executed by a coalition of Party members whose only common ground at times was their dislike of the Party leader. There was no evidence that Brezhnev conceived the plot, but undeniably he was a prime mover in its implementation on October 13, 1964. Brezhnev was a master at manipulating political infighting, and he exercised his talents to assure Khrushchev's political demise.

The Reign of Cautious Progress

BREZHNEV RULES AS PART OF A COLLECTIVE LEADERSHIP

A few days after Khrushchev's ouster, a lead article in *Pravda* tossed some final darts at the former leader and announced the Party's determination to create a collective leadership in the USSR:

> The Leninist Party is an enemy of . . . wild schemes; half-baked conclusions and hasty decisions and actions divorced from reality; bragging and bluster; attraction to rule by fiat. . . . The construction of

communism is a living, creative undertaking. It does not tolerate
armchair methods, one-man decisions or disregard for the practical
experience of the masses.[3]

The collective leadership that emerged was headed by Brezhnev,
chief of the CPSU, and Alexis Kosygin, Premier of the Council of
Ministers and leading spokesman for foreign affairs.

Behind the facade of collective leadership, the low-key and efficient Brezhnev initiated a slow, relentless drive toward domination of both Party and government bureaucracies. Evidence of his
initial success surfaced in 1966 at the Twenty-third Party Congress when it reinstated the title "General Secretary of the
CPSU." The Congress also restored the Presidium's original
name, "Politburo." Perhaps more revealing was that no second
secretary was appointed. General Secretary Brezhnev had maneu-
vered himself into the position of first among equals.

Brezhnev continued to amass power and prestige throughout
the 1970s. For example, in 1977, he became President of the Soviet
government. He never, however, established the type of one-man
rule characteristic of Stalin or even Khrushchev. Powerful interest groups like the military competed for available resources, and
Brezhnev remained in power because he managed to keep the interest groups content. The General Secretary accumulated ceremonial titles during the decade, but in practice his leadership
rested on an intricate system of support from high-echelon Party
members, who were content to wield influence in their respective
bailiwicks.

MATERIAL STANDARD OF LIVING OF PEASANTS AND
WORKERS IMPROVES STEADILY BUT SLOWLY

Brezhnev and the new leadership believed, like Khrushchev
before them, that communism was nothing if it did not provide
plentiful food, better clothing, and comfortable housing for the
citizens of the Soviet Union. Typical of the third generation of
communists, the new leaders committed their energies to improving the material standard of living of peasants and urban
workers.

Particularly in its early years, the leadership made changes which greatly benefited peasants. Organizational changes included restoration of the pre-Khrushchev agricultural system, with the Ministry of Agriculture in Moscow directing production through state organizations in rural areas. Gone was the idea of having the agricultural planners work in the fields with peasants to better understand their problems. Gone, too, were the Regional Economic Councils, which had spread confusion throughout the countryside. The Brezhnev changes reestablished a chain of command that had withstood constant assault under Khrushchev.

Other changes directly enhanced peasant working conditions. The move from *kolkhoz* to *sovkhoz,* begun under Stalin, continued under Brezhnev. In 1940 there were more than 200,000 *kolkhoz*es, while by 1976 there were 27,000; comparative figures for *sovkhoz*es were 4,000 and 20,000. Peasants preferred life on *sovkhoz*es because they worked regular hours and received a steady wage instead of waiting for income from the sale of surplus at year's end. Peasants remaining on *kolkhoz*es also profited during the Brezhnev era from a guaranteed minimum salary, with the possibility of an annual bonus if the collective finished the year in the black.

During the Brezhnev years peasants continued to devote intensive care and time to fifteen million private plots, the kitchen gardens that comprised 1.4 percent of all Soviet farmland. To rural residents the plots generated extra income, and for the country the gardens produced in the late 1970s approximately one-quarter of its agricultural products, one-third of its livestock products, and almost half of its vegetables and potatoes. Brezhnev was forced to admit publicly that the kitchen gardens played a vital role in feeding the Soviet people. He also did an about-face from previous policy by officially promoting small-scale private farming. He permitted agricultural machines, among other things, to be sold to private farmers!

Agriculture under Brezhnev revealed two contrasting systems of organization. On the one hand, agricultural policies flowed from the Ministry of Agriculture in Moscow to the *sovkhoz*es; the Ministry also influenced, to a lesser extent, the *kolkhoz*es. At no other time in Soviet history had communal agriculture been so centralized. On the other hand, kitchen gardens functioned as private enterprises, virtually free of Moscow's policy directives. The two systems, agriculture by central planning and agriculture by family initiative, existed side by side with Brezhnev's official blessing. In the 1970s the mix of state and collective farming and limited private farming was working well. An indicator of this success was the distribution of internal passports to peasants. In the past these passports, necessary for travel from city to city, had been issued routinely to urban dwellers. The internal passport for peasants, if nothing else, affirmed that the financial lot of rural residents had improved to the point of at least making travel possible. More palpable measurements of the success of the Brezhnev policies were grain yields. The highest yields during the Khrushchev era had occurred in 1962 and 1964 with 140 and 152 million tons respectively; during Brezhnev's rule, the figures were 224 and 237 in the late 1970s. Even Brezhnev's two worst years in the 1970s equalled the best years under Khrushchev: 168 million tons in 1972 and 140 in 1975. A factor that contributed significantly to the high grain yields in the 1970s was the increased use of artificial fertilizers, a practice initiated by Khrushchev and intensified under Brezhnev.

Life in the countryside might have improved during the Brezhnev years, but agricultural production remained the Achilles' heel of the Soviet Union. To offset sudden and uncontrolled fluctuations in grain yield (for example, 237 million tons in 1978 and 179 the following year), the USSR negotiated costly, long-term import agreements with the United States and Argentina. Part of the problem with agriculture in the Soviet Union traditionally has been unfavorable climatic conditions, a situation beyond the influence of Party leaders. Another factor has been the inefficiency of the peasants themselves. In comparison with United States farmers, the Soviet peasantry in the 1970s tilled 70 percent more land with seven times more manpower, but it produced only four-fifths of the food. True, it utilized less sophisticated machinery than American farmers and possessed only one-third the tractors; nonetheless, one cannot avoid the thought that more energetic and determined peasants could have produced higher grain yields. In improving peasant efficiency, Brezhnev could claim no more than Khrushchev could: the USSR fed itself more or less adequately, but its agricultural system could hardly be held up for emulation.

The Brezhnev leadership procured more for peasants than it

Grain Harvest (million tons)

Comparison Table: 1886–1988

Year	Harvest	Year	Harvest	Year	Harvest
1886–1890	36[1]	1937	96	1969	162
1900	56	1940	96	1970	187
1910	74	1945	47	1971	181
1913	80	1950	81	1972	168
1916	64	1953	82	1973	222
1920	46	1954	86	1974	195
1921	38	1955	104	1975	140
1922	50	1956	125	1976	224
1923	57	1957	103	1977	196
1924	51	1958	135	1978	237
1925	73	1959	120	1979	179
1926	77	1960	126	1980	189
1928	73	1961	131	1981	150
1929	72	1962	140	1982	180
1930	84	1963	108	1983	190
1931	70	1964	152	1984	170
1932	70	1965	121	1985	192
1933	68	1966	171	1986	210
1934	68	1967	148	1987	211
1935	75	1968	170	1988	215[2]

Note: Population figures were 125,000,000 in 1897 and 275,000,000 in 1985.

[1] Average annual production in European Russia

[2] Projected yield

Sources: Alec Nove, *An Economic History of the U.S.S.R.* (Baltimore: Penguin, 1969), pp. 94, 186, 226, 293, 336.

J. N. Westwood, *Endurance and Endeavor, Russian History, 1812–1980,* Second Edition (New York: Oxford University Press, 1981), pp. 420, 492, 496, 497.

was able to gain for urban workers. The main problem facing industry was the same one that had plagued agriculture: productivity. The Regional Economic Councils had served industry just as poorly as they had agriculture, and so the Party leadership reinstated the pre–1957 system of industrial ministries that centralized planning and supervision. Centralization might not be a panacea, but it was superior to the disorganization and confusion wrought by the Economic Councils.

The leaders also introduced "market socialism," the concept of profitability in limited areas. If they could tolerate limited private enterprise in agriculture, they could live with it in industry and business too. The Brezhnev leadership, in a controlled experiment, liberated a few hundred enterprises from most government controls. These businesses could now assign wage increases and bonuses on the basis of profitability or the sale of products rather than on the fulfillment of production goals. Where market socialism was introduced, it was successful. But to numerous Party conservatives, the profit incentive smacked of capitalism or at the very least "goulash communism."* Many CPSU members also feared that Party control of industry would diminish if managers severed their ties with Party planners. In the face of these criticisms, Brezhnev and the leadership retreated by terminating most of the experiments involving market socialism. This retreat from an apparently successful program indicated that leadership was still a collective one, marked by compromises among powerful Party personnel.

Inevitably the growing conservatism of the Brezhnev years affected the economy negatively. The Soviet Union's gross national product (GNP) showed a significant slowdown after the 1960s. The average GNP growth rate reached 5.2 percent during the Eighth Five Year Plan (1966–70), then declined steadily during the remainder of Brezhnev's tenure: 3.7 percent during 1971–75, and 2.7 percent for 1976–80. These dismal figures adversely affected the material existence of citizens, since defense and heavy industry expanded faster than the rest of the economy and siphoned resources from the consumer sector.

Despite the problems attached to a sluggish growth rate, the Brezhnev leadership supplied more and better quality goods and services for the people than they had enjoyed at any other time in the century. For example, during Brezhnev's first full year as Party chief, production of television sets and refrigerators was 68,000

---

*"Goulash communism" was an expression applied to the economic policy of Hungarian Party leader Janos Kadar. It featured a cautious economic liberalism that was based on the theory that economic growth was a prerequisite for social progress. By 1959 he had abolished a planned economy in favor of private initiative and provided a legal framework for small-scale entrepreneurship. This mixture of socialist and capitalist economic features (hence the term "goulash") continues in Hungary to this day.

and 29,000 units respectively. In 1970 the corresponding figures were 143,000 and 89,000; in 1977 they were 229,000 and 210,000. But despite these investments in the consumer sector, the Soviet people continued to live simple existences by Western standards. Indeed, the material standard of living of the Soviet citizenry during the Brezhnev years remained the lowest among the major industrial nations. Also, the costs of most consumer goods were prohibitively high in relation to wages; in 1980, for example, it took a factory worker more than five months of wages to purchase a twenty-four inch color television set. But the fact remained that TV sets, refrigerators, and other consumer goods were available, and families were managing to save enough rubles to purchase them.

MILITARY BUILDUP DETRACTS FROM DÉTENTE

For the material existence of the Soviet people to improve, more resources had to be invested in the consumer sector. For more resources to be available, the USSR had to remain at peace with the capitalist world. To that end, the Brezhnev leadership followed Khrushchev's direction in foreign affairs: peaceful coexistence with the West and the easing of international tensions, a policy which became known as détente.

When Brezhnev and Kosygin assumed power, they wanted to improve the Soviet Union's relationship with other nations, and particularly with the rival ones. They blamed the acrimony some nations displayed toward the USSR on the petulance and poor diplomacy of Khrushchev. But the finger-pointing at Khrushchev proved to be of limited value when the old tensions and animosities resurfaced within a year or so.

Relations with China, the thorn in Khrushchev's side, reappeared as a nagging problem to the Brezhnev leadership. Ideological disputes had plagued relations between the Soviet Union and China since the late 1950s. After the USSR had launched its first intercontinental rocket and *Sputnik I*, Mao had declared that "the east wind (is prevailing) over the west wind."[4] To him, the communist bloc had demonstrated its technological superiority over the West; it ought to act on that strength. But the Soviet Union feared nuclear holocaust, and it continued to spread communist ideology through economic, not military, means. Generally the conflict between the two communist giants remained a war of words until 1969. On Damansky Island, on the southeastern boundary between the USSR and China, a fistfight between two border patrols escalated into a pitched military battle in which fifty-one soldiers died. Tensions between the two countries increased again in 1974 when the USSR moved fifty armed divisions through Mongolia to the Chinese frontier, a mere six hundred miles from Peking. Near the end of Brezhnev's rule, the Red Army had almost one-third of its forces stationed along the world's longest and most disputed frontier, the border between the USSR and China.

Trouble with the communist states in eastern Europe also continued during Brezhnev's reign. In 1968 the hot spot was Czechoslovakia. Attempting to create "socialism with a human face," the Czech Communist Party allowed a free press and radio, stripped the secret police of most of its powers, initiated steps to sanction a multiparty political system, and improved relations with the West. These liberal political changes were threatening because they occurred in a communist country bordering the Soviet Union. Brezhnev and the CPSU hierarchy feared that Czech leadership might lose control of events, that is, Czech liberal ideas might influence the people of other eastern European countries or the Soviet Union. Thus the Red Army, with token troops from other communist bloc states—400,000 all together—invaded the country and forced the creation of a government more favorably disposed to Moscow. The invasion took place without a credible pretext or without the cooperation of any Czech group. A stunned world objected but offered little more than verbal protests. The CPSU elite later justified its move into Czechoslovakia with a statement which became known as the Brezhnev Doctrine: the USSR may intervene in the affairs of any Soviet-bloc nation if communist rule is threatened. Though the Brezhnev Doctrine would not be invoked again during the leader's tenure, it served notice to other eastern European nations that any movement toward liberalization had to proceed slowly and with the consent of the USSR.

Brezhnev and the military intervened one more time with the invasion of Afghanistan in 1979. When the pro-Moscow People's

Democratic Republic of Afghanistan, after an existence of little more than a year, toppled at the hands of Afghan Muslim leaders, the Red Army marched in to suppress the rebellion and restore communist leadership. The invasion of Afghanistan was the first advance into an area not recognized by informal World War II acknowledgments as lying within the Soviet orbit.

Brezhnev and the Party hierarchy risked the dangerous move into Afghanistan for several reasons. For centuries Russian leaders had hoped to expand southward in order to control year-round warm weather ports. The 1979 invasion brought Soviet troops to within a few hundred miles of the Persian Gulf and the Arabian Sea. Also, the Party elite could not swallow the bitter pill of a pro-Soviet regime overthrown by subject peoples. Whatever prompted the Politburo to proceed with the invasion, the gains probably did not equal the drawbacks since the war drained valuable resources and personnel from the USSR. In the international arena, the Soviet Union also lost prestige and money due to the war. The United States immediately suspended commercial relations with the country and led a forty nation boycott of the 1980 Olympic Games held in Moscow. But the war continued. Despite overwhelmingly superior Soviet forces and armaments, Afghan rebels have fought eight years for independence. In 1988, Mikhail Gorbachev began the withdrawal of Soviet forces from the country.

What had happened to Brezhnev's policy of détente? The conflict with China and the invasions of Czechoslovakia and Afghanistan certainly reversed Soviet attempts at easing international tensions in parts of Asia and eastern Europe. The involvement of the Red Army in these areas also proved that the supporters of the military in the Politburo had clout in determining foreign policy. Nonetheless, Brezhnev had mitigated the power of the military by limiting actual combat and by preventing local conflicts from escalating into nuclear war with Western nations. In the end, the Brezhnev leadership had scored moderately well in implementing a policy of détente.

Unfortunately for the Soviet people, détente did not improve their economic well being. True, the Brezhnev leadership had limited the gargantuan expense of widespread and protracted warfare. But money continued to pour into the military anyway. Soviet citizens continued to subsist at the lowest material standard of living among major industrial nations. The allocation of resources to the military was astounding for a nation in peacetime. A few comparisons with the United States will serve to clarify the enormous investment in the Soviet military during these years. At the time of the Cuban missile crisis in 1962, the United States enjoyed a three to one advantage in strategic nuclear weapons. Brezhnev neutralized this advantage in less than ten years. In the late 1970s the armed forces of the USSR had twice the personnel of the United States military, and the total defense budget of the Soviet Union was the largest in the world. The country devoted about 15 percent of its GNP to defense, while the United States, whose GNP was almost twice that of the USSR, allocated 6 percent to defense. The only bright light in this dismal picture was that Brezhnev, like Khrushchev before him, comprehended the insanity of a nuclear confrontation.

During Brezhnev's reign, Americans lived under five different Presidents: Lyndon Johnson, Richard Nixon, Gerald Ford, Jimmy Carter, and Ronald Reagan. The Soviet leader met with Nixon, Ford, and Carter and formally discussed limitations on nuclear armaments with them. Nothing significant was accomplished during these talks, due in no small measure to the lack of continuity in the White House. However, the leaders at least sat face to face and listened to each other's anxieties, concerns, and priorities. The fact that numerous crises over two decades never escalated into a nuclear war is evidence that Brezhnev and the American presidents clearly recognized the necessity of consultation and cooperation.

DISSENT RAISES ITS HEAD

By the early 1980s, the Soviet people experienced a more secure and comfortable material life than at any other time in the history of the USSR or the Russian Empire. They enjoyed virtual insulation from their official enemies, the capitalist nations of the West. Though China and some eastern European nations displayed ill feelings and, occasionally, open hostility toward the Soviet Union, there was no evidence that this hostility, albeit threatening and volatile, was anything other than an expression of nationalism. These countries were claiming their right as nations to determine internal policy and to cultivate and even display their national identities. In addition to their European buffer zone, the Soviet people endured the mixed blessings of a nuclear arsenal. On the one hand, nuclear arms protected their way of life from real or imagined encroachment by Western nations, while on the other hand, the possibility of nuclear annihilation eroded this sense of security.

The people also reaped benefits from the consumer programs developed by Khrushchev and Brezhnev over three decades. These leaders sufficiently buoyed the economy and provided free medical assistance, inexpensive housing, double the amount of food than what was consumed in 1950, four times more clothing, and enough televisions and refrigerators for 85 percent of Soviet families. Unfortunately, alcohol was available in large quantities also. In the early 1980s, alcohol consumption was rampant in the country, with people spending one-third of their food budget on alcohol and consuming twice as much hard liquor as Americans. The result was the creation of almost ten million alcoholics. Of course, alcoholism adversely affected the people's health and contributed significantly to declining standard of living indicators such as infant mortality (over 40 deaths per 1000, the highest in Europe) and life expectancy for men (about 62, the lowest in Europe, a figure which has also declined five years in two decades). This is a trend for which there is no modern historical precedent in peacetime. Improved standards of material existence do not always guarantee longer life expectancy.

But most Soviet people were not alcoholics and most profited from the improvements of these years. Far from squelching human aspirations, these improvements lessened for Soviet people the demands of daily survival, and permitted them to turn their attention to more philosophical—and political—matters. In the Soviet Union these questions inevitably centered on one issue: the right to express opinions divergent from Party ideology. Diversity of opinion could not receive CPSU support since the Party promulgated one opinion, the Party line. Contrary opinion could only come from a few courageous people, and it appeared in the form of dissent.

Dissent emerged for the first time when Brezhnev attempted to rehabilitate Stalin. After Khrushchev's ouster in late 1964, influential military figures and prominent *apparatchiki*—Brezhnev among them—believed that de-Stalinization had weakened the Party's authority. They pressed for the rehabilitation of Stalin's legacy. But what Khrushchev had dismantled, Brezhnev and his cohorts could not restore. Khrushchev had curtailed the role and power of the political police by striking down Beria and by exposing Stalin's cult of the individual. He had released intellectuals from Siberia's deep freeze, and he had permitted the publication in 1962 of Solzhenitsyn's *One Day in the Life of Ivan Denisovich*, an account of life in a Stalinist labor camp. Khrushchev and the CPSU had never relinquished their control of society, but the signs of the time indicated that restraints on Soviet artistic expression were lessening. When Brezhnev and the Party leadership attempted to rehabilitate Stalin, protests streamed in from intellectuals and even Party members who feared that the memory of those days would squelch the new voices of diversity. Faced with this dilemma, Brezhnev responded in his typical fashion—he compromised. Thus, at the Twenty-Third Party Congress in 1966, Stalin was not officially rehabilitated but two conventions of his era were, as Brezhnev assumed the title of General Secretary of the CPSU and the Presidium became the Politburo once again.

Brezhnev was not comfortable with the voices of diversity, and so he tried to muzzle them. The first prominent dissidents of the Brezhnev era were Andrei Siniavsky (pseudonym Abram Tertz) and Yuli Daniel (pseudonym Nikolai Arzhak), who were arrested for allowing some of their works considered critical of the USSR to be published abroad. The charge of treason, the media blitz against the two men, the courtroom packed with carefully selected spectators, the guilty verdict, the harsh sentences for Daniel and Siniavsky were events which shocked people in the Soviet Union and abroad. The entire spectacle was reminiscent of Stalin's show trials in the 1930s. The Siniavsky-Daniel hearing created in the USSR widespread dissent in the form of antigovernment demonstrations by the intelligentsia and by students, workers, and housewives. It also supplied impetus for the flourishing of *samizdat*, small clandestine presses. The two intellectuals received clamorous support from their countrymen not simply because the courts had awarded them harsh punishments, but also because the pair had refused—for one of the first times in Soviet history—to plead guilty and to admit to any complicity.

Other dissidents quickly followed Siniavsky and Daniel into forced labor camps or the dreaded insane asylums. But there were always more courageous people to take their places. None were more outspoken and more forceful than Alexander Solzhenitsyn and Andrei Sakharov. After writing *One Day in the Life of Ivan Denisovich*, Solzhenitsyn continued to produce searing indictments of the Soviet penal system such as *The First Circle* and *The Cancer Ward*. Excluding *One Day*, these masterpieces never appeared in the USSR in Party-approved publications. They were smuggled out of the Soviet Union and published abroad. Solzhenitsyn received the Nobel Prize in Literature in 1970, and after publication of *The Gulag Archipelago* in the West in 1973, the CPSU could tolerate him no longer. Fortunately for Solzhenitsyn his reputation was too prominent for the Party to risk arresting him, but it found another way to punish him. In 1974 Soviet authorities seized the Nobel laureate, put him on a plane, and deported him to the West. The punishment was perpetual banishment from his beloved homeland.

Sakharov, physicist and father of the hydrogen bomb, spoke out prominently and irrepressibly against government policies limiting the rights of citizens. His 1968 manifesto, *Thoughts on Progress, Peaceful Coexistence, and Intellectual Freedom*, called for freedom of expression and a multiparty system in the Soviet Union, and two years later he co-founded the Moscow Committee for Human Rights. In a less spectacular but just as effective manner, Sakharov's voice loudly supported the right of Soviet Jews to emigrate to Israel and Western countries. His protests and those of others helped persuade the government to let 200,000 Jews leave the USSR during the 1970s. For all his work, Sakharov received little reward. In 1975 the Nobel Committee awarded him its Peace Prize, which Soviet authorities did not permit him to receive. The ban on foreign travel was the only punishment the government dared to impose on Sakharov throughout the 1970s. His international reputation protected him from arrest and the dire fate meted out to lesser political prisoners. But by 1980 Soviet authorities no longer feared condemnation from the world community. They gave Sakharov his second "reward" by arresting and exiling him to Gorki, a city several hundred miles from Moscow that was closed to foreigners. He remained there until his release in 1987 as part of Mikhail Gorbachev's new policy of "openness."

Solzhenitsyn and Sakharov both have seized the imagination of the Western media, but in the Soviet Union they symbolize the weakness of the dissident movement as a whole. The two protesting voices are resounding and unyielding, but they are not in unison, and worse, they articulate contrary philosophies. A classic Slavophile, Solzhenitsyn believes that a return to Russia's Slavic roots would cure present ills. He would eradicate from the USSR all Western influences, especially Marxism, and promote values derived from Russia's Orthodox Church and from its peasant traditions. Sakharov, on the other hand, is a modern-day Westernizer, advocating reform of the Soviet system according to Western democratic ideals, such as freedom of speech and multiparty elections. This lack of common ground, combined with the intimidating influence of the secret police and the traditional Russian apathy in the face of authority, has prevented the dissident movement from gathering momentum.

Despite the small, disorganized, and ineffective character of the dissident movement, it is worthy of scrutiny because of the traditional role of dissent in Russian society. In the nineteenth century, the intelligentsia represented the voices of dissent in the country, and like Sakharov and Solzhenitsyn these social critics were divided into Westernizers and Slavophiles. The dissident movement in Brezhnev's time continued a centuries-old tradition in Russian society: it challenged governmental authority, and it asked the vital question, "What is to be done?" But neither Solzhenitsyn nor Sakharov has, thus far, formulated an answer that has captured the loyalty of the Soviet people.

Brezhnev died on November 10, 1982 at the age of seventy-five. Despite his partial success in giving the Soviet people more and better commodities, he clearly chose guns over butter. The USSR in 1982 might rightly claim the title of the world's greatest military power, but its farms still struggled to feed 270 million people, and its industries could not supply sufficient goods so that the people could enjoy a material standard of living equal to that of other industrialized nations.

Summary and Comment

The CPSU Politburo during the Brezhnev era upheld in theory and in practice the principle of collective leadership. It did not want another Stalinist cult of the individual or even the strong-man rule of a Khrushchev. Brezhnev led the CPSU for almost two decades and he accumulated numerous Party and government titles, but he never wielded power with a free hand in the manner of his predecessors. The policies he promulgated were the result of compromise.

If more resources had been invested in consumer industries, would the Soviet people have enjoyed in time the highest material standard of living in the world? Probably not. The Brezhnev leadership continued to centralize the economy as Stalin had done. All production plans originated in Moscow, leaving factory managers and workers no freedom or incentive in their work. Khrushchev had understood this problem, and he had attempted to decentralize the economy with Regional Economic Councils. But the Brezhnev leadership wanted nothing to do with de-centralization, and it cancelled the Economic Councils and other experimental ventures in the 1960s aimed at stimulating worker productivity. Even if more resources had been available to invest in the consumer sector, the Soviet people might not have had the motivation to create a higher material standard of living.

In the 1980s the problems facing the USSR were manifest. The military could not continue to take a gargantuan bite out of the country's economic resources, and centralization was not an effective method for improving the productivity of farmers and urban workers. The communist society envisioned by Karl Marx seemed to be, according to many Western observers, a dream that would never be realized.

Further Reading

Like his predecessor Khrushchev, Brezhnev wrote nothing of phil-osophical or intellectual merit. Publications in English on the man or his era are not abundant, primarily because of the uneventful and plodding character of his leadership and because of the return to a closed society that restricted information in a manner reminiscent of the Stalin period.

ON BREZHNEV AND HIS ERA

Bialer, Seweryn. *Stalin's Successors: Leadership, Stability, and Change in the Soviet Union.* New York: Cambridge University Press, 1980. The book provides an overview of how Soviet politics has changed since Stalin's death and particularly during Brezhnev's rule.

Breslauer, George W. *Khrushchev and Brezhnev as Leaders: Building Authority in Soviet Politics.* London: George Allen and Unwin, 1982. This scholarly work explores the development of authority of the two leaders through the appeal of their policies.

Carrère d'Encausse, Hélène. *Confiscated Power: How Soviet Russia Really Works.* Trans. George Holoch. New York: Harper and Row, 1982. The book is a highly readable account of the Soviet Union's political system as seen through its institutions and especially through the people who represent those institutions.

Cohen, Stephen, et al., eds. *The Soviet Union Since Stalin.* Bloomington, Indiana: University of Indiana Press, 1980. Leading scholars, most of them with firsthand knowledge of the USSR, address continuity and change in politics, the economy, and other areas in the twenty-five years since Stalin's death.

Dornberg, John. *Brezhnev, The Masks of Power.* New York: Basic Books, 1974. The biography is an early one but still good.

Gelman, Harry. *The Brezhnev Politburo and the Decline of Détente.* Ithaca, N.Y.: Cornell University Press, 1984. The book examines the Politburo as the center of Soviet politics, and discusses Soviet policy toward the United States during the Brezhnev era.

Murphy, Paul J. *Brezhnev, Soviet Politician.* Jefferson, N.C.: McFarland, 1981. The biography selects significant events from each period of Brezhnev's life to provide a portrait of his political growth.

Sakharov, Andrei. *Progress, Coexistence, and Intellectual Freedom.* Trans. *The New York Times.* New York: W. W. Norton, 1968. This intellectual manifesto analyzes nuclear war, hunger, pollution, and other international problems.

Smith, Hedrick. *The Russians.* New York: Quadrangle, 1976. The book provides an outstanding account of the personal lives of the Russians during the early 1970s.

"What is at stake is the ability of the
Soviet Union to enter the new millennium
in a manner worthy of a great and prosperous power."

—Mikhail Gorbachev

6

THE THIRD GENERATION OF COMMUNISTS: MORE BUSINESSMEN LEAD THE SOVIET UNION INTO THE TWENTY-FIRST CENTURY

Between the November Revolution in 1917 and Brezhnev's death in 1982, a period of sixty-five years, the Soviet people knew only four leaders—Lenin, Stalin, Khrushchev, and Brezhnev. Three years after Brezhnev's death, between 1983 and 1985, the country listened to the promises and aspirations of three successive leaders, Yuri Andropov, Konstantin Chernenko, and Mikhail Gorbachev. Andropov and Chernenko were not robbed of power by a vote of the Politburo as had happened to Khrushchev two decades earlier. Both leaders were old and sickly, and each died within two years of taking office. Their deaths spotlighted the advanced age of most Politburo members. In 1980 a Politburo gerontocracy with an average age of seventy ruled the country. The new Soviet leader, Gorbachev, on the other hand is much younger (fifty-four in 1985), and he appears sufficiently strong both physically and politically to hold power for a longer period than had his immediate predecessors.

Despite the rapid succession of leaders in the early 1980s, no debilitating infighting apparently occurred among members of the CPSU hierarchy. The smooth transitions to power were evidence that a collective leadership still controlled the CPSU. But this leadership will undoubtedly be tested as a young, dynamic Gorbachev attempts to lead his country closer to communism, the promised land of bountiful goods and services.

Yuri Vladimirovich Andropov

Less than three days after Brezhnev died, the CPSU hierarchy chose Yuri Andropov as General Secretary. At age sixty-eight, Andropov was expected to rule the world's second superpower for years to come. But the prospect of a lengthy Andropov tenure as Party boss was shattered fifteen months later when the General Secretary died of complications resulting from kidney disease.

ANDROPOV RISES FROM PROLETARIAN ROOTS TO KGB HEAD

Yuri Andropov was born on June 15, 1914, in the Caucasus province of Stavropol, in south Russia near Georgia. As the son of a railway worker, he came from humble beginnings. And like his immediate predecessors, Andropov devoted his entire life to Party work in one form or another.

Western observers began noticing Andropov first when he served as ambassador to Hungary and later when he was chairman of the Committee for State Security, better known by its Russian intials KGB. Appointed ambassador to Hungary in 1954, Andropov, by Kremlin accounts, assisted the Soviet military in staging a successful invasion of the country in late 1956. As Soviet troops broke through Budapest's defenses, Ambassador Andropov visited Hungarian Premier Imre Nagy's offices to assure him of the USSR's peaceful intentions and to urge him to refrain from any defensive action. For his efforts the ambassador received a new position, head of the foreign relations (socialist) department of the Central Committee in Moscow.

In 1967 Andropov, now a secretary of the Central Committee, accepted the chairmanship of the KGB on the condition that he also become a member of the Politburo. In the CPSU during the 1960s, the KGB head ranked lower than a Central Committee secretary. Thus to satisfy Andropov's demand, the Party leadership promoted him to candidate member of the Politburo, answerable directly to Brezhnev.

Andropov led the KGB for fifteen years, longer than any previous chairman, and he also became the most successful and so-

phisticated head of the secret police. Abandoning the brutal terror
tactics initiated by Stalin, Andropov and his police employed
more subtle techniques to quash the dissident movement. They
carefully prepared cases for trial, infiltrated organizations, and
used modern technology in surveillance. To control well-known
dissidents, the police avoided the courts and exercised control
through forced deportation or internal exile, as happened to Alexander Solzhenitsyn and Andrei Sakharov respectively. The KGB's
sophisticated methods proved effective, virtually crushing the
dissident movement by 1982. Andropov resigned as KGB chairman six months before the death of Brezhnev vaulted him into
the position of General Secretary of the CPSU and leader of the
nation.

ANDROPOV ASSUMES POWER TOO LATE IN LIFE

Fifteen months as Party boss was too little time for Yuri
Andropov to demonstrate his leadership abilities, especially since
Soviet leaders must first consolidate their power to ensure their
continuance in office. But Andropov moved with speed, accepting
the presidency of the Soviet government seven months after becoming General Secretary. Poor health, however, undermined his
ability to rule vigorously, and he disappeared from public view
after August 1983.

While healthy, the General Secretary addressed some of the
nation's troubled areas. For example, he initiated a campaign to
improve industrial productivity by penalizing drinking on the job
and by sending police to bars and public baths to round up absen-
tee workers. He added young blood to the Party hierarchy by pru-
ning the ruling gerontocracy and firing thousands of elderly,
poorly educated *apparatchiki*, replacing them with young, highly
trained officials. In foreign affairs Andropov continued Brezhnev's
policy of détente. But when a Soviet jet downed a South Korean
commercial airliner with 269 people aboard in September 1983
and the Party elite refused to acknowledge the incident for nearly
a week, world leaders questioned Andropov's ability to make
sound diplomatic judgments. Nevertheless, the General Secretary
in less than a year had attacked perennial domestic and Party

The Government of the USSR

There has always existed in the USSR an uneasy relationship among the more than one hundred different nationalities which comprise the nation. These nationalities can be clustered into more than a dozen major language groups totaling one hundred thirty languages. The cause of the tension is traceable to the domination of one national group, the Great Russians, who constitute approximately half of the population but claim a preponderance of power within government and Party ranks.

For administrative purposes, the diverse nationalities are organized into fifteen Soviet Socialist Republics, nineteen autonomous republics, and nine autonomous regions. The structure of government is pyramidal in form. At the base of the structure are village soviets, then, hierarchically, soviets of cities and districts, territories and provinces, autonomous and constituent republics. The highest organ of governmental power and the only legislative body in the USSR is the Supreme Soviet, a bicameral legislature with co-equal houses: the Soviet of the Union, comprised of constituencies elected on the basis of the general population, and the Soviet of Nationalities, which represents national groups. Deputies to the Supreme Soviet are chosen every five years in single candidate elections with voter participation in the 99 percent range. (Since 1986 the government has permitted two candidates to vie for office in a few designated elections.) Citizens either approve a selected candidate or they express dissatisfaction by crossing the name off the ballot or by writing in a substitute; candidates lose when "strike outs" or substitute names exceed the number of unchanged ballots. No candidate to the Supreme Soviet has ever lost an election. Since the Supreme Soviet meets only briefly twice a year, formal legislative power rests with its Presidium, which is chosen by the two houses at a joint session. To provide executive and administrative leadership between its brief sessions, the Supreme Soviet also chooses a Council of Ministers, which is accountable to it and to the Presidium between sessions. The chairman or Premier of the Council of Ministers directs its proceedings. The chairman of the Presidium is often referred to as the President, and he is the titular head of government; the position, however, is mainly honorific.

problems. But Yuri Andropov had reached the top too late. He died on February 9, 1984.

Konstantin Ustinovich Chernenko

Four days after Andropov's death, Konstantin Chernenko assumed power in the Soviet Union. Brezhnev had originally chosen

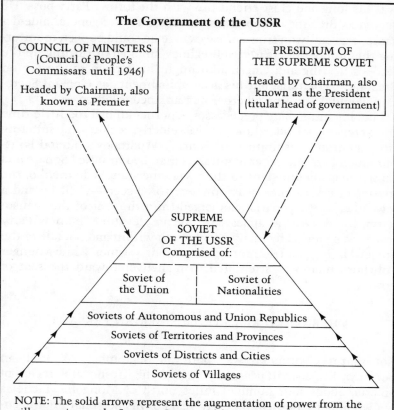

The Government of the USSR

COUNCIL OF MINISTERS
(Council of People's
Commissars until 1946)

Headed by Chairman, also
known as Premier

PRESIDIUM OF
THE SUPREME SOVIET

Headed by Chairman, also
known as the President
(titular head of government)

SUPREME
SOVIET
OF THE USSR
Comprised of:

Soviet of | Soviet of
the Union | Nationalities

Soviets of Autonomous and Union Republics

Soviets of Territories and Provinces

Soviets of Districts and Cities

Soviets of Villages

NOTE: The solid arrows represent the augmentation of power from the
village soviets to the Supreme Soviet, and from the Supreme Soviet to
the Presidium and Council of Ministers. The broken arrows point to the
bodies to which the Council of Ministers and Presidium are responsible.

Chernenko to succeed him, but in the power struggle after
Brezhnev's death Andropov had won. Now, the second time
around, Chernenko became General Secretary. Never before had a
number-two man of a former leader survived politically for another chance at the Party's top position. Chernenko's ascendancy
revealed his most important qualities, patience and persistence.
He had worked more than fifty years for the Party, thirty-two of
those years with Brezhnev. Undoubtedly Chernenko's major asset

was his long and close friendship with the former Party boss. He served as Brezhnev's appointment secretary and general aide-de-camp, especially on trips abroad, where he could be seen monitoring the number of cigarettes Brezhnev smoked or turning up the leader's hearing aid. Chernenko might have risen to the top on Brezhnev's coattails, but his accomplishments as General Secretary would determine whether he remained in office.

Like his immediate predecessor, Chernenko had too little time to exercise his leadership. He was elderly, feeble, and suffering from a chronic respiratory ailment. At Andropov's funeral Politburo members and other dignitaries marched into Red Square and up the mausoleum steps to the reviewing stand. Chernenko, the master of ceremonies, was nowhere to be seen—until he and a few other septuagenarians emerged from the rear of the mausoleum, lifted by what appeared to be an elevator. The new Party leader was viewed by many people both within and outside of the Soviet Union as little more than a chair warmer while younger Politburo members attempted to maneuver toward the seat of power.

CHERNENKO RISES FROM SIBERIAN PEASANT TO BREZHNEV PROTÉGÉ

Konstantin Chernenko was born on September 24, 1911, in Bolshaya Tes, a small peasant village in the Krasnoyarsk region of Siberia, about four hundred miles north of Mongolia. Little is known about Chernenko's early years or his personal life in general. He came from a large and poor peasant family, lost his mother while a young boy, and at the age of twelve worked for kulaks to earn a living. His life was grim and uneventful until he joined the Komsomol as a teenager. Chernenko later revealed the feeling of vitality he experienced when he cast his lot with the communists: "New Soviet life was just coming into its own, and I felt its fresh winds when I had joined the Young Communist League [Komsomol]."[1] At age twenty he joined the Communist Party and embarked on a slow but steady rise through Party ranks.

The watershed in Chernenko's career occurred in 1950 when Brezhnev arrived in Moldavia to become the republic's First Secretary. Chernenko was already working in the republic as the Party's local director of propaganda and agitation. The two men quickly struck up a comfortable professional relationship, and in 1956 Chernenko, under Brezhnev's patronage, moved to Moscow to take a post in the propaganda department of the Central Committee. The climb up the Party ladder continued for the peasant from Siberia when he became a full member of the Central Committee in 1971 and of the Politburo in 1978.

CHERNENKO CONTINUES BREZHNEV'S POLICIES

It took Yuri Andropov seven months to consolidate his position as leader of the USSR, and by Soviet standards he had moved with lightning speed. Chernenko accumulated the titles symbolic of power in the USSR even faster; after becoming General Secretary, he assumed the presidency of the country two months later in April 1984. The speed with which Chernenko became president suggested that Party leaders had decided to award the position to the General Secretary as standard practice. Politburo members harbored no fear that the feeble septuagenarian would launch any programs which would threaten their positions. As one Soviet source remarked, "What they were looking for when they picked Chernenko was a quiet life."[2] What they would get from Chernenko was Brezhnevism without Brezhnev, the quintessence of status quo politics.

In his first months as Party leader, Chernenko functioned as Brezhnev's ideological clone. He advocated détente and peaceful coexistence, promised to raise the cultural and living standards of Soviet citizens, and praised the competent and experienced people in the Party's upper echelon. He also vowed continuity with Andropov's reforms, though it seemed apparent from public statements that one reform, the introduction of young blood into the ruling hierarchy, had been interred with the former leader. Considering his age and state of health, Chernenko could do little more than serve as a transitional figure. He died shortly thereafter on March 10, 1985.

Mikhail Sergeyevich Gorbachev

While a startled population was still absorbing the news of Chernenko's death, the Soviet media announced four hours later the

The Communist Party of the USSR

Like the government, the Party resembles a pyramid with primary Party organizations at the base and powerful party organs at the apex. Theoretically, the Party Congress is the most powerful organ of the CPSU, but while Stalin was leader Party Congresses were called irregularly and then only to rubber-stamp policies generated by the more powerful bodies of the Party. A similar fate befell the Party's Central Committee, which on paper is responsible for directing the work of the Party between Congresses.

In practice, the Secretariat and Politburo hold power in the CPSU. The Secretariat represents the second most important body in the Party, and its General Secretary (or First Secretary, as it was called at one time) is the leader of the Soviet Union. The position of "leader" is not a formal one, but rather a convention started by Stalin and continued by his successors. As the administrative arm of the CPSU, the Secretariat selects Party personnel and verifies compliance with Party decisions. The most powerful organ of the Party and the only policymaking body in the country is the Politburo, headed by the General Secretary, who directs its meetings. This body is responsible for the initiation, formulation, and implementation of all domestic and foreign policies of the USSR. Politburo members and other high-ranking elements of the Party populate the Presidium of the Supreme Soviet and the Council of Ministers (known as the Council of People's Commissars until 1946), thus assuring the proper and consistent administration of Party policies by the government. Top level CPSU members also hold leadership positions in the communist parties of the union republics. There is only one voice in the USSR, and it is the CPSU.

election of Mikhail Gorbachev as General Secretary by the CPSU Central Committee. Never before had a successor moved to the CPSU top position so quickly following the demise of a predecessor. But Gorbachev was the fourth General Secretary in twenty-eight months, and the third one in that span to have been elected by the Central Committee. Gorbachev's ascendancy as General Secretary was marked by other "firsts" too. He was the first Party leader born after the November Revolution of 1917, the first leader from the post–World War II generation, and the first one since

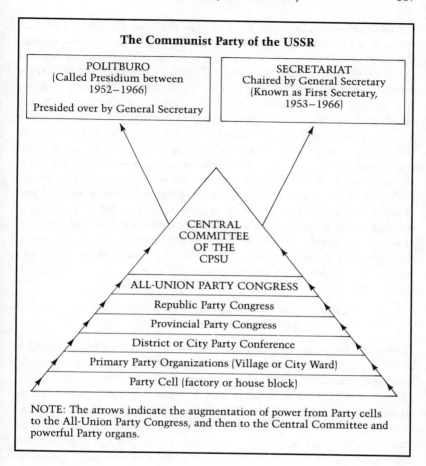

The Communist Party of the USSR

POLITBURO
(Called Presidium between
1952–1966)

Presided over by General Secretary

SECRETARIAT
Chaired by General Secretary
(Known as First Secretary,
1953–1966)

CENTRAL
COMMITTEE
OF THE
CPSU

ALL-UNION PARTY CONGRESS

Republic Party Congress

Provincial Party Congress

District or City Party Conference

Primary Party Organizations (Village or City Ward)

Party Cell (factory or house block)

NOTE: The arrows indicate the augmentation of power from Party cells to the All-Union Party Congress, and then to the Central Committee and powerful Party organs.

Lenin with a law degree. Western politicians and journalists described Gorbachev as witty, sophisticated, and well-informed, but invariably their talk focused on his relative youth (fifty-four) when compared to previous Party leaders. As Strobe Talbott explained:

Here, finally, was a General Secretary who could go on vacation to his native northern Caucasus without the world wondering whether he was on a dialysis machine or a respirator.[3]

Mikhail Gorbachev has held center stage on the international scene since March 1985. Is he a revolutionary like Peter the Great, the eighteenth-century tsar who recognized that Russia had to catch up with the West, or like Stalin, the General Secretary who drove his nation into the twentieth century through forced industrialization and collectivization? To a growing number of Sovietologists, Gorbachev is now more frequently labelled as a reformer rather than a revolutionary. As his objectives come under the scrutiny of an interested world, he is perhaps more accurately compared to Tsar Alexander II, the nineteenth-century Russian autocrat who saw clearly the dangerous weaknesses in the country's social, political, and economic systems but who settled instead for a patchwork of unsuccessful reforms. Whether he is a revolutionary or reformer, Mikhail Gorbachev has already talked of a new era for the USSR, an era that will certainly see change in the entrenched bureaucratic system that is now seriously impeding the development of a communist society.

GORBACHEV RISES FROM TRACTOR DRIVER TO ANDROPOV PROTÉGÉ

With the exception of Lenin, who was born into an upper middle class family, Soviet leaders have originated from the peasant or working class. Mikhail Gorbachev is no exception. Born on March 2, 1931, to a peasant family in the village of Privolnoye in the Stavropol region of the Caucasus, he attended local schools, survived the Nazi occupation of Stavropol during the Great Patriotic War, and in the postwar years finished his high school education while spending long, hard summers driving a combine in the grain fields of the region. Like most of his countrymen, he knew the meaning of hardship and poverty as the nation struggled to recover and rebuild after the terrible devastation of both city and countryside in World War II. It was during this grim period that the young Gorbachev attracted the favorable attention of local Party officials, not only as a diligent tractor operator but also as a bright and energetic member of Komsomol.

A major turning point in Gorbachev's life was his matriculation in 1950 at the prestigious Moscow State University law school. Apparently he possessed not only the intelligence but also the right recommendations from Party officials in his region. While working toward a law degree, Gorbachev continued his Komsomol work, eventually assuming leadership of the campus organization. Classmates remember him as an average student who was an adept glad-hander within the university community. His affability and his knack for making contacts characterized Gorbachev's style during his school years and continue to be his hallmarks today. Soviet citizens are becoming accustomed to a General Secretary who, on occasion, mingles with them, encourages their questions, even informally lectures them on the need for total commitment to hard work and sobriety if the communist goal of the good life is to be achieved.

His image is often enhanced by the presence of his wife, Raisa. Just as he represents what is certainly a new type of Soviet leader—comparatively young, vigorous, and adept at diplomacy—Raisa is her husband's equal in many respects. Possessing a doctorate in philosophy and a demonstrated command of Marxist-Leninist ideology, this slender, fashionably dressed, and vibrant woman is comfortable in the public eye. An attractive, sophisticated pair, they have done much to erase the stereotype of elderly Soviet leaders and their reclusive, dowdy wives.

Among Gorbachev's foremost mentors during his Stavropol years was Mikhail Suslov. As the Party's leading ideologist for several decades, Suslov was known as a maker and breaker of careers. In the 1960s he had played a key role in the dethronement of Nikita Khrushchev and in the choice of Leonid Brezhnev as Khrushchev's successor. During his years of Party work in the Stavropol region, Suslov had come in contact with Gorbachev. It was with his recommendation that Gorbachev left Stavropol in 1978 for work in the Central Committee's secretariat, where he was in charge of agriculture. A decade earlier in 1967, Gorbachev had earned a degree in agronomy at the Stavropol Agricultural Institute, an important addition to his resume. However, his record as the nation's coordinator of agricultural policy was a poor one, since during his years in this post (1978–84), the Soviet Union suffered a series of disastrous harvests and was forced to import millions of tons of grain.

Another important personal connection enhanced the career of young Gorbachev. Arriving in Moscow, he developed an almost filial relationship with the powerful Yuri Andropov, whose roots were also in Stavropol. Andropov was credited with the election of Gorbachev to full Politburo membership in 1980 despite the latter's youthful forty-nine years, two decades younger than most of his Politburo colleagues. The strong relationship between the two men continued through Andropov's brief tenure as General Secretary. Indeed, during this period, Gorbachev quietly served as the leader's closest ally. Though Gorbachev was unable to win Party leadership after his friend's untimely death in 1984, he continued to play an important role in the nation's affairs by operating as the aged Chernenko's number-two man, and by chairing Politburo meetings in the General Secretary's absence. Thus Gorbachev's acquisition of the Party's top position after Chernenko's death in 1985 was merely formal acknowledgment of his ascendancy.

With the selection of Mikhail Gorbachev, the USSR has gained a highly intelligent, tough, dynamic chief officer, a man skilled at the negotiating table and coolly aggressive in the pursuit of his goals. He must now employ all of his leadership qualities if the Soviet Union is to continue to hold its place as a world power as the next century begins.

GORBACHEV USES NEW WORDS AND SOME OLD POLICIES

Since coming to power in 1985, Mikhail Gorbachev has not only commanded an unprecedented share of the world's attention through his plans for restructuring his nation's economic system and for modifying aspects of the electoral system, but he has added three Russian words to the international vocabulary—*glasnost, perestroika,* and *demokratizatsia.* An analysis of these three words as Gorbachev uses them provides insights into the character of Mikhail Gorbachev and reveals the implicit limits he places on his plans for the nation. Unlike Peter the Great, who brutally shook off Russia's past, General Secretary Gorbachev has carefully structured his proposed changes to fit within the traditional framework of socialist ideological goals. Openness, restructuring, and a more fully developed democracy, as officially interpreted by Gorbachev, are words of reform and not of revolution.

Glasnost. Already, *glasnost,* or openness, has led to an un-

precedented outpouring of information to Soviet citizens and to
the world concerning current Soviet political, economic, and social problems. People at home and abroad are hearing about alcoholism, absenteeism in the workplace, juvenile delinquency, corruption within Party and government ranks, and unrest among
the country's many nationalities. Not only are the nation's weaknesses being aired in the Soviet media, but the formerly banned
works of Russian writers like Boris Pasternak and Vladimir Pla-
tonov are now available to delighted Soviet readers. A thaw is dis-
cernible in the works of current Soviet writers and artists as well,
and this permissiveness is encouraging a limited flourishing of
the arts in the Soviet Union. As a political strategy *glasnost* has
worked well, drawing to Gorbachev's side many people in the intelligentsia, the scientific communities, and the professions. But
such freedom is feared and resented by both Party and government conservatives, who view *glasnost* as a threat to the bureaucratic structure made permanent in the Stalin era, a structure that
has maintained them in positions of power and relative affluence.

Perestroika. The term *perestroika*, or restructuring, points to
the basic problem not only for Gorbachev's leadership but for the
future of the USSR as a world power. Since the turbulent years of
Lenin's rule, the Communist Party has ruled the country; the government has existed only as a means of implementing Party policy. Under Stalin, the Party machine expanded as a growing number of subservient appointees carried out the General Secretary's
directives. This officialdom became the true Soviet ruling class.
Today, all important governmental, economic, and cultural positions within the USSR are filled from the ranks of this ruling
class. In carrying out its will, the Party has total power over all
the means of production and, as Wolfgang Leonard states, ". . . its
members have the power to organize these means of production
in their own interest."[4] Thus Gorbachev's *glasnost*, by opening
the door to public criticism of the regime's failures and inequities,
and *perestroika*, by decentralizing the economy, threaten the monopoly of Party power.

Perestroika would diminish Party control over aspects of the
economy. A few examples illustrate the extent of this decentralization. In a June 1987 address, Gorbachev called for the disman-
tling of the present state planning commission (Gosplan) and the

central ministries, thus freeing factory managers from the old restrictions and thus encouraging and challenging local initiative. Each enterprise would develop its own five year plan and would negotiate the best prices for its raw materials and seek the most profitable markets for its finished products. In 1987, the state controlled all industrial contracts. Gorbachev's plan would reduce state control of these contracts to 25 or 30 percent by 1990. Restructuring would also apply to agriculture. Gorbachev has already called for a major increase in the size of peasant kitchen gardens in order to augment the nation's food supply. Perhaps limited private enterprise with a profit incentive will improve agricultural production where state-directed agriculture has faltered. Even collective farms are feeling Gorbachev's reforming efforts. In the farming areas close to major population centers like Moscow and Leningrad, collective farms are selling produce directly to customers instead of selling through the state's official agricultural stores. If the kitchen gardens grow, if the collectives continue to sell directly to customers, if Gosplan and the central ministries are dismantled, elites in the Party and state bureaucracies will have much to lose since the new policies will seriously weaken the entrenched, centralized system.

Perhaps Gorbachev has given notice, though, that the Party will remain the center of power. In his political report at the 1987 CPSU Congress, he stated that "the Party can resolve new problems successfully if it is itself in uninterrupted development, free of the 'infallibility' complex, [if it] critically assesses the results that have been attained, and clearly sees what has to be done."[5] In his closing remarks at that same Congress Gorbachev invoked Lenin's words to underscore the importance of the present challenge to the Party:

> All the revolutionary parties that have perished so far, perished because they became conceited, because they failed to see the source of their strength and were afraid to discuss their weaknesses. We, however, shall not perish, because we are not afraid to discuss our weaknesses and will learn to overcome them.[6]

Demokratizatsia. An examination of the third word, *demokratizatsia*, provides another insight into the General Secretary's plans for reform of the Soviet state. At the January 1987 Plenum of the Central Committee, Gorbachev told his audience, ". . . the serious, deep democratization of Soviet society . . . will enable us to involve in reconstruction its decisive strength—the people."[7] This democratization could take the form of secret ballots and choice between candidates in some, if not all, elections of Party and government representatives. But when Gorbachev made these proposals to the Central Committee, it roundly rejected them. The General Secretary counterattacked in a February 1987 speech to a convention of trade unions:

> We are not moving away from socialism. Through reconstruction we are developing the potential of the socialist system. . . . We need such powerful forms of democracy as *glasnost,* criticism and self-criticism, to change radically every area of social life. . . . The more democracy we have, the faster we shall advance along the road of reconstruction and social renewal, and the more order and discipline we shall have in our socialist house. So it is either democracy, or social inertia and conservatism.[8]

Nonetheless, Gobachev's democratization of the electoral system has advanced slowly, with only a few two-candidate elections thus far. It remains to be seen how much of "democratization" is oratory and how much is true reform.

Foreign Policy, Old Policy. Since taking office Gorbachev has released an almost uninterrupted stream of surprising policy statements which have startled the Soviet people and caught the attention of the world media to an unprecedented degree. His words have been analyzed, criticized, doubted, praised, and puzzled over by an intrigued public. However, in the crucial area of foreign policy, Gorbachev is no innovator. Despite his refreshingly blunt and candid style and his openness in stating painful truths about national problems, Gorbachev's foreign policy, at least in these early years, seems firmly grounded in expansionism.

During the three hundred years of Romanov rule, the Russian Empire pursued expansionist policies, and its military bureaucracy played an important role in setting the nation's course. Throughout these tsarist centuries, Russia expanded to the north, to the west, and to the south. In the east, Russia had completed its Asiatic expansion by the mid-nineteenth century, establishing the city of Vladivostok on the Pacific edge of the Asian continent in 1860. Religious influence during these centuries was also an important factor in support of Russia's military posture. Calling Moscow the Third Rome*, the Orthodox Church considered itself the one true repository of Christian beliefs, and, as such, preached Russia's messianic role in the salvation of the world. Since the Bolshevik takeover in late 1917, the USSR has continued to expand its influence. Now, instead of purely military conquest, the goal is ideological dominance.

Basic to Soviet foreign policy is the officially proclaimed belief in a "world revolutionary process." According to this tenet, the contemporary world is in a transitional phase marked by declining capitalism, the growth of socialism, and the inevitability of world communism. Certainly this aspect of Soviet foreign policy is no longer voiced as stridently as it was during Lenin's years. The Comintern, formed in 1919, insisted on the unification of communist parties throughout the world and espoused the goal of world conquest. But Lenin also needed cooperation with the capitalist West to help the economy, and Stalin needed to join forces with the West to neutralize the Nazi threat. Thus in Lenin's and Stalin's time the immediate needs of the Soviet state muted the calls for communist revolutions throughout the world. Khrushchev was no different from his predecessors. He boldly predicted that America would one day live under communism. Nevertheless Khrushchev, too, was aware of national needs and declared at his Party's Twentieth Congress that the principle of peaceful coexistence would govern his country's foreign policy. Gorbachev so far has downplayed more than the previous leaders the international dimension of communism. Not only is communist triumphalism conspicuously absent from the General Secretary's speeches, but his Party's official program in 1987 contained only a modest reference to world communism when it stated that "mankind's movement toward socialism and communism" could not

---

*Russian religious leaders had proclaimed Moscow to be the "Third Rome," i.e. the center of Christendom, in the fifteenth century. They believed that because Roman Catholicism had fallen into heresy, and because Eastern (or Byzantine) Christianity had betrayed its sacred trust when it reunited temporarily with Rome, only Russian Orthodoxy remained untainted and worthy of spiritual leadership.

be reversed.[9] The oratory on Soviet socialism as the vanguard of world communism may be absent from the leader's speeches and programs, but there is no indication that Mikhail Gorbachev is anything but a true Marxist-Leninist. He is a product of the Party system, from his Komsomol days in Stavropol to his appointment to the Moscow Politburo and, finally, to General Secretary of the CPSU. In an interview with members of the Soviet press in the summer of 1987, he made clear his orthodoxy by stating that "we intend to make socialism stronger, not replace it with another system."[10]

Thus today, the continuity from the traditional expansionist foreign policy of the tsars to the foreign policy of Gorbachev is unbroken, though of course expansionism today is linked to a different political and ideological system. This reality must be taken into consideration in any analysis of the foreign policy aims of the Gorbachev administration. At any given time, based on the state's needs and global circumstances, the expansionist policy may be put on temporary hold, but the nations of the world would be wise to recognize its continuing existence.

Summary and Comment

Yuri Andropov, Konstantin Chernenko, and Mikhail Gorbachev are members of the third generation of communists. Andropov and Chernenko died before they could influence substantially the course of Soviet history. Gorbachev, younger and healthier, has already ruled the USSR longer than the combined tenures of Andropov and Chernenko. A consummate businessman, Gorbachev has initiated a new vocabulary of change to motivate his people, and he has downplayed age-old Russian expansionism to ease worldwide tensions and to divert resources from defense to the domestic sector. The new vocabulary and the disarmament treaties support the traditional goals of third generation communists: more goods and better services for the Soviet people.

Gorbachev's ambitious plans to rejuvenate the Soviet economy will constantly encounter opposition from different quarters of the ruling elite. *Glasnost, perestroika,* and *demokratizatsia* will threaten the power of the Party, and they may be permitted to

flourish only to the extent that Party power is preserved. Comprehensive arms control agreements will reduce the exorbitant costs
of the Soviet military but, as a consequence, will threaten its
power within the Soviet hierarchy. Will Gorbachev survive
staunch opposition from conservative members in the Party, government, and KGB who advocate military spending? In 1987 the
closing words of Gorbachev's political report at the Party Congress were words of a leader sure of himself, his Party, and his
people:

> The Soviet people can be confident that the Party is fully aware of
> its responsibility for our country's future, for a durable peace on
> Earth, and for the correctness of the charted policy. Its practical im-
> plementation requires above all persistent work, unity of the Party
> and the people, and cohesive actions by all working people.
>   That is the only way we will be able to carry out the behests of the
> great Lenin—to move forward energetically and with a singleness of
> will. History has given us no other destiny. But what a wonderful
> destiny it is, comrades![11]

Should he succeed, Mikhail Gorbachev will have earned the
mantle of a great revolutionary, indeed, a man of destiny. He may
become the first representative of a yet unseen generation of communists who will live in the promised land of plenty. Should his
ambitious program fall short, history will record him as a reformer who, like Nikita Khrushchev, had a clear understanding of
the problem but who lost the battle against the forces of conservative obstructionists, and perhaps against the lethargy of the Soviet people.

Further Reading

Typical of the third generation of communists, Andropov, Chernenko, and Gorbachev have written no works of enduring value.
The best scholarship on them and their era remains to be written,
so contemporary is their leadership. The following books are
chosen not so much on the strength of the scholarship, which is
still under evaluation, but on the reputation of the authors.

ON THE POST—BREZHNEV LEADERS AND THE
EMERGING ERA

Bailer, Seweryn. *The Soviet Paradox: Eternal Expansion, Internal Decline.* New York: Knopf, 1986. The author explores the numerous problems facing Gorbachev, and he argues that after reaching its zenith under Brezhnev, the USSR will decline unless the leadership introduces sweeping reform, including decentralization.

Ebon, Martin. *The Andropov File.* New York: McGraw-Hill, 1983. Half of the book examines Andropov's political rise in the 1970s, and the other half is a collection of Andropov's speeches.

Gorbachev, Mikhail. *Perestroika.* New York: Harper and Row, 1987. There is a propagandistic slant to this book, especially when Gorbachev presents his views on arms control and superpower relations.

Johnson, D. Gale, and Karen McConnell Brooks. *Prospects for Soviet Agriculture in the 1980s.* Bloomington: Indiana University Press, 1983. The book examines the current status and trends in Soviet agriculture.

Leonhard, Wolfgang. *The Kremlin and the West, A Realistic Approach.* Trans. Houchang E. Chehabi. New York: W. W. Norton, 1986. The author takes a contemporary look at the USSR—its power pyramid, domestic problems, foreign policy objectives—and raises important issues for Western nations to consider.

Medvedev, Zhores A. *Andropov.* London: Basil Blackwell, 1983. There are a few dozen pages of biography, but the book primarily addresses the political rise of Andropov during the 1970s and the initial months of his rule as General Secretary.

———. *Gorbachev.* New York: W. W. Norton, 1986. The book has two parts: the making of a General Secretary and Gorbachev in power.

NOTES

Chapter One

1. Friedrich Engels, *Ludwig Feuerbach and the Outcome of Classical German Philosophy* (New York: International Publishers, 1941), pp. 42–43.

2. Karl Marx and Frederick Engels, *Karl Marx/Frederick Engels: Collected Works*, vol. 3 (New York: International Publishers, 1975), p. 329.

3. "Letter of Moses Hess to Berthold Auerbach in 1841," in *The Portable Karl Marx*, ed. Eugene Kamenka (New York: Penguin, 1983), p. 22.

4. "Letter of Arnold Ruge to Ludwig Feuerbach in 1844," in *The Portable Karl Marx*, p. 26.

5. Marx and Engels, *Collected Works*, vol. 39, p. 181.

6. Ibid., vol. 40, p. 217.

7. This reference was recounted by Engels in several of his letters in 1882 and afterwards. See in particular Engels' letter to Eduard Bernstein in 1882 as cited in Wolfgang Leonhard, *Three Faces of Marxism: The Political Concepts of Soviet Ideology, Maoism, and Humanist Marxism*, Trans. Ewald Osers (New York: Holt, Rinehart and Winston, 1974), p. 45.

8. Marx and Engels, *Collected Works*, vol. 5, p. 5.

9. Karl Marx, *Capital*, vol. 1, Trans. S. Moore and E. Aveling (New York: International Publishers, 1967), p. 178.

10. Marx and Engels, *Collected Works*, vol. 5, p. 4.

11. Karl Marx, *A Contribution to the Critique of Political Economy*, Trans. S. W. Ryazanshaya (London: Lawrence & Wishart, 1971), p. 21.

12. Marx, *Critique of Political Economy*, pp. 20–21; italics ours.

13. Marx and Engels, *Collected Works*, vol. 6, p. 166.

14. Marx, *Critique of Political Economy*, p. 21.

15. Marx, *Capital*, vol. 1, p. 363; tense change ours.

16. Ibid., p. 360; tense change ours.

17. Marx and Engels, *Collected Works*, vol. 6, p. 482.

18. Ibid., p. 497.

19. Karl Marx and Friedrich Engels, "Preface to the Russian Edition of 1882," in *The Communist Manifesto* (Middlesex, England: Penguin, 1967), p. 56.

20. Marx and Engels, *Collected Works*, vol. 39, pp. 62–65.

21. Kamenka, ed., *The Portable Karl Marx*, p. 541.

22. Marx and Engels, *Collected Works*, vol. 5, p. 256.

Chapter Two

1. Quoted in Bertram D. Wolfe, *Three Who Made a Revolution* (New York: Dial, 1964), p. 249.

2. Ibid., p. 78.

3. V. I. Lenin, *Collected Works*, vol. 23 (Moscow: Progress Publishers, 1964), p. 253.*

4. Quoted in Robert C. Tucker, ed., *The Lenin Anthology* (New York: W. W. Norton, 1975), p. xxxi.

5. V. I. Lenin, *Collected Works*, vol. 5 (Moscow: Foreign Languages, 1961), p. 369.

6. Ibid., p. 375.

7. Karl Marx and Friedrich Engels, "Preface to the German Edition of 1872" in *The Communist Manifesto* (Middlesex, England: Penguin, 1967), p. 53.

8. Quoted in Edmund Wilson, *To the Finland Station* (Garden City: Doubleday, 1940), p. 453.

9. Quoted in Louis Fischer, *The Life of Lenin* (New York: Harper and Row, 1964), p. 86.

10. Quoted in Wilson, *Finland Station*, p. 462.

11. Lenin, *Collected Works*, vol. 24, pp. 21–24.

12. Ibid., vol. 25, p. 404.

13. Ibid., p. 464.

14. Ibid.

15. Ibid., p. 469; tense change ours.

16. Ibid., pp. 469–70.

17. Ibid., vol. 26, p. 21.

18. Quoted in John Reed, *Ten Days That Shook the World* (New York: Random House, 1960), p. 172.

19. Ibid., pp. 171–172.

---

*The volumes of the *Collected Works* are from Progress Publishers unless otherwise noted.

20. Lenin, *Collected Works*, vol. 26, p. 382.
21. Ibid., vol. 32, p. 200.
22. Ibid., p. 185.
23. "Constitution and Rules of the Communist International," in Basil Dmytryshyn, *USSR, A Concise History*, Fourth Edition (New York: Charles Scribner's Sons, 1984), p. 456.
24. Quoted in Fischer, *Life of Lenin*, p. 600.
25. "Letter to Vera Zasulich," in *Karl Marx: Selected Writings*, ed. David McLellan (Oxford, England: Oxford University Press, 1977), p. 580.

Chapter Three

1. J. V. Stalin, *Works*, vol. 6 (Moscow: Foreign Languages, 1953), p. 49; the entire quotation is in capital letters in the *Works*.
2. Isaac Deutscher, *Stalin, A Political Biography*, Second Edition (New York: Oxford University Press, 1967), p. 326.
3. Quoted in Robert C. Tucker, *Stalin as Revolutionary: 1879–1929* (New York: W. W. Norton, 1973), p. 73.
4. Quoted in Tucker, *Stalin*, p. 86.
5. Quoted in Tucker, *Stalin*, p. 91.
6. Quoted in Tucker, *Stalin*, p. 108.
7. "Declaration of the Rights of the Peoples of Russia," in Dmytryshyn, *USSR, A Concise History*, p. 430.
8. Lenin, *Collected Works*, vol. 10 (Moscow: Foreign Languages, 1962), p. 443.
9. Lenin, *Collected Works*, vol. 36 (Moscow: Progress Publishers, 1966), p. 595.
10. Ibid.
11. Ibid., p. 596.
12. Quoted in Dmytryshyn, *USSR, A Concise History*, p. 141.
13. Stalin, *Works*, vol. 6, p. 111.
14. Ibid., p. 387.
15. Ibid., vol. 8, p. 22.
16. Ibid., p. 33.
17. Bruce Franklin, ed., *The Essential Stalin: Major Theoretical Writings, 1905–52* (Garden City, N.Y.: Doubleday, 1972), p. 444.
18. Quoted in Dmytryshyn, *USSR, A Concise History*, p. 170.
19. Quoted in John Scott, *Behind The Urals* (Bloomington: Indiana University Press, 1973), p. 18.
20. Quoted in Merle Fainsod, *Smolensk under Soviet Rule* (New York: Random House, 1958), p. 311.

21. Stalin, *Works*, vol. 13, p. 41.
22. Quoted in Leonhard, *Three Faces of Marxism*, p. 108.
23. Stalin, *Works*, vol. 6, p. 191.
24. Ibid., p. 193.
25. Ibid., p. 192.
26. *History of the Communist Party of the Soviet Union*, Second Edition (Moscow: Foreign Languages, 1962), p. 486.
27. Quoted in Wolfe, *Three Who Made a Revolution*, p. 253.
28. Quoted in Adam B. Ulam, *Stalin, The Man and His Era* (New York: Viking, 1973), p. 371, 373.
29. Ibid., p. 371–72.
30. Nikita Khrushchev, "De-Stalinization Speech" quoted in Dmytryshyn, *USSR, A Concise History*, p. 537.
31. Quoted in Donald W. Treadgold, *Twentieth Century Russia*, Fourth Edition (Chicago: Rand McNally, 1976), p. 282.
32. *History of the Communist Party of the Soviet Union (Bolsheviks), Short Course* (New York: International Publishers, 1939), p. 111; tense change ours.
33. Ibid., p. 121; tense change ours.
34. Quoted in Ulam, p. 541.
35. Generalissimo Stalin, *War Speeches* (London: Hutchinson, no date), p. 10.
36. Wolfe, *Three Who Made a Revolution*, p. 12.
37. Found in William G. Rosenberg and Marilyn B. Young, *Transforming Russia and China: Revolutionary Struggle in the Twentieth Century* (New York: Oxford University Press, 1982), pp. 213–14.
38. Stalin, *War Speeches*, p. 139.
39. Quoted in Treadgold, *Twentieth Century Russia*, p. 447.
40. Quoted in Rosenberg and Young, *Transforming Russia and China*, p. 212.
41. Nikita Khrushchev, "De-Stalinization Speech" quoted in Dmytryshyn, *USSR, A Concise History*, p. 556.

Chapter Four

1. Quoted in Mark Frankland, *Khrushchev* (New York: Stein and Day, 1966), p. 141.
2. Edward Crankshaw, *Khrushchev, A Career* (New York: Viking, 1966), p. 287; tense change ours.
3. Frankland, *Khrushchev*, p. 15.
4. Quoted in Crankshaw, *Khrushchev*, pp. 12–13.
5. Quoted in Frankland, *Khrushchev*, p. 32.

6. Dmytryshyn, *USSR, A Concise History*, p. 274.

7. Nikita Khrushchev, "De-Stalinization Speech" in Dmytryshyn, *USSR, A Concise History*, p. 536.

8. Ibid., p. 536.

9. Ibid., p. 547.

10. Ibid., p. 548.

11. Ibid., p. 564.

12. Ibid., p. 561.

13. Ibid., p. 526.

14. Ibid.

15. Quoted in Frankland, *Khrushchev*, p. 124.

16. Michael Kort, *The Soviet Colossus, A History of the USSR* (New York: Charles Scribner's Sons, 1985), p. 222.

17. "Excerpts From Speech by Khrushchev to 20th Congress of Soviet Communist Party" in *The New York Times*, February 15, 1956, p. 10.

18. Ibid.

19. Ibid.

20. Ibid.

21. Quoted in Thomas P. Whitney, ed., *Khrushchev Speaks* (Ann Arbor: University of Michigan Press, 1963), p. 4.

22. "The Program of the Communist Party of the Soviet Union (Draft), 1961" in *The New York Times*, August 1, 1961, p. 20.

Chapter Five

1. John Dornberg, *Brezhnev, The Masks of Power* (New York: Basic Books, 1974), p. 11.

2. Ibid., p. 15.

3. Quoted in Dornberg, *Brezhnev*, p. 184.

4. "Speech at the Moscow Meeting of Representatives of Communist and Workers' Parties of Socialist Countries on November 18, 1957" in *Mao Tse-tung and Lin Piao, Post-Revolutionary Writings*, ed. K. Fan (Garden City, N.Y.: Doubleday, 1972), p. 240.

Chapter Six

1. Quoted in *Time*, February 27, 1984, p. 36.

2. Quoted in *Newsweek*, February 27, 1984, p. 33.

3. Strobe Talbott, "The Soviets, Both Continuity and Vitality" in *Time*, March 25, 1985, p. 22.

4. Wolfgang Leonhard, *The Kremlin and the West, A Realistic*

Approach, trans. Houchang E. Chehabi (New York: W. W. Norton, 1986), p. 19.

5. Mikhail Gorbachev, *Political Report of the CPSU Central Committee to the 27th Party Congress* (Moscow: Novosti Press, 1986), p. 98.

6. Mikhail Gorbachev, "Speech at the Closing of the 27th CPSU Congress" in *Political Report*, p. 125.

7. Quoted in Peter Reddaway, "Gorbachev the Bold" in *New York Review of Books*, May 28, 1987, p. 23.

8. Ibid.

9. Ibid.

10. Quoted in *Time*, July 27, 1987, p. 31.

11. Gorbachev, "Speech at 27th CPSU Congress" in *Political Report*, p. 122.

Index

Lenin to Gorbachev: Three Generations of Soviet Communists was copyedited and proofread by Michael Kendrick. Production manager was Judith Almendáriz. The cartographer was Valerie Krejcie. This book was typeset by G & S Typesetters, Inc., and the first run was printed and bound by Edwards Brothers, Inc.

Cover and book design by Roger Eggers.

EPILOGUE 1994

EPILOGUE 1994

Library of Congress Cataloging-in-Publication Data

Crowley, Joan Frances.
    Lenin to Gorbachev: three generations of Soviet communists / Joan Frances Crowley and Dan Vaillancourt.
        p.   cm.
    Originally published: Arlington Heights, Ill.: Harlan Davidson, 1989. With new epilogue.
    Includes bibliographical references and index.
    ISBN 0-88295-863-1
    1. Statesmen—Soviet Union.   2. Communism—Soviet Union—History.   3. Soviet Union—Politics and government.   4. Communists—Soviet Union—Biography.   5. Communism—History—20th century. 6. Post-communism.   I. Vaillancourt, Dan.   II. Title
HX311.5.C76   1994
947.084'099—dc20
[B]   93-47041
                                                                                  CIP

Manufactured in the United States of America

98 97 96 95 94 1 2 3 4 5 MG

Head of Yeltsin courtesy of Wide World Photos, Inc.

EPILOGUE CONTENTS

"*Profound transformations must be carried-out in the economy and in the entire system of social relations, and a qualitatively higher standard of living must be ensured for the Soviet people. . . . This, comrades, is a problem of truly huge scale.*"

— Mikhail Gorbachev

"*There has been a noticeable increase in what I can only call adulation of the General Secretary by certain full members of the Politburo. I regard this as impermissible.*"

— Boris Yeltsin

THE LAST GENERATION OF COMMUNISTS:
MIKHAIL SERGEYEVICH GORBACHEV, THE REFORMER WHO KILLED THE CPSU AND USSR

Introduction

C hapter 6 of *Lenin to Gorbachev*, written in 1988, stated that Mikhail Gorbachev might become "the first representative of a yet unseen generation of communists." This new generation would face the enormous challenge of trying to raise the Soviet standard of living, a feat requiring the liberation of the nation from Stalinism, the political and economic system that had evolved under Joseph Stalin. Chief among the characteristics of Stalinism were the police state directed by a Party monolith, isolationism, the powerful military presence at home and abroad, Great Russian nationalism disguised in Marxist-Leninist idiom, and the highly centralized command economy controlled by an enormous bureaucracy—an *apparat*—under leadership of the CPSU. Would Gorbachev be the communist to dismantle Stalinism in the Soviet Union? Yes, but in the process he would wreck the economy, and he would lose his Party, his country, and his job.

Gorbachev never intended to scrap communism, only to restructure it, to reform its Stalinist character. His motto might have been: "De-Stalinize society, but keep it communist." To eliminate the lies and fears perpetuated by the Soviet police state, he advocated openness; the people finally learned the truth about their past and felt free to voice their concerns about the present. For this achievement, Gorbachev became one of the most popular leaders of the Soviet Union—for a few years at

least. To reduce other countries' fears of Soviet expansionism
and nuclear war, he negotiated historic nuclear arms agreements
with the United States and withdrew Soviet troops from
Afghanistan, Eastern Europe, and Mongolia, thus winning the
Nobel Peace Prize in 1990 and the plaudits of people around the
world. To break the monopoly of CPSU power, he instituted
contested elections by secret ballot for a parliament, the
Congress of People's Deputies, thereby becoming the first Soviet
leader to champion Western-style democracy.

But Gorbachev's strengths and successes were matched by
weaknesses and failures, and nowhere did he fail more miserably
than with the economy. At first he tried to implement policies
to decentralize it; the Enterprise Law, for example, allowed local
enterprise managers, as opposed to Moscow ministers, to control
part of production and to reap a profit. Unfortunately, Gorbachev and his aides overlooked the need for a middle echelon of
wholesalers to supply enterprise managers with raw materials
for manufacture and to help market the products. Therefore, the
scheme failed. Numerous other economic policies never worked
well either, since they did not constitute a comprehensive economic plan, and the *apparatchiki*, whose job it was to implement the policies, did not support decentralization, fearing loss
of their own prestige, power, and jobs. Yet another failure of
Gorbachev was his inability to represent the hundred-plus
diverse nationalities constituting the USSR. His Politburo, the
de facto ruling body of the country, should have included non-
Russian voices to guide his decision-making, but instead it was
populated mainly by Slavs, except for Eduard Shevardnadze, a
Georgian. Moreover, Gorbachev believed that the multinational
state, which had evolved over centuries as the Russian Empire
and now the USSR, was a legitimate political entity, whereas
the non-Russians—half of the population—believed differently:
the Soviet Union was a political façade that Russia used to dom-
inate them. Finally, Gorbachev's repeated poor choices of aides
and associates, people who could not see the wisdom of his policies and would not try to implement them, may make him the
only twentieth-century leader who handpicked all the men who
later betrayed and tried to oust him.

Gorbachev's uninspired moves opened a Pandora's box of
forces he did not always understand, could not always control,

and whose consequences he could not anticipate. In 1991, after six years as head of the USSR, Gorbachev was a man alone, disliked by virtually everyone in the country. Consumers could not find the food and clothing they wanted in state stores. The republics had distanced themselves from the Union by declaring their sovereignty in 1990. CPSU members were abandoning their Party. Given the extreme situation, something had to change, and so the leading government officials, all communists, tried to oust Gorbachev in an August 1991 coup. Though the putsch failed, Gorbachev was virtually finished. In one of the most ironic turns of events in modern history, the coup attempt accomplished the opposite of what it set out to do. Instead of augmenting the power of the Party in government and strengthening the Union, it precipitated the demise of Marxism-Leninism as the ruling party and dominant ideology and accelerated the dissolution of the USSR, as the republics, one after the other, declared their independence from the Union. Gorbachev, now a man with no country to lead, resigned the presidency of parliament on December 25, 1991, and slipped quietly into retirement. He never became the leader of a new generation of communists. Instead, Gorbachev will be known as a committed communist whose policies so stressed the USSR and CPSU that they suffered deadly strokes.

Three Tactical Weapons: *Glasnost, Perestroika, Democratizatsia*

IN 1985 THE ECONOMY IS FALTERING

On March 11, 1985, a confident Mikhail Gorbachev became General Secretary of the CPSU. Like other prominent Party leaders, he understood the dire situation of his sixty-seven-year-old nation. The economy was still faltering from the stagnant 1970s and early 1980s of the Brezhnev era, and the military was devouring 15–20 percent of the GNP.[1] The 1984 grain harvest had totalled only 173 million metric tons, the third lowest amount in a decade, forcing grain imports to reach 55 million metric tons, the largest import of grain in Soviet history. A stagnant economy, an exorbitant military bill, and a gargantuan grain importation combined to drive down even further the Soviet standard of living. Work was available, as it always was in the USSR, but state-set wages were so low that workers quipped, "They pretend to pay us, so we pretend to work." There were few goods to purchase in any case, since those sold in state stores were meager in both quantity and quality. The Soviet people were disillusioned and cynical, many turning to alcohol for consolation. At the beginning of the Brezhnev era, the legal sales of alcoholic beverages totalled about 15 billion rubles; twenty years later, legal sales had skyrocketed to more than 50 billion rubles, contributing to the increase in the country's overall death rate from 6.7 deaths per 1,000 citizens in 1964 to 10.8 per 1,000 in 1984. Gorbachev knew these trends and statistics, and he also realized that a profound economic and social transformation would be necessary to improve the living standard of the Soviet people.

Such a transformation would mean reform of the Stalinist institutions, especially the highly centralized command economy. Most businesses and industries were monopolies led by professional bureaucrats—*apparatchiki*—put in place by and answering to CPSU ministers in Moscow. This system enabled the Party to centralize the economy, thereby controlling it, and in the mind of CPSU leaders, making it efficient. The scheme also produced Soviet giganticism with individual mammoth factories sometimes employing as many as 40,000 workers and being responsible for the raw materials, production, or storage of a single commodity for the entire country. So pervasive was this form of economic organization that Gossnab (the government supply agency responsible for storing, delivering, and receiving industrial goods) reported during the Gorbachev era that 5,884 of 7,664 products (77 percent) in machine building, metallurgy, chemicals, timber, and construction were each manufactured by one producer.[2]

In some areas, the command economy enabled some goals to be accomplished. During the 1930s, Stalin effectively quashed opposition to his policies—both real and imagined—and his five-year plans developed the industrial infrastructure of the nation quickly, though with little regard for the safety, comfort, and livelihood of the people. In other areas, the Soviet economy failed abysmally. Standards of quality in production stayed low since there were no competitors to manufacture better products: for example, government stores sold shirts with buttons missing. Additionally, the command economy was unresponsive to consumer demands and feedback since there were no channels for consumers to communicate with Moscow planners; thus such bizarre inefficiencies as production of the chandeliers so heavy that they tore from their ceiling moorings occurred year after year (see p. 149). Supply disruption surfaced as another weakness of this economy; whenever a single source did not produce or deliver its product, the factories dependent on the missing product could not produce their own commodities—a disruption in the delivery of tires would cause the tractor factory to halt its shipment of tractors to farms or to send them without tires.

Gorbachev marshalled his forces for change around three banner words: *glasnost* (openness), *perestroika* (restructuring), and *democratizatsia* (democratization). The words were not unfamiliar to his countrymen. *Glasnost*, he often pointed out, had been used by Lenin in his writings and speeches twenty-three times, while *perestroika* had referred to agricultural and transportation changes during the early Stalin years, and now was part of the vocabulary of economists, writers, and journalists. *Democratizatsia* was a staple word for the Soviet people since Party leaders championed socialist society as the only true democratic society. For Gorbachev, the words not only defined his strategy for attacking the nation's problems but they also became tactical weapons in his campaign to transform the Stalinist socioeconomic system. He believed that "people . . . with all their creative diversity are the makers of history,"[3] but unfortunately the Soviet people, silenced for generations, had fallen into a torpor. *Glasnost* would help energize them by confronting them with present realities and their newly revealed history—the fabrications in the purge trials, the unjust executions, the forced deportations—and *democratizatsia* would help them reclaim their country. Only an alert, critical people wanting to transform their country would work energetically on the new economic programs, the *perestroika* programs, proposed by Gorbachev. *Glasnost*, *perestroika*, and *democratizatsia* were the

tactical weapons that would succeed over the next six years in
radically altering Soviet society, but not always in the manner
Gorbachev had hoped for.

GLASNOST RESTORES THE PEOPLE'S VOICE

Traditionally, tight controls hampered all forms of free expression in the Soviet Union. Journalists, for example, were stifled
by a five-page list of topics not to be discussed in the press; they
could not report on economic problems, the private lives of
Party and government officials and their families, accidents and
natural disasters, nor even on censorship itself. The people, too,
did not speak out. Fearful of reprisals, they kept their grievances
to themselves or shared them only with trusted friends and relatives. *Glasnost*, however, irrevocably transformed the political
climate in the USSR. By encouraging openness about the Soviet
Union's history and present conditions, Gorbachev served
notice that the people could be open about their daily concerns,
too. He hoped they would criticize corrupt Party and government officials, thus opening the way for him to dismiss the inefficient and unworthy and to replace them with officials who
shared his reform goals. Little did he know that the people
would extend their criticism to the Party, the Union, and even
to Gorbachev himself.

In 1985–86, *glasnost* moved slowly and within limits. The
media reported daily on the nation's social and political shortcomings, increasing alcoholism, rampant worker absenteeism,
the declining life expectancy for males, the soaring death rate
among the newborn, and the flagrant corruption among Party
officials and businessmen. *Glasnost* even encouraged a limited
flourishing of the arts as the works of previously banned writers
like poet Nikolai Gumilev and Nobel laureate Boris Pasternak
were published to the delight of Soviet readers. Even Soviet dissident Andrei Sakharov received a phone call from Gorbachev,
inviting him and his wife, Elena Bonner, to return to Moscow
from their involuntary exile in Gorki. But *glasnost* only went so
far; the people were not hearing all the truth about their past,
such as the fabrications in the purge trials. Gorbachev must
have come to realize that openness only within limits, besides

being oxymoronic, would probably not encourage the Soviet people to voice their concerns about the country's current affairs. Without the people's critical voice, he would lose vital assistance in the campaign to weed out corrupt Party and government officials.

In February 1987, Gorbachev swept away the limits to *glasnost* when he asserted unequivocally, "There must be no forgotten names, no blank spaces, either in history or in literature."[4] Now *glasnost* skyrocketed in Soviet society, showering citizens with an unprecedented openness. They heard "Voices of America" (jamming of the radio waves stopped in May 1987) and saw on television the Easter services of the Russian Orthodox Church—in a country that was the world's torchbearer for state-sponsored atheism. They read anti-Stalinist pieces like Anatoli Rybakov's *Children of the Arbat* and Mikhail Bulgakov's *The Master and Margarita*, Nikolai Bukharin's "Last Testament," in which he warned of the human blood that would stain the march to communism, and the secret protocols of the 1939 Nazi-Soviet Pact. The people also learned that the Supreme Soviet was annulling the sentences of thirty-three Party leaders, including Grigory Zinoviev, Lev Kamenev, and Bukharin, all purged and executed under Stalin, and that Alexander Solzhenitsyn and twenty-two other dissidents who had been forced to emigrate from the USSR during the 1970s and 1980s were having their citizenship restored. In the first year of Gorbachev's *glasnost*-without-limits, the revelations about the USSR's past varied so widely from the history depicted in official textbooks that in late May 1988, the end-of-year high school history exams throughout the USSR were canceled pending an accurate rewriting of the texts.

The new *glasnost* did create a freer atmosphere in which the people no longer had to be afraid to exercise their critical voice. The increase in the number of letters to the feature "A Word From the Reader" in *Ogonyok* (Small Fire) magazine, testified to this phenomenon. In 1986, readers' letters totaled 12,000; in 1989, 150,000. Gorbachev had hoped that the people, not fearing to speak their minds, would articulate support for him and criticism of *apparatchiki* opposing his policies of restructuring. Although some citizens did rally behind Gorbachev, many eventually turned their criticism directly on the CPSU for its power monopoly, on the Soviet Union for its stranglehold on the republics, and on Gorbachev himself for his inability to fill the shelves in state stores with food and clothing.

PERESTROIKA INFLUENCES FOREIGN POLICY

Restructuring, of course, was geared toward the economy. But *perestroika* without peaceful foreign relations would inevitably fail since too much of the nation's limited resources would be committed to arms and military personnel instead of domestic programs. Gorbachev constantly made this point in discussions with Western statesmen: "I always ask bluntly if they [people from the West] want the Soviet Union to have a chance to direct more resources to its economic and social development through cuts in its military spending."[5] In essence, Gorbachev was proposing a less-is-more foreign policy similar to that introduced thirty years earlier by Nikita Khrushchev who had pushed peaceful co-existence to free resources needed for domestic reform. Gorbachev, to his credit, would score far more foreign policy successes than Khrushchev had.

Through negotiations with President Ronald Reagan, Gorbachev ended the Cold War era and significantly reduced the nuclear arms threat that had menaced world peace for forty years. The 1987 INF treaty (intermediate-range land-based nuclear forces) between the two nations, for example, eliminated all medium-range and shorter-range nuclear missiles, and provided for on-site inspection by Soviet and American technicians stationed on each other's territory. Gorbachev also announced in 1987 that his country had abandoned the manufacture of chemical weapons, another class of weapons that could cause large-scale horrendous deaths.

Perhaps the most dramatic implementation of the General Secretary's less-is-more foreign policy occurred in the area of Soviet troop withdrawal from foreign soil. In early 1988 Gorbachev promised to pull all Soviet troops out of Afghanistan within the year, and he kept his word, ending a ten-year Vietnam-type nightmare for the USSR. He also withdrew from Mongolia the 75,000 Soviet troops facing the seventy-division

Chinese force along the border. (The last 12,500 Soviet service personnel went home in 1992.) In Eastern Europe he withdrew tank divisions and other combat units from the communist countries and announced in March 1989 that the future of these countries lay in their own hands, a virtual renouncement of the Warsaw Pact.

Without the Warsaw Pact or the presence of Soviet combat troops in Eastern Europe, the reform movements in these countries gathered momentum and changed the political face of the area. Within two years, the communist governments of the eight Eastern European countries had resigned or been overthrown, the Romanian President, Nicolae Ceausescu, had been executed for crimes against the people, the Berlin Wall had crumbled, and the two Germanies had reunited. Not since World War II had the world political map marked such swift and widespread changes, most of them achieved democratically. The German Federal Republic's democratic institutions expanded to include East Germany; in Poland, after a decade of Solidarity-led movements toward full democracy, unconditionally free parliamentary elections were held in October 1991. Even Hungary approved a new constitution based on the rule of law with popularly elected representatives to make up its National Assembly. But in countries like Albania, Bulgaria, and Romania, general strikes and riots forced the new transitional governments to resign and interim governments to restore order; democracy did not begin to take hold in these nations until 1992 when general elections for representative governments were held. In the remaining two Eastern European countries, Czechoslovakia and Yugoslavia, representative governments did not prevent powerful ethnic groups from forming their own nations. On January 1, 1993, Czechoslovakia split into two nations, the Czech Republic and Slovakia. In Yugoslavia, ethnic groups carved five independent states, Slovenia, Croatia, Bosnia and Herzegovina (one nation), Macedonia, and Yugoslavia (comprising Serbia and Montenegro). The new Yugoslavia demonstrated its ruthless aggressiveness by waging war on its neighbors, Croatia and more recently Bosnia and Herzegovina. Change in this part of the world, a virtual tinder box, will undoubtedly continue for many years.

Gorbachev could claim no credit for initiating or leading these transformations in Eastern Europe, and he might not have been able to thwart them in any case. By allowing events to follow an uninterrupted democratic or nationalistic course, he accomplished much, if only by default. He did not add to the turbulence inside these countries, and he did not increase the human death toll, which would have risen dramatically if Soviet troops had tried to quash the reform movements. For his judiciousness in allowing Eastern European countries to decide their own fate, his courage in withdrawing Soviet troops from Eastern Europe, Afghanistan, and Mongolia, and his initiative in proposing Soviet nuclear arms reductions, Gorbachev was awarded the Nobel Peace Prize in 1990.

His foreign policy successes notwithstanding, Gorbachev never realized a peace dividend at home. He successfully reduced the overall size of the armed forces from more than five million in 1984 to four million in mid-1990, but this personnel reduction never translated into a substantial defense budget reduction. In 1988, military spending increased 3 percent in real terms, and in 1989 (the last year for reliable figures) it decreased 1.5 percent.[6] This minuscule reduction yielded few liberated resources to invest in the *perestroika* programs. Gorbachev's less-is-more foreign policy meant fewer troops abroad, fewer nuclear and chemical weapons, more peace around the world, and more peace of mind as a result of reduced risk of nuclear holocaust, but not abundant resources for domestic investment, the goal that had motivated him to restructure the USSR's foreign policy in the first place.

PERESTROIKA RUINS THE ECONOMY AND THE FINANCES OF THE COUNTRY

Although Gorbachev changed the world, he did not improve the living standard of his own people. He never implemented a comprehensive economic and financial plan, and even if he had done so, the plan probably would not have worked, since the *apparatchiki*, who had their own agenda, and the people themselves, who were psychologically unprepared, would have sabotaged it. In no other areas did Gorbachev want to advance more rapidly, and in no other areas did he stumble more frequently. At the end of six years, the economy and the finances of the country were in a shambles.

Gorbachev tried economic and financial experiments that frequently were poorly conceived and isolated from one another, two major flaws for economic and financial entities which, like the strands of a spider's web, derive strength from their place in the whole. Two brief case studies poignantly illustrate these shortcomings.

On January 1, 1988, the Enterprise Law went into effect, its goal being to decentralize the administrative system for the economy by transferring decision-making from the central ministries to local enterprises. Essentially, the Law empowered plant managers, who would now be elected by workers, to produce and sell an increasing percentage of goods each year (starting with 15 percent the first year) at whatever price they could negotiate in the marketplace. Profits from these sales would be shared by managers and workers alike. In theory, by increasing the managers' control over the manufacture of more goods each year, central planning would wither away and a market economy would develop. Unfortunately, the Enterprise Law did not work. First, its creators failed to develop a country-wide echelon of wholesalers for enterprise managers to buy supplies from and to sell products to. In the Soviet Union, the leadership had traditionally prevented the rise of middlemen since they profited from the sweat of other people, an anathema in a communist society. Also, managers opted to increase the production of high-price items (for more profit), thereby creating shortages of cheaper products, a cycle that increased consumer demand and encouraged mass panic-buying and hoarding. For example, if given the choice, managers would produce high-ticket items like tractor tires rather than bicycle tires because they could earn more profit per ruble on tractor tires. (In theory, the quantity of these tires would be less than the quantity of bicycle tires, so tractor tires could command much higher profit margins). In the end, the Enterprise Law undermined the economy instead of bolstering it.

The second case study deals with Soviet finances. The Soviet system has always subsidized consumer goods and services such as food, rent, medicine, and education, at a yearly cost of 130 billion rubles. In the late 1980s, for example, consumers paid 20 kopecks (100 kopecks = 1 ruble) for a two-pound loaf of bread, the government absorbing the difference between the 20 kopecks and the real cost to produce bread, perhaps one ruble. Subsidization, coupled with a flagging economy during Gorbachev's tenure, increased budget deficits from a not uncommon 17 billion rubles in 1985 to an astronomic 200 billion rubles in 1990. How did the Soviet government finance these deficits? It printed more money, a strategy that not only fueled inflation (raising prices of goods) but created shortages since there was more paper money available to purchase goods, even at higher prices. In spring 1990, Gorbachev also decided to reduce the budget deficit by slashing agricultural subsidies and by letting the prices of bread and other foodstuffs rise closer to their true costs. When Soviet officials announced the strategy, consumers flocked to state stores and emptied the shelves while prices were still low. To purchase these goods, people even withdrew part of their bank savings, which created a run on banks. The Ministry of Finance tried to control the situation in 1991 by calling in all 50- and 100-ruble notes and by raising prices again, but it was too late. The people had lost confidence in the ruble, state store shelves were bare, and barter had become a popular form of transaction among individuals. In the midst of this chaos, in October 1990, Gorbachev admitted that he had handled Soviet finances poorly: "We lost control over the financial situation in the country. This was our most serious mistake in the years of *perestroika*."[7]

Even if Gorbachev had conceived a master plan for the economy, he would have wanted for the necessary enthusiastic support of the *apparatchiki* and the people to implement it. The *apparatchiki*, who enjoyed such material privileges as access to summer cottages, special stores with the best cheese and salami, and automatic admittance of their children to first-rate schools, wanted to safeguard their jobs and lifestyles. They undermined economic reforms intended to decentralize the economy because such reforms would eliminate their jobs. The people, on the other hand, had lived for decades with minimal material comforts and an ideology that mandated equal access to material goods; they resented neighbors-turned-entrepreneurs who succeeded in the marketplace and then enjoyed a privileged material existence. The following case study demonstrates well the sabotaging efforts of the *apparatchiki* and of the people.

One of the most promising economic reforms of the Gorbachev era involved privatization. Beginning May 1, 1987, individuals could work their own leased farms or they could collaborate with others to form, operate, and draw profit from their own businesses, known as co-operatives. Restaurants, beauty salons, tailor shops, and a variety of other co-ops quickly sprang up, from 14,000 in early 1988 to 133,000 in July 1989. The increase was statistically significant, but in a society with 287 million people, the co-ops, which employed about three million, did not alter the big picture of Soviet economic life. In the countryside, private leased farms did not sprout up as quickly as did co-ops in the cities. As late as April 1990, there were only 20,000 such farms. The story of Alexander Bozhko helps explain why the majority of the Soviet people did not rush to form co-ops or to try their hand at private farming, despite the sputtering economy and the opportunity for them to control their economic lives while earning a profit.[8] In 1989 Bozhko leased thirty acres of state farm land in the Rybinsk region, 200 miles northeast of Moscow. With the lease came a multitude of problems. First the *apparatchiki* loaded the law with so many stipulations that Bozhko could not turn a profit. He was obligated to purchase his equipment and supplies from the local state farm, whether or not the state farm could provide the materials. The steers he was obliged to raise were to be sold only to the state, and at half price. The produce he grew could not be sold on the open market. When Bozhko began raising his own animals on the side to clear a profit, the local state farm *apparatchik* accused him of violating the terms of the lease and demanded the land back. If the *apparatchik* had not canceled the lease, Bozhko's jealous neighbors would have ruined him anyway, since they had already slashed his tractor tires and run a harvester through his wheat field, crushing part of the crop. Life for the Bozhkos of the Soviet Union was difficult and dangerous, discouraging many like-minded people from continuing as entrepreneurs and serving as a warning to others who might contemplate private enterprise.

Gorbachev's *perestroika* programs frustrated the Soviet people, who showed displeasure with their leader in early 1991 by giving him a 10 percent or less support rating in opinion polls.

DEMOCRATIZATSIA PUTS THE COUNTRY IN THE HANDS OF THE PEOPLE

Gorbachev's third tactical weapon to reform the Stalinist socio-economic system was *democratizatsia*. The Soviet people had for decades voted "yes" or "no" for the governmental candidates preselected by the Party. This unusual form of democracy harbored glaring weaknesses: there was no choice of candidates since each election featured only one, and the elected person served in the government which was only a façade for the real seat of power, the CPSU. In proposing *democratizatsia*, Gorbachev did not have in mind this traditional form of Soviet democracy. Instead he advocated contested, secret ballot elections of a broad spectrum of leaders in society, governmental representatives, delegates to Party Congresses, and even factory managers and shop foremen. Through this broad democracy, Gorbachev expected to accomplish two things. He planned to transfer the locus of power from the CPSU to an elected government based on the supremacy of law. He also believed that widespread democracy would create among the people a sense of ownership of their country, motivating them to work enthusiastically with their leader to bring it prosperity.

The first tentative but incomplete steps toward broad democracy occurred in 1988 with the Enterprise Law, which sanctioned the election of enterprise managers by their workers (though this right to elect managers was annulled in June 1990), and with the election of delegates to the Nineteenth Party Conference. But the breakthrough to widespread, secret ballot, multicandidate contests occurred with the election of a new parliament, the Congress of People's Deputies, on March 26, 1989.

The Congress included 2,250 members, of which 750 were elected by special organizations like the CPSU (100 delegates— Gorbachev came to the Congress from this group) and the Academy of Sciences (twenty delegates including Andrei Sakharov). The remaining 1,500, elected by the people, represented constituencies around the country. When an election matched a reformer against an *apparatchik*, the reformer invariably won, a startling revelation of the disdain in which the people held their officials. (For example, reformer Boris Yeltsin trounced the Moscow Party machine candidate, Yevgeny Brakov, 5,118,745 votes to 392,633.)

The inaugural session of the Congress took place on May 25, 1989, marking the first time the Soviet people were represented by their own elected officials since the one and only meeting of the Constituent Assembly in January 1918. A population of 287 million could now turn on their televisions and watch their representatives at work. In fact, the television broadcasts were so popular that worker absenteeism shot up, and the government resolved to show future meetings on tape in the evening.

Two items dominated the agenda of that congress: the election of a new Supreme Soviet chairman, in effect the Soviet President, and the elections to the Supreme Soviet itself. Before Gorbachev was elected chairman by a vote of 2,123, he faced a barrage of challenges, questions, and severe criticisms from the parliamentarians. Some of them requested that he give up his post as CPSU General Secretary since the offices of the Presidency and General Secretaryship together would place too much power in the hands of one person; a delegate scolded Gorbachev for what was perceived by some as the too pervasive influence of his wife, Raisa; while still another representative asked for the truth regarding the rumor that the Gorbachevs were building a Crimean dacha (vacation home). Gorbachev demonstrated his political skill in handling such effronteries, unheard of among a population that had for centuries silently accepted the dictates of the ruler. He hedged on the dacha question by explaining that many of the Crimean dachas had been opened for public use but some were necessary for high officials, and he firmly rejected the suggestion that he resign as General Secretary, reminding them that the Soviet people were learning democracy and that they might need to lean on the Party for support.

The second major agenda item was the elections to the Supreme Soviet. Officially the state's chief organ of government, it had served merely as a rubber-stamp, giving pseudo-legality to the dictates of the Party. Now it would become a true parliament with 542 members chosen from Congress deputies, and would perform the day-to-day legislative functions between the two sessions of the Congress each year. The debate to decide how to set up the elections took an entire day, and the talk was marked by clashes between reformers and conservatives. In the end the conservatives prevailed, though last minute political maneuvering enabled a leading reformer, Boris Yeltsin, to become a Supreme Soviet member.

The Congress lasted twelve days, enough time for Soviet representative democracy to be born. So powerful were the television images of delegates formulating opinions, defending viewpoints, even shouting at each other and chairman Gorbachev that the people would never again submit unquestioningly to the fist of the CPSU. Boris Yeltsin described the Congress as a watershed event for the Soviet people: "On the day the Congress opened, they were one sort of people; on the day that it closed, they were different people. . . . Almost the entire population was awakened from its state of lethargy."[9]

The sessions of the Congress of People's Deputies so transformed Soviet society that even the CPSU realized that its days of monopolistic rule were over. On February 7, 1990, the Central Committee of the CPSU, after a bitter debate, voted favorably on a proposal by Gorbachev that the Party give up its leading role in society and become a participant in a multiparty system. Five months later, at the Twenty-Eighth Party Congress, the new Politburo relinquished its role in government. The transfer of power from the CPSU to the Congress of People's Deputies was now complete.

Democratizatsia, like *glasnost*, galvanized the spirit of the Soviet people, but *perestroika* drained their bodies. Freedom and openness are fundamental to the life of the human spirit, but they don't nurture the body. For that, bread and milk are necessary. *Perestroika* was ruining the economy, and the staples necessary to support physical existence were dwindling instead of increasing. As the dissonance between the programs to nurture the spirit and those to feed the body increased, opposition to Gorbachev grew and spread throughout the country.

The Fall of the CPSU, USSR, and Gorbachev

YELTSIN AND LIGACHEV CRITICIZE GORBACHEV

Two names, Boris Yeltsin and Yegor Ligachev, became synonyms for the contending forces of liberalism and conservatism in Gorbachev's early struggle to shape the country's future. In several ways the two Party men shared a similar background. Neither was a Muscovite, and each had a reputation for being a straight arrow—not a bribetaker. At the time of their summons to Moscow they were serving as Party bosses, Ligachev in Tomsk and Yeltsin in Sverdlovsk. Both were Gorbachev appointees to the Politburo and both publicly formulated their outspoken critical positions in early 1987. There the similarities ended.

In April 1987, Yeltsin chose his local *Pravda* newspaper as the place to carry out his assault on *apparatchiki*: "Many leaders have outdone even the clergy in ritualism. They know at what point to clap, when to say what, how to greet the authorities, and what decor to put up for an event. This is the invention of wheeler-dealers and toadies who are trying to keep afloat."[10] He continued to voice his displeasure of Party leaders as a group until October when, at a Central Committee plenum, he openly criticized two individuals, Ligachev and Gorbachev: "I cannot help remarking that although five months have passed since then (the June plenum of the Central Committee), nothing has changed in the style of work of . . . Comrade Ligachev."[11] Of Gorbachev he said: "There has been a noticeable increase in what I can only call adulation of the General Secretary by certain full members of the Politburo. I regard this as impermissible."[12] The comments were forthright and severe, accusing the Party's number-two man of footdragging on *perestroika* programs, and the Party leader of slipping into a Stalin-like cult of personality. Yeltsin concluded that he could not work with such leaders, and he closed his speech with a shocking request: "I must put before you the question of my release from the duties and obligations of a candidate member of the Politburo."[13] His resignation from the ruling body was accepted a few weeks later, and Gorbachev then appointed him to the modest post of deputy chairman of the State Construction Committee.

Boris Nikolayevich Yeltsin

Yeltsin was born in 1931 in a village near Sverdlovsk, 900 miles east of Moscow. Poverty, mischief, and physical activity characterized his formative years. Poverty: The Yeltsins were so poor that the nine family members from three generations slept on the floor of a one-room hut with a goat. Mischief: At eleven, Yeltsin sneaked into a church-turned-armory and stole two grenades, which he tried to dismantle with a hammer. One of the grenades exploded, mangling his left thumb and little finger, which were later amputated since gangrene had set in. Physical activity: An intelligent young man who earned A's on his report cards, Yeltsin preferred athletics to book work. At the Urals Polytechnic Institute, he studied engineering but "majored" in volleyball, which he played six hours a day. And later, he spent thirteen years as a physically active construction engineer in Sverdlovsk.

Yeltsin's CPSU career did not begin until he was thirty, but then it moved quickly. He became Sverdlovsk's Party chief in 1976, and nine years later (7/1/1985) Gorbachev brought him to Moscow as a Central Committee secretary because Yeltsin's liberal stance would strengthen Gorbachev in his struggle with conservative Moscow Party officials. Gorbachev promoted Yeltsin to first secretary of the Moscow Party Committee by the end of 1985, and he became a Politburo candidate a few months later.

Yeltsin's flamboyant provincialism delighted Muscovites. He rode public transportation instead of Party limousines, and he boasted that his shoes were a product of a Tomsk factory rather than a purchase from a fashionable Moscow store. He openly criticized local *apparatchiki* after unannounced visits to their stores, clinics, and housing units. But his hardhitting criticism went too far in October 1987 when he unleashed his displeasure on Gorbachev and Ligachev at a Central Committee plenum. He resigned from the Politburo, but his popularity among Muscovites never waned, as evidenced by his March 1989 landslide election in the city as a delegate to the Congress of People's Deputies. In late June 1991 he won the popular election for President of Russia.

Yeltsin towered literally (6 feet tall and over 200 pounds) and figuratively over most politicians in the twilight of the Soviet era. He accomplished numerous historical firsts: he was first to build a grassroots political organization, first to challenge the communist establishment and win a seat in parliament from the nation's most populous district, first high-profile Soviet politician to resign voluntarily from the CPSU (July 1990), first to be elected President of Russia, and first to turn back a coup. Boris Yeltsin has secured a unique place in Russian history, no matter what ultimately happens during his presidency of the country.

This resignation episode, much of it reported in Moscow newspapers, increased Yeltsin's reputation as a daring outsider, and he became a popular speaker at the political and cultural clubs that were springing up throughout the country. He surfaced again as a major player in the continuing struggle between conservative and liberal forces when he was elected in 1989 to the Congress of People's Deputies. From there, Yeltsin's political star rose to match and eventually surpass that of Gorbachev.

Ligachev's opposition to some of Gorbachev's policies followed a more serpentine path than Yeltsin's cannon shots, but not in 1987 when he spoke his mind. In March, he broadcast his remarks on national television. He praised the general direction of *glasnost* and *democratizatsia*, but in some areas, he said, the reforms had gone too far. He opposed "attempts to reduce the leading role of state management in the cultural sphere . . . the wholesale disparagement of everything . . . elements of mass bourgeois culture." His jargon concealed a genuine fear: the Party elite was losing control over an important aspect of society, culture. [14]

But Ligachev's most forceful move against Gorbachev occurred with the publication of the Andreyeva letter. On March 13, 1988, as Gorbachev was preparing to leave for his trip to Yugoslavia, Nina Andreyeva, a chemistry instructor at the Leningrad Technology Institute, attacked Gorbachev's policies in a 4,500-word letter published in the national daily, *Soviet Russia*, which also served as Russia's official government newspaper. The letter amounted to a manifesto against *glasnost*, particularly against criticisms of Stalinism.

> Take the question of J. V. Stalin. . . . [His] era is one of an unexampled rise of a whole generation of Soviet people who only now are gradually leaving the social and political arena. The formula of the period, 'a cult of personality,' is supposed to describe [those achievements] of industrialization, collectivization, and cultural revolution that brought our country the status of a superpower. All that is being questioned.[15]

Andreyeva made numerous other points, most of them critical of Gorbachev's policies. The letter was disturbing, but more shocking was the lack of official response to it for almost a month, encouraging people to conjecture that Gorbachev and his reforms were lacking support within the Politburo and the Central Committee.

What was the connection between the Andreyeva letter and Ligachev? The letter had been sent to him months earlier by the newspaper editor. For publication it was severely edited, its contents mirroring Ligachev's views; however, no evidence existed that Ligachev himself had taken a pen to the original pages. Even if he had had no hand in the writing, the permission to publish and the timing pointed to Ligachev. Certainly, the wide circulation the letter received was due to Ligachev. After the letter's publication, he convened a meeting of mostly conservative newspaper editors to sell them on the importance of the letter; also, Tass, the official news agency, sent word to regional newspapers to pay attention to the letter, and at least forty-three of them printed it. Even Party lecturers began to praise it in CPSU meetings. Ligachev and his conservatives were on the offensive.

On April 5 Gorbachev finally responded to the letter. An official article in *Pravda*, probably written by Gorbachev's close aide, Alexander Yakovlev, reprimanded *Soviet Russia* for giving so much attention to the backward-looking views of one person. "There is no going back,"[16] the article averred; *glasnost, perestroika,* and *democratizatsia* would continue. Stalin's cult of personality was described as an aberration of socialism: "It is alien to the nature of socialism and only became possible because of deviations from fundamental socialist principles."[17] With widespread publication of the strongly worded response, Gorbachev and his reformers regained control. Within two weeks, the General Secretary, backed by the Politburo and Central Committee, isolated Ligachev politically. Though Ligachev retained his Politburo seat, he lost his important posts within the Party hierarchy. In 1990 he retired from the Politburo to write his memoirs.

By mid-spring 1988, Gorbachev had outmaneuvered Yeltsin and Ligachev, representatives of two opposing Party factions. He seemed politically invincible, and the suggestion that in forty-four months he would be politically irrelevant in the USSR would have been judged as lunacy. But in that time, the elections to the Congress of People's Deputies humiliated scores of high-ranking CPSU *apparatchiki*, communism in Eastern

Europe toppled, and the economy worsened considerably. Many Party leaders wondered whether Gorbachev was leading them and their country into an abyss from which they might never return. The safety net holding them back, they believed, was the unity of the USSR. They were still governing a multinational empire, but, alas, even this safety net was not intact. Growing nationalism within the republics was inciting violence throughout the country and leading most republics to reconsider their legal ties to the Union.

NATIONALISM LEADS TO THE DEMISE
OF THE USSR AND GORBACHEV

The phrase "nationalities problem," whether employed at the community or republic level, was a catch-all term to cover the complex and multifaceted tensions that existed among the more than 100 nationalities in the USSR. These various nationalities were not conveniently located in distinct territorial units. Due to Stalin's mass deportations in the 1930s and the CPSU's priority given to industrialization which forced millions of educated and skilled Russians to work and live outside their native land, ethnic minority groups existed in nearly all the republics. In mid-1991, 65 million people—including 25 million Russians—lived, according to University of Wisconsin scholar Mark Beissinger, "outside their titular national territory, or were members of an ethnic group that had no territorial unit."[18] These people were so evenly distributed throughout the Soviet Union that each republic (except Armenia) was accommodating two ethnic groups numbering at least 100,000 each, and some republics like Moldova, Georgia, Kirghizia, and Kazakhstan were working to keep the peace among four such groups as well as within their own nationality group.

No doubt Gorbachev knew these statistics, but throughout his tenure as General Secretary he inaugurated no major programs to address the racism, prejudice, religious intolerance, and other problems that normally exist when people with different languages and cultures live in the same communities. He continued the traditional Russification programs—to teach in schools the Russian language and Russian history—as mandated under Stalin and supported by succeeding leaders. In a sense, to be ethnic-sensitive and ethnic-responsive might have been asking too much of Gorbachev, since in Stavropol and as a member of the Central Committee (responsible for agriculture) he had dealt with few ethnic issues; and later as General Secretary he received counsel on nationalities from an almost all-Slav Politburo (the only exception being the Georgian, Shevardnadze). Consequently, when ethnic conflict erupted in communities throughout the USSR in the late 1980s, the violence was quashed in the usual way, by police and troops. This strategy was about as effective as trying to smother a fire by pouring gasoline on it. And so, the ethnic rioting in Alma-Ata, Kazakhstan, in 1986 left an undisclosed number of police and demonstrators dead; the Moslem Azeri pogrom against the Christian Armenian residents in Sumgait, Azerbaijan, in 1988, killed thirty-one and wounded hundreds; army troops in Tbilisi, Georgia, in 1989 fired poison gas into a crowd of demonstrators and killed nineteen people, most of them women. Scores of similar examples could be given, each one involving casualties. The incidents of ethnic turmoil spread death and violence throughout the Soviet Union and increased confusion, anger, economic disruption, and social chaos among the populace.

Gorbachev dealt no better with the nationalities problem at the republic level. He truly believed in the multinational Soviet state: "We are one country, a single people. . . . Whether we like it or not, this is the way things have turned out for us. If we begin to split up, there will be a war, a terrible war. . . . We cannot split up."[19] Unfortunately for Gorbachev, the people did not agree with him. While the Soviet Union comprised nationalities that went back hundreds of years (through the Russian Empire), these ethnic groups had not joined the Empire or the Union voluntarily. What Lenin had said of the Tsarist Empire applied equally to the Soviet Union: it was a "prison of nationalities." Now *glasnost* was making it possible for people to say this, even to articulate aspirations of independence, some people quoting Article 76 of the 1936 Soviet constitution: "Each Union republic shall retain the right freely to secede from the USSR."[20]

Talk of seceding from the Soviet Union turned to action on

May 18, 1989. Lithuania and Estonia, through their own legislatures, declared their republics sovereign; minimally this meant that the laws of the republics would supersede those of the Union. Within nineteen months, the other republics had done the same, serving notice to Gorbachev that they wanted decisions about their lives to be made by them, not by *apparatchiki* in Moscow. The secessionist movement took a quantum leap forward in 1990 when Lithuania (in March) and Armenia (in August) declared independence from the USSR. Political decentralization was gaining momentum, and Gorbachev tried to check the pace by forming a new Union.

In late November 1990 he circulated a draft of a new Treaty of the Union, which would keep the republics together while guaranteeing political freedoms for the restive nationalities. But this Treaty of the Union was wishful thinking on Gorbachev's part, since the momentum of republican independence movements had already outstripped the President's proposals—Lithuania and Armenia wanted no part of any Union. Gorbachev recognized that the time for reconciliation had passed. A few months later he turned to the people for a popular mandate to support the Union, hoping a favorable vote would put pressure on republican leaders. He conducted a national referendum on March 17, asking the people to answer "yes" or "no" to the ballot question, "Do you consider it necessary to preserve the Union of Soviet Socialist Republics as a renewed federation of equal Soviet republics, in which the rights and freedoms of people of any nationality will be fully guaranteed?" Gorbachev won and lost the referendum: three-quarters of the people who voted supported it, but six republics—Lithuania, Latvia, Estonia, Georgia, Armenia, and Moldova—chose not to participate officially in the voting.

The following month Gorbachev accepted the inevitable—a Union with fewer than fifteen republics. He and the leaders of the nine republics that had conducted the referendum met and signed the "nine-plus-one" agreement. There would be a new nine-republic Union, greater republican autonomy, a new Union treaty and constitution, and new elections. The signing of the Union treaty would take place August 20, 1991.

Though the "nine-plus-one" agreement satisfied the drive for national autonomy of many republican citizens, it did not please leading Party *apparatchiki*. The country of Lenin and Stalin would be legally dissolved, and the new elections would surely bring fresh faces to the central government. The *apparatchiki* would eventually slide into oblivion, and the ones most likely to disappear first would be holding the highest positions in Gorbachev's government in 1991. To protect themselves and the country, these *apparatchiki* moved against Gorbachev in August and initiated a series of events that, in a few months, would drive the President from office.

Ironically, this new opposition had emerged via Gorbachev's own hand. With the USSR collapsing, ethnic violence escalating, and the economy spiraling downward, Gorbachev, incredibly, surrounded himself with hard-line Party conservatives to help him restore order in the country, thus demonstrating once again his poor judgment of character. Perhaps the five worst government officials he selected near the end of his years in power were Vice-President Gennadi Yanayev, Prime Minister Valentin Pavlov, KGB Chairman Vladimir Kryuchkov, Minister of the Interior Boris Pugo, and Minister of Defense Dimitri Yazov— these were five of the people who spearheaded the August coup against him.

Fateful Choices: Gorbachev's Last Cabinet

Gennadi Yanayev: Selected Vice President in December 1990, and confirmed by the Congress of People's Deputies on the second ballot after Gorbachev pleaded for confirmation. Undoubtedly, many delegates were unimpressed with Yanayev's statement, "I am a Communist to the depths of my soul," and with his activities months earlier trying to create opposition among workers to Gorbachev's reforms.

Valentin Pavlov: Appointed Prime Minister in January 1991 and known as a staunch opponent of radical economic reform. In a bizarre published interview in February he claimed to have foiled a Western and Soviet bank conspiracy to oust Gorbachev and to bring capitalism to the USSR. In June he attempted a constitutional coup by requesting from the Supreme Soviet that he and his ministers be given power over the state bank and nearly all economic matters.

Vladimir Kryuchkov: Appointed KGB chief in September 1988 and recognized as a die-hard supporter of Union integrity. He said in December 1990, "National chauvinism is being encouraged, and mass rioting and violence have been provoked [but the KGB will fight] with all the means at their disposal [against these] anti-Communist elements."[22]

Boris Pugo: Installed December 2, 1990, to replace Minister of the Interior, Vadim Bakatin, a leading liberal whom Gorbachev fired. A former KGB chief known as a conservative and an enforcer, Pugo would not hesitate to use his 700,000 police and 400,000 troops to crush ethnic violence.

Dimitri Yazov: Promoted to Minister of Defense in May 1987 when Gorbachev fired 200 military officers after the penetration of Soviet defense systems by a West German teenager, who, as a stunt, flew a rented Cessna Skyhawk from Finland to Moscow's Red Square, apparently undetected by Soviet radar. The new Minister proved to be a lackluster man with mediocre abilities.

AUGUST COUP ACCOMPLISHES CONTRARY GOALS

The coup started unofficially Sunday night, August 18, 1991, when five high-placed government officials, including one general, arrived at Gorbachev's dacha in the Crimea where he and his family were vacationing. The officials presented Gorbachev with two options: to cede his Presidency to Vice President Yanayev or to step down. Of course, Gorbachev refused both options. The men placed the President under estate arrest (he could not leave the grounds) with no live telephone lines to communicate with the outside world. In the next three days, the world outside Gorbachev's estate would change so rapidly the President would lose his grasp of it.

On Monday morning, eight senior government officials announced publicly that they had constituted themselves into a "State Committee for the State of Emergency in the USSR." The eight were Yanayev; Pavlov; Kryuchkov; Pugo; Yazov; First Deputy Chairman of the Defense Council, Oleg Baklanov; Chairman of the Peasant's Union, Vasily Starodubtsev; and President of the Association of State Enterprises, Alexander Tizyakov. The announcement attempted to veil the takeover as a constitutional devolution of power, claiming that Yanayev was taking charge of the government because Gorbachev was too ill to discharge his duties as President. The State of Emergency would last six months, enough time the Committee hoped "to prevent society from sliding into national catastrophe and insure law and order."[23]

In theory, the putsch should have succeeded since it was planned, it included all the leaders of the Soviet power institutions, and the people in Moscow seemed to accept the idea. The planning of the coup had begun in the summer when top government officials and Gorbachev himself met numerous times to discuss the creation of just such an emergency committee and other measures to halt the country's slide into chaos. In a sense the Gang of Eight preempted the emergency plan and then sought Gorbachev's cooperation on the night prior to the takeover. Moreover, KGB chief Kryuchkov had begun engineering a coup for almost a year by tapping phone lines (including Gorbachev's), compiling a list of people to be arrested, and so on. The putsch was not a haphazard affair.

Behind the attempted coup were the two leaders of government, Yanayev and Pavlov; the heads of intelligence and police, Kryuchkov and Pugo; and the heads of the military and defense-industrial complex, Yazov and Baklanov. Below this power echelon, the overwhelming majority of ministers from the government's Council of Ministers supported the coup, as did nearly 70 percent of the local governments in the Russian republic. Kryuchkov had even anticipated possible opposition to the coup and issued orders to arrest sixty-nine Russian politicians, including Yeltsin. Therefore all the power brokers either supported the coup or else were earmarked for arrest; success seemed inevitable.

On the first day, Muscovites seemed to take the news of the coup in stride. They heard about it on the news network Tass Monday at 6:00 A.M. Instead of rushing to the Kremlin to protest or erecting barricades to prevent troop movements, the people in Moscow swarmed to local stores to buy bread, canned food, and whatever else was available, and then they set up street "booths" to re-sell the merchandise at ten times its cost. In state stores and restaurants shoppers were pleasantly surprised to find vodka and cognac in abundant supply, a detail anticipated by the putschists to divert attention from the takeover. Initially, most people in Moscow thought of their stomachs and pocketbooks, not their political rights.

Despite everything in its favor, the coup did not succeed. The putschists were typical *apparatchiki*: incompetent, uninspired, and weak. To take control of an entire country far exceeded their abilities; the most they could do was to issue orders to key Moscow bureaucrats and then hope the commands were obeyed. Two vignettes speak volumes about the character of these usurpers.

At an early Monday morning meeting, Yazov ordered his chief generals to use no force in the takeover: "Don't do anything stupid. There will be people in the crowd who will throw themselves in front of tanks or throw Molotov cocktails. I want no bloodshed or carnage."[24] Tanks and armored personnel carriers were deployed to strategic locations throughout Moscow, including Russia's parliament building, where they sat motionless, sometimes in the midst of angry protest crowds. How could leaders with no stomach for blood crush opposition?

Another incident that illuminates the character of the putschists occurred late Wednesday afternoon when it became clear that the coup had failed. In a piece of burlesque, Yazov, Kryuchkov, and Baklanov flew to the Crimea to meet with Gorbachev, apparently to bargain with him to retain their positions in government or to beg his forgiveness; he refused to see them. Yanayev drank himself into a stupor in his Kremlin office; Pavlov had already admitted himself into a hospital for high blood pressure and signs of a heart attack; Pugo went home, shot himself in the head, and died. The arrested surviving putschists pointed fingers of blame at one another for leading the plot and even claimed they were acting on orders from Gorbachev.

Despite the impotent leadership of the putschists, the coup also failed because key power brokers just did not obey their orders. For example, commanders of the KGB's elite antiterrorist unit known as Alpha Group refused to attack the Russian White House (Parliament) early Tuesday morning. Another commander, General Yevgeni Shaposhnikov, head of the air force, ordered fighter planes on alert in case assault helicopters moved against the White House. He ordered that the helicopters be stopped by any means. Minister of Defense Yazov noted this insubordination but was incapable of forcing his will on the commanders. Indeed, on Wednesday morning, at a meeting with his top generals, Yazov was informed by Shaposhnikov and others that the coup attempt was over—troops would be withdrawn from Moscow at 3:00 P.M.

Timetable of the August Coup

Sunday, August 18
5:00 P.M. Government officials arrive in the Crimea and give Gorbachev two options: to hand over his Presidential powers to Yanayev or to step down. Gorbachev refuses to comply. KGB units sever his telephone lines and keep him under estate arrest for the duration of the coup.

Monday, August 19
6:00 A.M. The news agency Tass announces that Gorbachev is ill and that Yanayev is taking over the government under a new entity, The State Committee for the State of Emergency in the USSR.
12:30 P.M. Yeltsin climbs on a tank in front of the Russian Parliament and denounces the coup before television cameras and a few thousand people.

Tuesday, August 20
12:30 P.M.–5:30 P.M. Outside the Russian Parliament the crowd now numbering 50,000 swells to 150,000.
7:00 P.M. More armored vehicles roll toward the Russian Parliament, but stop a mile away.
9:00 P.M. Yanayev announces that troops will not attack the White House.

Wednesday, August 21
3:00 P.M. The army does not cooperate with the putschists, and troops withdraw from the center of Moscow.
4:00 P.M. Three coup leaders fly to the Crimea to meet with Gorbachev; he has nothing to do with them.

Thursday, August 22
2:15 A.M. Gorbachev's plane lands in Moscow, and he takes charge of the government.

Finally, the coup attempt failed because of Yeltsin's courage and luck. He had been listed as one of the sixty-nine Russian politicians to be arrested, and the KGB did drive to his house on Monday morning to arrest him, arriving thirty minutes too late—he had already left for the White House. At 12:30 P.M. on the same day, he risked arrest or, worse, a sniper's bullet, when he ventured outside the safety of the Parliament building and climbed onto one of the T-72 tanks to denounce the coup. This image of Yeltsin atop a tank was broadcast on the evening news in the Soviet Union and later around the world. It became an icon for resistance, popularizing Yeltsin, who began to draw to him a huge crowd, at times in excess of 150,000 people.

With the coup crumbling, the putschists hiding or scattering, and Gorbachev in the Crimea, a power vacuum existed in Moscow, and Yeltsin stepped in, asserting his authority as elected President of Russia. Late Wednesday he dispatched his people to the Crimea to free Gorbachev and to bring him back to the capital. Later (Friday), when the two men made a joint appearance before the Supreme Soviet of the Russian Federation, the person giving orders was Yeltsin. He forced Gorbachev to read a long list of government ministers who had supported the coup (all Gorbachev appointees), and he signed a decree banning the Russian Communist Party in front of a stammering Gorbachev. The Party that had spearheaded the November 1917 coup was now dead in Russia, itself the victim of a coup, though a botched one. The next day Gorbachev resigned as CPSU General Secretary and ordered the government to seize all buildings, dachas, and other property belonging to the Party. Yeltsin had already upstaged Gorbachev, and so the move did little to enhance the latter's popularity among the Soviet people.

For the rest of 1991, Yeltsin remained one political step ahead of Gorbachev, and in no area was this more evident than in the controversy over Union integrity versus Republican independence. The coup dealt a mortal blow to the Union. Between August 19 and 31 more than half of the republics declared their independence from the Union, and several others did the same in September and December. With the CPSU outlawed in Russia and other republics, there was no center to hold the Union together. "The center is dead, the center committed suicide,"[25] said Armenian President Levon Ter-Petrosyan after the coup. Gorbachev never understood this point. At the September meeting of the Congress of People's Deputies he changed the constitution to permit the creation of a looser Union, and in November he rallied seven republics around a new banner, the Union of Sovereign States. But no new Union would rise from the deathbed of the USSR, and Yeltsin knew this.

Requiem For Soviet Marxism-Leninism

Karl Marx's vision for human beings and society was simple: human beings would freely exercise their physical and intellectual talents, and society would supply them with the material goods required for their existence—food, shelter, clothing, medical and educational facilities, and so on. This is what he meant by the maxim identified with the higher phase of communism, "From each according to his ability, to each according to his needs." Not pie-in-the-sky, this higher phase of communism would occur at the conclusion of a lengthy historical process, one that would give rise to capitalist society, the necessary antecedent to communism since capitalism would, among other things, create the industry that would permit communist society to produce an abundance of material goods.

In late 1917 Russia, Lenin and the socialists usurped political power prematurely according to Marx's view of history—the country had not yet developed a strong industrial base. Lenin's pivotal use of an elite and highly organized political party to gain governmental power added his name to Marxism (now known as Marxism-Leninism), but it did not nullify Marx's original insight about the necessity of industrialization to make a communist society viable.

The Soviet leaders, particularly Stalin, employed the Communist Party as a powerful tool to industrialize the Soviet Union, and in the process they created a partocracy,[26] a state in which the party attempts to control and direct everything, the government, economy, military and police, media, arts, culture, and in the extreme, even the thoughts of its citizens. When partocracy is strong, society develops in the intended direction of its leaders, as happened under Stalin when he industrialized and collectivized the USSR in the 1930s and after World War II; but when partocracy falters, society stagnates, as happened under Brezhnev; and when partocracy attempts to reform itself by decentralizing its power, society implodes under the weight of its own leaderless institutions, as happened under Gorbachev. Marxism-Leninism in the USSR died when its heart, the CPSU, collapsed. Its epitaph might read:

Soviet Marxism-Leninism
Born 11/7/17
Died 8/23/91

> "A success in crushing political opposition
> and constructing heavy industrial base.
> A failure at accommodating individuality of people
> and vicissitudes of marketplace."
>
> Soviet Marxism-Leninism did not work, and ultimately it did not survive. Marx's vision, however, is still alive, even among many people in the fifteen nations constituting the former Soviet Union—human beings should develop their talents freely, and society should supply them with vital goods.

With the leaders of the Ukraine and Belarus, Yeltsin founded the Commonwealth of Independent States (CIS) on December 8, 1991, and two weeks later the organization expanded to eleven members. (Of the original fifteen republics, the four missing included the three Baltic states and Georgia, the latter expressing interest but being told to resolve its virtual civil war before signing on.) The CIS did not serve as a substitute for the Soviet Union, since it functioned like an elite debating society. Every agreement had to be a consensus and, even then, no decision was binding on the members. Nonetheless, the CIS provided a forum for the republican leaders to dismantle the USSR peacefully and to address other concerns. They agreed to honor current national borders, to place ex-Soviet strategic nuclear weapons and their support services under Russia's command, and to award the USSR's permanent seat in the United Nations Security Council to Russia. The members did not resolve all problems among themselves, but in all discussions they insisted on treating each other as leaders of independent, sovereign nations. The Soviet Union was de facto dead.

Gorbachev criticized the founding of the CIS, claiming the leaders had no legal authority to create the organization. He lagged one giant step behind Yeltsin and the others, who viewed Soviet legal authority as irrelevant. With the republics functioning as new nations, the USSR existed in name only, and so Gorbachev resigned as President on December 25. The next day the Congress of People's Deputies dissolved itself.

Gorbachev had relinquished his Presidency, a goal the August putschists had tried to achieve four months earlier. Their actions

had also led to other achievements, ironic ones. They had wanted
to strengthen the leading role of the CPSU in the government, but instead they brought about the Party's demise. They
had wanted to safeguard the unity of the USSR, but instead they
hastened its breakup. So monumental were these achievements
that the August coup and its aftermath marked a watershed in
Soviet history, and prompted foreign policy expert Michael
Mandelbaum to compare the events to the American Revolution
of 1776 and the French Revolution of 1789.[27]

	Size[1] (square miles)	Population[2] (millions)	Date of Independence
The New Republics			
Russian Federation	6,592,800	148 82% Russians 4% Tatars 3% Ukrainians	none[3]
Republic of Armenia	11,490	3.3 93% Armenians 3% Azeris 2% Kurds 2% Russians	8/23/90
Democratic Republic of Azerbaijan	33,430	7.1 83% Azeris 6% Russians 6% Armenians	8/30/91
Republic of Belarus	80,134	10.3 78% Belarusans 13% Russians 4% Poles	8/25/91
Republic of Estonia	17,413	1.6 62% Estonians 30% Russians 3% Ukrainians	8/20/91
Republic of Georgia	26,900	5.5 70% Georgians 8% Armenians 6% Russians 6% Azeris 3% Ossetians	4/9/91

	Size[1] (square miles)	Population[2] (millions)	Date of Independence
Kazakhstan	1,049,155	16.7 40% Kazakhs 38% Russians 6% Germans 5% Ukrainians 2% Uzbeks 2% Tatars	12/16/91
Republic of Kirghizia	76,640	4.4 52% Kirghizs 22% Russians 13% Uzbeks 3% Ukrainians 2% Germans	8/31/91
Republic of Latvia	24,595	2.6 52% Latvians 34% Russians 5% Belarusans 4% Ukrainians	8/21/91
Republic of Lithuania	25,170	3.7 80% Lithuanians 9% Russians 7% Poles	3/11/90
Republic of Moldova	13,000	4.4 65% Moldovans 14% Ukrainians 13% Russians 4% Gagauzi 2% Bulgarians	8/27/91
Republic of Tajikistan	55,240	5.4 62% Tajiks 24% Uzbeks 8% Russians	9/9/91
Republic of Turkmenistan	186,400	3.6 72% Turkmens 10% Russians 9% Uzbeks 2% Kazakhs	10/27/91
Republic of Ukraine	231,990	51.9 73% Ukrainians 22% Russians 1% Jews	8/25/91

	Size[1] (square miles)	Population[2] (millions)	Date of Independence
Republic of Uzbekistan	172,741	20.3 71% Uzbeks 8% Russians 5% Tajiks 4% Kazakhs	8/31/91

[1] Statistical source is *The Statesman's Year Book*, 1993–94.
[2] Population figures are for 1990 except for Estonia (1992), Latvia (1993), Tajikstan (1991), and Ukraine (1991); statistical source is *The Statesman's Year Book*, 1993–94.
[3] Russia declared its sovereignty on 6/8/90, but it never made a proclamation of independence.

Summary and Comment

Gorbachev tried to reform the three dominant institutions of Stalinism in the Soviet Union—the centralized economy, Party monopoly, and the police state. To dissipate the fear created by decades of wanton police arrests, torture, and executions, he introduced *glasnost*; the bald and painful truth about the nation's past and present might encourage the people to voice their concerns freely and openly. To fracture the monopoly of Party power, he advocated *democratizatsia*; secret and contested elections might move the people to take charge of the collective life of their country. To diminish the impact of the centralized command economy, he presented *perestroika*; farms and industries controlled by individuals or small groups permitted to earn a profit might produce quality goods at reasonable prices. As a result of these programs, the Soviet people would prosper, and communism would reign supreme as an economic model. With his blueprint for Stalinist reform so clear, why did Gorbachev fail?

Gorbachev might have thought that he could perform only cosmetic surgery to reform these entrenched Stalinist institutions. He apparently hoped that the police, the Party, and the centralized economy did not need to be eliminated, only reshaped here and there. He was wrong. As St. Petersburg Mayor Anatoli Sobchak said, "Our great mistake during those six years had been to try to reform what was unreformable."[28] The Party had insinuated itself into every facet of society, making reform of institutions like the police and the economy impossible without removing Party *apparatchiki* from them (decentralization), an operation akin to removing blood vessels from a body. When enough vessels are torn out, the heart dies; when enough institutions were decentralized, the Party became powerless. And without its heart—the CPSU—the body politic of the Soviet Union collapsed.

Gorbachev's poor judgment also contributed to his failure. He needed like-minded people to carry out his policies effectively, but he chose his comrades poorly. Even after the coup, the knowledge that he had handpicked the people who betrayed him did not sharpen his judgment in making appointments. He still chose his people poorly, picking as heads of Defense, the Interior, and the KGB the very men who had participated in the coup. The appointments lasted a mere twenty-four hours but the image of Gorbachev indulging in old habits seemed farcical.

Finally Gorbachev had an inability to separate himself from his Stalinist heritage. He constantly advocated restructuring, but he could not restructure his own thinking. For example, he intended to decentralize the economy, to base it on market forces instead of commands from *apparatchiki* in Moscow, but he could not accept two pillars of a market economy: private property and private enterprise. Of private property he said, "I do not accept . . . private ownership of land—do with me what you will."[29] Of private enterprise he stated, "They say, 'Let's have free enterprise and give the green light to all forms of private enterprise . . . ,' but I cannot accept these ideas . . . they are impossible ideas."[30] A market economy by definition requires the economic decision-making of millions of individuals. Gorbachev expected such an economy to flourish without individuals owning property and controlling their own enterprises. Further, there could be no individual economic decisions if *apparatchiki* were still deciding how the resources would be allocated and the enterprises run. The impossibility of the situation evidences Gorbachev's flawed thinking.

Mikhail Gorbachev's judgments and policies so stressed the CPSU and the USSR that both the Party and the Union collapsed. His good intentions were consistently undermined by flawed thinking and his vision marred by lack of scope. To his credit though, he helped make the world safer by arms limitation; and ironically, the former Soviet peoples were politically awakened, enabling them to rise from the rubble of the USSR and start carving their own places in history as new republics. Although Gorbachev had said that "profound transformations must be carried out," he was not able to do so and save the Soviet Union as well. But the transformation that did occur was indeed profound and ultimately gives cause for hope.

Further Reading

Gorbachev's *glasnost* has assisted Sovietologists around the world. Scholars have gathered information on Gorbachev and his era through firsthand observation, newspapers, government reports, media stories, interviews, and so on. Even the major personalities, Gorbachev and Yeltsin, have given their own spin to events in speeches and books. The result has been strong—though not definitive—scholarship on the last years of the USSR despite the closeness of the era to our own time.

Cerf, Christopher and Marina Albee, editors. *Small Fires: Letters from the Soviet People to "Ogonyok" Magazine, 1987–1990.* Translated by Hans Fenstermacher. New York: Summit, 1990. Selections from 500,000 letters sent by Soviet citizens to *Ogonyok*'s Letters Department, giving firsthand evidence of the effectiveness of Gorbachev's *glasnost.*

Goldman, Marshall I. *What Went Wrong with Perestroika.* New York: W. W. Norton, 1992. Economist and Associate Director of the Russian Research Center at Harvard, Goldman reviews the entire Gorbachev era with a critical eye on the economy and why the General Secretary failed to restructure it.

Gorbachev, Mikhail. *Perestroika: New Thinking for Our Country and The World.* New York: Harper and Row, 1987.

The propaganda is unmistakable, but so is the genuineness of Gorbachev's beliefs in his policies to restructure the USSR and the role of his country in world affairs.

Kaiser, Robert G. *Why Gorbachev Happened: His Triumphs, His Failure, and His Fall.* New York: Simon and Schuster, 1992. Managing Editor of *The Washington Post* and frequent foreign correspondent in Moscow, Kaiser weaves an intricate and engrossing portrait of the Gorbachev years based on reports of events, Gorbachev's own words, and eyewitness accounts.

Ulam, Adam B. *The Communists: The Story of Power and Lost Illusions: 1948–1991.* New York: Charles Scribner's Sons, 1992. Director of the Russian Research Center at Harvard, Ulam explores the decline and disintegration of communism around the world, beginning after World War II with Eastern Europe and China and concluding with a hundred pages on the USSR under Gorbachev.

Yeltsin, Boris. *Against the Grain, An Autobiography.* Translated by Michael Glenny. London: Jonathan Cape, 1990. An intriguing, fast-paced look at Yeltsin, the book includes anecdotes about his early years as well as letters and documents, such as his resignation speech from the CPSU Politburo.

NOTES

1. Michael Dobbs, "Gorbachev Bares Budget For Military" in *The Washington Post*, Wednesday, May 31, 1989, pp. 1 and A17. Gorbachev announced that the Soviet Union spends 9 percent of the GNP on defense. The CIA has estimated defense expenditures between 15 to 20 percent of the GNP. The discrepancy is due to the amount the CIA attributed to soldiers' salaries, at the American GI level instead of the Soviet level ($12 per month).

2. Marshall I. Goldman, *What Went Wrong With Perestroika* (New York: W. W. Norton, 1992), p. 154.

3. Mikhail Gorbachev, *Perestroika: New Thinking For Our Country and The World* (New York: Harper and Row, 1987), p. 15.

4. Quoted in Goldman, p. 102.

5. Gorbachev, p. 115.

6. Robert Toth, "Soviet Defense Cut 1.5%, Scientist Says" in *Los Angeles Times*, Part 1, Friday, April 28, 1989, p. 6.

7. Quoted in Goldman, p. 136.

8. The Bozhko story was reported by Michael Dobbs in *The Washington Post*, Sunday, July 9, 1990, pp. A1 and A21.

9. Quoted in Robert G. Kaiser, *Why Gorbachev Happened: His Triumphs, His Failure, His Fall* (New York: Simon & Schuster, 1992), p. 288.

10. Quoted in Kaiser, p. 165.

11. Boris Yeltsin, *Against the Grain: An Autobiography*, Translated by Michael Glenny (London: Jonathan Cape, 1990), p. 145.

258

12. Yeltsin, p. 147.

13. Yeltsin, p. 147.

14. Quoted in Kaiser, p. 165.

15. Quoted in Adam B. Ulam, *The Communists: The Story of Power and Lost Illusions: 1948–1991* (New York: Charles Scribner's Sons, 1992), p. 419.

16. Quoted in Kaiser, p. 210.

17. Quoted in Kaiser, p. 210.

18. Mark R. Beissinger, "The Reconstruction of the USSR and the Search for a Post Soviet Community" in *Problems of Communism*, Nov.-Dec. 1991, p. 32.

19. Quoted in Kaiser, p. 375.

20. Quoted in Ulam, p. 477.

21. Quoted in Kaiser, p. 390.

22. Quoted in Kaiser, p. 379.

23. "Announcement of Ouster" in *New York Times*, August 19, 1991, p. A6.

24. Quoted in Jeff Trimble and Peter Vassiliev, "Three Days That Shook The World" in *U.S. News and World Report*, November 18, 1991, p. 57.

25. "End of an Empire" in *Newsweek*, September 9, 1991, p. 20.

26. The word "partocracy" was coined by Abdurakhman Avtorkhanov; it appears, for example, in his two-volume work, *Proishhozhdeniye partokratii* (The Origins of the Partocracy) Frankfurt am Main: Prosev, 1973.

27. Michael Mandelbaum, "Coup de Grace: The End of the Soviet Union" in *Foreign Affairs*, Vol. 71, No. 1, 1992, p. 183.

28. Quoted in Ulam, p. 491.

29. Quoted in Goldman, p. 241.

30. Quoted in Goldman, p. 241.

INDEX TO EPILOGUE

(Also see main Index, p. 205)